One
Bible
Only?

One Bible Only?

Examining Exclusive Claims for the King James Bible

ROY E. BEACHAM & KEVIN T. BAUDER

GENERAL EDITORS

kregel
PUBLICATIONS

Grand Rapids, MI 49501

One Bible Only? Examining Exclusive Claims for the King James Bible

© 2001 by Roy E. Beacham

Published by Kregel Publications, a division of Kregel, Inc., P.O. Box 2607, Grand Rapids, MI 49501. For more information about Kregel Publications, visit our web site: www.kregel.com.

Library of Congress Cataloging-in-Publication Data
Beacham, Roy E.
   One Bible only?: examining exclusive claims for the King James Bible / Roy E. Beacham.
      p.   cm.
   Includes bibliographical references.
   1. Bible. English—Versions—Authorized. I. Title.
BS186 .B43   2001   220.5'2038—dc21   00-048734
                                                                                    CIP
ISBN 0-8254-2048-2

Printed in the United States of America
2 3 4 5 / 03

Contents

Contributors

Kevin T. Bauder, Th.M., D.Min., Ph.D. (candidate), is director of Postgraduate Studies and serves as department chairman and associate professor of Systematic and Historical Theology at Central Baptist Theological Seminary, Plymouth, Minnesota.

Roy E. Beacham, M.Div., Th.M., Th.D., serves as the department chairman and professor of Old Testament at Central Baptist Theological Seminary, Plymouth, Minnesota.

W. Edward Glenny, M.A., M.Div., Th.M., Th.D., was director of Postgraduate Studies and professor of New Testament at Central Baptist Theological Seminary, Plymouth, Minnesota, and now serves as professor of Biblical Studies and New Testament at Northwestern College, St. Paul, Minnesota.

Douglas K. Kutilek, M.A., Th.M., serves as adjunct professor in the Romanian extension of Central Baptist Theological Seminary, Plymouth, Minnesota.

Douglas R. McLachlan, M.Div., D.D., is senior pastor of the Fourth Baptist Church, Plymouth, Minnesota, and is president of Central

Seminary, serving as the department chairman and professor of Practical Theology at Central Baptist Theological Seminary, Plymouth, Minnesota.

ROBERT W. MILLIMAN, M.Div., Th.M., Th.D., is assistant to the dean and serves as the department chairman and associate professor of New Testament at Central Baptist Theological Seminary, Plymouth, Minnesota.

LARRY D. PETTEGREW, M.R.E., M.Div., Th.M., Th.D., was academic dean and professor of Historical and Systematic Theology at Central Baptist Theological Seminary, Plymouth, Minnesota, and now serves as professor of Theology at The Master's Seminary in Sun Valley, California.

The Richness of Scripture

Douglas R. McLachlan

APART FROM THEIR RELATIONSHIP to God Himself, nothing is more precious to the people of God than the text of Scripture. In 2 Timothy 3:15–17 Paul celebrates the incredible value of the Scripture by identifying its impeccable virtues:

1. it is *sacred* in its character—because it is "the Holy Scriptures" (v. 15),
2. it is *salvatory* in its goal—because "it is able to make you wise for salvation through faith which is in Christ Jesus" (v. 15),
3. it is *sterling* in origin—because "all Scripture is given by inspiration of God" (v. 16), and
4. it is *sensational* in its impact—because "it is profitable for doctrine, for reproof, for correction, for instruction in righteousness" (v. 16).

Further, this value is mission driven because the *objective* toward which all of it is moving is the thorough equipping of the people of God for ministry (v. 17). In Paul's mind, to exaggerate the riches of God's Word is impossible. Its sacred character, saving goal, sterling origin, and sensational impact clearly set it apart from all other volumes.

Christians celebrate, in particular, the *trustworthiness* of Scripture as a breathed-out, written-down document from God Himself. Paul's phrase

9

given by inspiration of God means literally "God-breathed" *(theopneustos),* meaning that the content of Scripture was conceived in God's mind and sourced in the inner recesses of His being. This being true, certainly no document on earth is so trustworthy as Scripture, for indeed "the mouth of the Lord has spoken it" (Isa. 40:5).

But Scripture is not only breathed out but also written down. Peter instructs us here. He says that "holy men of God spoke as they were moved [picked up and borne along] by the Holy Spirit" (2 Peter 1:21). He means that the omniscient Spirit supernaturally superintended both the reception and the recording of the divine revelation by the human authors so that they were preserved from mental and mechanical blunders. This miraculous synergism of divine control and human cooperation is a process that defies logical explanation and empirical analysis. It did not demean the human authors into machines, as though they were Dictaphones, and yet it preserved from error the text of Scripture as originally given by God. The end result was a book that manifests the imprint of both God and man and that was both inerrant and infallible *in the autographs.* Such "perfections of utterance" are inexplicable apart from divine intervention. In the production of the *original documents* of Scripture, it was the work of the Holy Spirit supernaturally to superintend the work of the human authors so that flawed agents in a flawed world could produce a flawless manuscript. The original text of Scripture could not have been any more perfect.

The unfortunate reality is that in the intervening years we have lost access to the original manuscripts of Scripture. None of them has survived. Notwithstanding, God in His grace and governance has ensured access to the original content of those documents by preserving for us a rich abundance of manuscript copies. Although many variants among the Greek manuscripts of the New Testament exist, the overwhelming majority of these variants are of minor importance. Significant variants number about two thousand, *none of which* affects the overall theology of Bible-believing Christians. Textual variants do no harm to one's overall theology because no element of theology is constructed on only one text of Scripture but on numerous texts, most of which have solid manuscript support.

David Alan Black was right to say, "These differences in Greek manuscripts are reflected frequently enough in the major English versions that the expositor will inevitably be called upon to make an informed judgment."[1]

Gordon D. Fee states well the need for probing the text of the New Testament systematically:

> The need for NT textual criticism results from a combination of three factors: (1) The originals, probably written on papyrus scrolls, have all perished. (2) For over 1,400 years the NT was copied by hand, and the copyists |scribes| made every conceivable error, as well as at times intentionally altering [probably with the idea of "correcting"] the text. Such errors and alterations survived in various ways, with a basic tendency to accumulate [scribes seldom left anything out, lest they omit something inspired]. (3) There are now [1993] extant, in whole or in part, 5,338 Greek MSS, as well as hundreds of copies of ancient translations [not counting over 8,000 copies of the Latin Vulgate], plus the evidence from the citations of the NT in the writings of the early church fathers. Moreover, no two MSS anywhere in existence are exactly alike.[2]

We consider this combination a very large "kettle" of "textual soup"—more than five thousand Greek manuscripts of the New Testament (in part or in whole)—plus all of the rest. We rest in the historical reality of this abundance and see it as God's way of preserving the integrity and accuracy of His Word.

This book began as a lecture series in the chapel services of Central Baptist Theological Seminary of Plymouth, Minnesota, a suburb of Minneapolis. Those lectures were designed to assist the students in understanding the historic position of Central Seminary and to incite those students to further well-informed study with regard to the growing Bible version controversy. Those lectures eventually were reworked and drafted into an initial printed publication that was produced by Central Seminary for the information and edification of graduates, alumni, and other interested students of Scripture. Now the work has reached a new plateau in this present form. The initial publication has been revised and edited, and new contributions have been made to further the discussion. All of the contributors to this work share a common association with Central Baptist Theological Seminary. Most of them are graduates of the seminary, and all of them have served at the school as either adjunct or full-time faculty members.

As you will see in the following chapters, the approach that these contributors take to the whole matter of textual criticism (the study of the original text of Scripture) and of translation issues has been very balanced. Dr. Richard V. Clearwaters, the founder and first president of Central Seminary and, for many years, its guiding light, was not an advocate of the King James-Only position. The faculty at Central Seminary never subscribed to such a view, and no evidence exists that previous generations of fundamentalists or evangelicals have used the translation issue as a hallmark of authentic faith. The contributors to this work have done an excellent job of laying out the factual data and addressing the various questions that seem to hover around this issue. I believe that you will find their answers to these questions to be accurate, fair, and charitable.

In our view, becoming frozen in time by anchoring to and absolutizing only one English translation or one narrow family of Greek manuscripts, while ignoring all of the rest of the textual evidence, does not seem to be a prudent course to follow. We believe that investigating and probing the abundance of available manuscript evidence that is accessible to the serious student has merit. Then we can preach and teach with the authority of true biblicists, speaking God's absolute truth accurately, passionately, and relevantly into the hearts and minds of our postmodern world. The following chapters are designed to help us do that at the highest levels of exegetical, historical, theological, and intellectual integrity.

Chapter Notes

1. David Alan Black, *Using New Testament Greek in Ministry* (Grand Rapids: Baker, 1993), 73.
2. Gordon D. Fee, "The Textual Criticism of the New Testament," in *Expositor's Bible Commentary,* ed. Frank E. Gaebelein (Grand Rapids: Zondervan, 1979), 1:420.

The Issues at Hand

Kevin T. Bauder

THIS IS ANOTHER BOOK about the King James Version debate. If you have followed the debate at all, you know that hundreds of volumes have been published on the subject over the last thirty years. These discussions range from comic books to scholarly treatises. So why do we publish yet another treatment of this issue? Let us explain.

A Bit of History

Most of the contributors to this book grew up in Baptist fundamentalism during the 1950s and 1960s. The foremost version of the Bible that we heard taught or preached in those years was the King James. The Revised Standard Version was uniformly denounced. Some of us were exposed to the American Standard Version of 1901 in college. Most other versions of the Bible—including the American Bible Union version, the Revised Version, and Young's Literal Translation—were unused or even unknown in our experience. In the late 1960s, the New Scofield Reference Bible was released, and fundamentalists broadly welcomed it. The editors of this revision had actually updated some of the difficult terms, a feature that was generally favored.

Soon, many fundamentalist preachers were purchasing and reading the *Living Letters* and other volumes of the series that would eventually become Kenneth Taylor's *Living Bible*. Because of their concrete language, these books were prized for use in deaf ministry—even at Wealthy

Street Baptist Church in Grand Rapids, under the pastorate of David Otis Fuller. Fuller would soon become the dean of the King James-Only movement, but in the late 1960s he welcomed Taylor's work.

Tremendous excitement greeted the introduction of the New American Standard Bible (NASB). The New Testament of this translation swept into fundamentalist churches, which then waited eagerly for the Old Testament to be released. The NASB quickly found a home in many fundamentalist Bible college and seminary classrooms, where professors valued it for its precision and faithfulness to the Greek and Hebrew. Another version, the *Amplified Bible,* never saw common use in church services, but most pastors and many laymen had a copy on their shelves, and they used it regularly.

Some disappointments did occur. The choice to market the *Living Bible* as a Bible version did not set well. Most conservative evangelicals also judged *Good News for Modern Man* to be objectionable for its lack of precision and its theological biases. When the New International Version (NIV) was released, however, it was welcomed as a faithful yet readable alternative, even by many people within fundamentalism.

If it seems that we are focusing inordinately upon fundamentalism to the exclusion of the rest of evangelicalism, we do so for two reasons. First, as was mentioned earlier, the contributors to this book have their theological roots in fundamentalism; this is where we have direct, personal, and experiential knowledge. Second, the contemporary King James-Only movement is often regarded as a branch of fundamentalism and is sometimes used to lampoon fundamentalism (or at least the conservative branches of fundamentalism) as a whole. Historic fundamentalists, however, were not King James Only,[1] and the mainstream of the fundamentalist movement continues to reject the King James-Only mentality. Moreover, not all of the figures connected with the King James-Only movement should be identified as fundamentalists.

Through the late 1960s, reverent attempts at producing modern translations of the Scriptures were greeted with praise, even by fundamentalists. That situation began to change during the early 1970s with the publication of *Which Bible?* by David Otis Fuller. Before *Which Bible?* a few isolated voices had spoken for the exclusive use or doctrinal superiority of the King James Bible. What Fuller did was to popularize the issue, employing a whole series of arguments that were designed to appeal to people with little background in biblical or theological studies. Soon, small pamphlets began to appear comparing the NASB and the NIV with the New World Translation of the Jehovah's Witnesses. It began to be noised abroad that these were not Bible versions but perversions. They were supposed to have removed the deity, bodily resurrection, and blood of Christ from the pages of Scripture.

The great majority of fundamentalists never found these allegations persuasive. The real question was what to do about the controversialists who began to push the King James Version as the only true Word of God in the English language. Although they were no more than a small minority, some of the King James–Only promoters held responsible positions in fundamentalist organizations. Therefore, an effort was made to accommodate their sensibilities. Churches and fellowships that had once been accustomed to hear the Scriptures read from one of the various newer versions began to pressure their preachers to use only the King James for public reading and teaching. Resolutions were passed honoring the King James Version and recommending its exclusive use. Some of these resolutions also questioned the value of modern, "distorted" versions of Scripture. Although such resolutions did not usually disparage the use of faithful, modern translations, that fact did not seem to matter to the controversialists, who quoted the resolutions as if they condemned all contemporary versions of the Word of God.

From the late 1970s through the 1980s, this policy of conciliation was combined with the occasional attempt to engage the King James–Only adherents in sober discussion of the issues. Those attempts produced little, if any, results. Supporters of the King James–Only viewpoint seemed to be interested in speaking to only those whom they hoped to convert to their position. Over the years, they came to portray their opponents (even their fundamentalist opponents) as enemies of the Christian faith. Words such as *heretic, apostate,* and *hypocrite* became weapons of choice in the effort to discredit anyone who disagreed with them.

By the end of the 1980s, most fundamentalists had grown weary of the controversy. They chose to ignore the King James–Only proponents. At just that time, however, a new generation of controversialists arose. Throughout the 1990s, these new leaders mounted an increasingly vocal campaign to attract fundamentalists away from the mainstream and toward the fringe. This increasing fervor sometimes resulted in the division of churches, the purging of school faculties, and the splitting or dissolution of fellowships.

With a few notable exceptions, mainstream fundamentalist leaders have been slow to respond to Bible version controversialists. Unfortunately, the policy of accommodation has often proven disastrous. Most Bible version enthusiasts, it seems, will not be accommodated. The granting of concessions has usually been met only by further demands.

The Purpose of This Book

At some point, silence becomes culpable. The writers of this book believe that the time has come to speak together on this issue. Our firm conviction is that most of the people who champion a particular edition or version of Scripture to the exclusion of all others have based their belief upon neither an accurate understanding of the Bible's own teachings nor the actual facts of the case. Rather, their position is founded on a misunderstanding of the Bible's own statements and a defective line of reasoning about the manner in which Scripture has been preserved.

Our principal intent is not to speak *to* the King James-Only adherents. Our chief aim is to isolate certain core issues for those who have come into contact with their writings and speeches. Our concern is for thoughtful pastors and church members who might not be in a position to examine all of the evidence first hand but are wondering about some of the accusations they have heard. Of course, in a book of this length, we cannot respond to every assertion, every bit of supposed evidence, or every speculation. But we hope to supply a core of information and a perspective that should be of help to those who are still thinking through the important questions.

Risks of This Book

Certain risks do attend our task. The first risk is the hazard of making sweeping generalizations about our friends in the King James-Only movement. We recognize that not all of them share every conclusion drawn, and not all of them would countenance every tactic employed by others in that movement. We do not intend to criticize the moderates (for the King James-Only movement does have a relatively moderate wing) by holding them accountable for the actions of extremists. In this book, we shall be more concerned with responding to the arguments and observations of the middle ranks than those of the extremists. Some references to the extremists will be impossible to avoid, but we shall attempt to make clear when we are discussing the extremes rather than the center of the King James-Only movement.

A second risk is that the mere publication of this book might raise the temperature of the debate. Unfortunately, the debate has too often descended to the level of name calling, guilt by association, bandwagoning, and truth-twisting. We will attempt to avoid such unchristian behavior. We also trust that this book will not receive such a welcome.

One final risk must be noted. We intend to write plainly about the King James-Only issue. We believe, sorrowfully, that this movement has propagated a seriously damaging doctrine within the Church of Jesus Christ. We also believe that the conduct of some people in that camp has been less than honorable. We intend to speak to these matters. The result is that we might seem to regard the King James-Only leaders as enemies. We do not. In our view, they are friends, but they are mistaken in doctrine and conduct and, in those cases, have become opponents of truth. We speak in the same spirit in which Paul withstood Peter and for the same reason. Our desire is to speak the truth in love. We have long-standing ties with some proponents of this viewpoint. We have labored side by side with them in the Lord's vineyard. In some cases, we have even been responsible for a portion of their education. We wish the Lord's blessing upon their ministries, but we wish for their ministries to be conducted according to truth in word and in deed. We pray the same for our own ministries.

What Is the King James-Only Movement?

Anyone who has spent much time reading or listening to the King James-Only advocates knows that they do not like the name "King James Only." The problem, as they see it, is that the name is too vague. What outsiders see as a single King James-Only movement, insiders see as three or four distinct movements. Although the whole King James-Only movement is quite vocal, some of the voices are extreme. The movement does have a wing that is *relatively* more moderate. These moderates resent being classed with the more extreme King James-Only controversialists. Therefore, a bit of definition is in order.

Here is what the King James-Only movement is *not.* People who use only the King James Bible are not necessarily part of the King James-Only movement. People who believe that the King James or its underlying Greek and Hebrew texts (the Textus Receptus and the Ben-Chayyim) are superior to other texts or translations are not necessarily part of the King James-Only movement. Even people who are willing to argue publicly for the superiority of the King James, the Textus Receptus, or the Ben-Chayyim are not necessarily the people to whom this book responds.

The authors of this book are willing to entertain the theory that asserts the superiority of the King James Version among English translations of the Bible, the Textus Receptus among editions of the Greek New Testament, and the Ben-Chayyim text among editions of the Hebrew Old Testament. We disagree among ourselves about how strong the case might be in support of that theory, but none of us would rule out the possibility. The main question is whether the debate is academic or doctrinal in nature.

Within the King James-Only movement the issue is regarded as doctrinal, although different doctrinal emphases might be discerned. At the extreme end of the movement are those who believe that God "reinspired" the King James Bible, or the Textus Receptus; that all versions that are translated into other languages should be translated from the King James rather than from the Greek or the Hebrew; that the King James is actually superior to the Greek and Hebrew texts and can correct them; or that people who have been led to the Lord from one of the modern versions of the Bible (they would say "perversions") are not really saved. The authors of this book recognize that these theories are variously held and are in the minority in the King James-Only movement. We do not mean to impute all of these views to all King James-Only advocates. Because the people who hold these views are quite vocal, however, we cannot afford to ignore them completely in our discussion.

The relatively moderate wing of the King James-Only movement recognizes, in principle, that more than one English version of the Bible might actually be permissible. These moderates insist, however, that all good versions of the Bible must meet four criteria.

1. They must be translated from the proper texts: the Textus Receptus of the Greek New Testament and the Ben-Chayyim text of the Hebrew Old Testament.
2. They must employ the proper translation technique: verbal and formal equivalence rather than dynamic equivalence.
3. They must be the work of superior translators, reverent men who have a thorough mastery of biblical languages and a superb command of English style.
4. They must manifest the proper theology, usually defined in terms

of rejecting the distinctive readings of two Greek manuscripts (Sinaiticus and Vaticanus) that are supposed to advocate heretical doctrines.

Given these strictures, the King James Version turns out to be the only translation that constitutes an acceptable version of the Bible.

Almost all of the King James-Only movement can be located on a continuum between these two poles. Obviously, adherents to these various views differ from each other in significant ways. The moderates can hardly be blamed for objecting when they are lumped together with the "reinspirationists," whom even they regard as heretics. Nevertheless, they still share one crucial point in common. For the moderates as much as for the extremists, the exclusive use of the King James Version and its underlying Greek and Hebrew texts is a doctrinal issue. They believe that the Christian faith is at stake in the Bible version debate. In advocates of the Nestle-Aland Greek Text or the New American Standard Bible they perceive not only academic opponents but also enemies of Christianity.

The boundary of the King James-Only movement is the willingness to treat the superiority or exclusive use of the King James Version, the Textus Receptus, or the Ben-Chayyim Hebrew text as a doctrinal matter in which some aspect of the Christian faith is at stake. This is the point that all King James-Only advocates share in common, regardless of their other differences. Those who hold to the use of the King James or its underlying texts as a matter of preference or academic debate should not be included in the King James-Only movement. Those who treat these matters as doctrinal questions, however, are part of that movement, even if they anathematize other King James-Only advocates.

The authors of this book do not wish to discourage anyone from using the King James Version, the Textus Receptus, or the Ben-Chayyim Hebrew text. Christians who are most comfortable with these authorities will find no controversy with us. In fact, we do not completely agree among ourselves on these matters. What we do agree on is this: the King James is not the only true Bible in the English language. In the following pages, we will assert that the critical Greek texts or the New American Standard Bible, for example, are in fact the Word of God. When King James-Only advocates make the rejection of certain Bible texts or versions a test of orthodoxy, they have gone too far. Their position on these matters ought to be opposed for the sake of the Bible itself. The errors of their view need to be exposed for the sake of souls who are being misled by them. Therein lies the burden of this book.

What Are the Issues?

Many times, the King James Version debate becomes sidetracked over subordinate issues. Controversialists on both sides argue about whether Erasmus was an apostate, whether Westcott and Hort were liberal Romanists, whether Codex Sinaiticus was written by Gnostics, or whether James I was a homosexual. Some of these questions do have a bearing on the debate, although they are not all equally relevant. None of them, however is really at the core of the controversy. The heart of the conflict may be summed up in a series of rather simple questions, including the following.

1. Must all of God's words be preserved to have God's Word?

Can a person consistently believe in the preservation of God's Word without believing in the preservation of *every* word of the original documents of Scripture? The King James-Only advocates usually answer this question with an emphatic negative. If we do not have all of God's actual words, they insist, then we do not have God's Word. We do not know what God said unless we know the exact words in which He said it. This belief commits the King James-Only people to a particular theory of preservation: the theory that all of the words, and only the words, of the original documents must be preserved somewhere. Most of these people also add two corollaries. First, the words must be preserved in one place (one manuscript, edited text, family of texts, or translation) rather than in the plurality of all manuscripts, texts, and translations. Second, the words must be preserved in a publicly accessible fashion; the preserved words must be those that the believing community has actually used throughout the history of the people of God.

The King James-Only theory of preservation, then, is a theory of *verbal* preservation. The writers of this book might at different times refer to this theory as verbal preservation, perfect preservation, exact preservation, or word-for-word preservation. Whatever nomenclature is used, the theory is understood to contain the same three elements: (1) preservation of all of the words of the original; (2) preservation in a single manuscript, text, textual family, or translation; and (3) public accessibility.

Anyone who has read the King James-Only materials will recognize these elements.

The importance of this definition cannot be emphasized too strongly. According to the King James-Only position, the doctrine of preservation requires the perpetuation of *all* the words of the originals, *only* the words of the originals, in a *singular* place, *publicly accessible* to the people of God. If we take the King James-Only theory at its word, then any manuscript, text, or translation that deletes a single one of the words of the originals is not the Word of God but a perversion. If we accept the claims of this theory, then any manuscript, text, or translation that adds a single word that was not in the original cannot be the Word of God but must be a perversion.

This book will dispute the King James-Only teaching by insisting that we can know what God said, even if we do not have every single word with which He said it. The authors of this book will address the very heart of the controversy. Can we hold up an imperfect manuscript copy, an imperfectly edited text, or an imperfectly translated version, and rightly say, "This is the Word of God"? The authors of this book, in harmony with the vast majority of Bible believers throughout history, will insist that we can. Humanity can know what God has revealed; we can know His works and His ways; we can know how He sees us and what He has done for us; we can know what He demands of us. Most of all, we can know Him, for the Bible is His Word, even when it contains some imperfectly copied or translated words.

"Not so!" insist the King James-Only advocates. If humans have lost any of the words, then they have lost the Word. It is not enough that the *meaning* has been preserved; if we do not have all of the exact words, then we do not have the Word. Without every one of the actual words of God, all we are left with is human guesses about what God might have meant to say.

This strict position suggests a test by means of which we will evaluate the King James-Only theory. Can the adherents to this view produce the single manuscript, text, or translation that contains all of the words, and only the words, of God? Can they demonstrate, scripturally, that this particular text does not delete a single word from or add a single word to the words of the original? Can they show that these precise words, *without addition or deletion,* have been recognized and employed by the masses of God's people throughout the millennia of Christian history? These questions will constitute a fundamental test of the King James-Only proposal. If a single addition or a single deletion invalidates a manuscript or a text, then the King James-Only proponents are obligated to produce the right text and to justify it as the right text. If, however, they back away from the criteria that *all* of the words must be perfectly preserved, then they are really denying the theory of verbal or perfect preservation. From that point, the discussion is simply an academic conversation about how many words have actually been changed, which words have been historically preserved, and in which manuscripts and texts (issues that concern the discipline of textual criticism, not theology). If preservation does not *really* have to include *every* word, then the whole controversy is no more than a debate over percentages. To put it plainly, the King James-Only people have established a very high criterion by insisting upon the preservation of *all* of the words and *only* the words of God. If they are willing to accept a manuscript or a text that might omit *any* words (even a single word) from the originals, or that might add *any* words (even a single word) to the originals, then their whole position is falsified. They turn out to be on the same side as those whom they oppose. These issues will be examined in detail in the following chapters.

2. Does the Bible promise that all of God's words will be preserved?

King James-Only proponents regularly admit that their theory is fundamentally a "faith position." What they mean is that their conclusions do not rest *primarily* upon reasons or evidences but upon biblical promises. God, they say, is responsible to preserve His words, for He has promised in the Bible that He will do so.

Can the King James-Only theory be justified by an appeal to faith in the teachings of Scripture? Obviously, many aspects of the Christian faith are received on exactly that basis. We affirm special creation, not because we saw it but because God said that it occurred. We believe in a substitutionary atonement and receive Christ as our Savior, not because we can see the atonement but because God announces it to us and promises us eternal life. Christians should not be in any hurry to dismiss the appeal to faith. We affirm with our King James-Only friends that if God says it, that settles it.

The question that this book will ask is, Did God say it? This question suggests a second test that will be employed for evaluating the claims of the King James-Only theory. If the theorists are going to justify their appeal to faith, they must first demonstrate that God has specifically promised the verbal (perfect) preservation of the text of Scripture. That demonstration hinges upon careful exegesis of the passages in which God is supposed to have made this promise. The question will not be settled by listing references or even by citing verses but rather by showing what those verses mean historically, grammatically, and contextually.

Those who oppose the King James-Only hypothesis are willing to concede that the Bible might contain promises that God will preserve His Word. That concession, however, does not end the debate. The specific issue is whether any of those passages constitutes a promise that God will preserve the actual *words* of the original documents of Scripture; that He will preserve *all* of those words and *only* those words; that He will preserve them in a particular manuscript, text, or translation; and that He will do so in a publicly accessible way. The authors of this book propose that any promise that is less specific than this is insufficient as a scriptural basis for the appeal to faith.

We recognize that the King James-Only advocates need to find only a single passage of Scripture that makes this promise. If they can offer us clear assurances from the Word of God that God has committed Himself to the business of perfect, verbal preservation in a particular text, text family, edition, or translation, then every author of this book is quite prepared to submit to the appeal to faith. If, however, the passages that they propose can be better understood to mean something else, then the appeal to faith is out of place. Having faith in God's promise is not quite the same thing as having faith in one's own interpretation of a passage. This line of reasoning will be examined in detail in the following chapters.

3. Does reason demand that all of God's words have been preserved?

As we have seen, the appeal to faith rests upon the assumption that God has promised perfect preservation in one particular, widely accessible document. This book will test this assumption against the claims of the Bible itself. But the appeal to faith is not the only argument upon which the King James-Only controversy hinges. Equally important is an appeal to reason.

What is this appeal? King James-Only advocates frequently propose that it would be unreasonable to think that God would inspire the Scriptures verbally and deliver them inerrantly if He did not also preserve them perfectly. Ironically, this is one of the arguments that liberals and leftward-leaning evangelicals have employed against the inerrancy of the original documents of Scripture. Inerrancy is worthless, they argue, if it applies only to originals that we do not have. Similarly, the King James-Only proponents argue that verbal inspiration is worthless unless the exact words are preserved. Whether employed by the far Left or the far Right, the argument is the same: what good are inerrant originals if all that we have are flawed copies?

On its face, this argument from reason has a certain appeal. It seems plausible. In this book, however, we will point out that it is a *logical* argument and not a *biblical* argument. As we shall show, the Bible nowhere explicitly links the doctrines of inspiration and inerrancy with a concomitant promise of perfect preservation. Therefore, the authority of Scripture does not stand or fall with the success of this one argument. A person who rejects this logical argument might not be guilty of rejecting Scripture. Because the argument is an attempt to reason logically rather than biblically, it must be evaluated on logical grounds. Here, then, is our third test of the King James-Only proposal. When the King James-Only advocates make their appeal to reason, are they advancing a valid and sound argument? If so, then they might be able to found their case on this argument. On the other hand, if they are simply suggesting what seems plausible to them, then their argument has a much weaker force. Later chapters of this book will offer an extended evaluation of this argument.

4. Does empirical evidence exist to demonstrate that all of God's words have been preserved?

The last question at the heart of the King James-Only debate is about a simple matter of fact: does the actual, empirical evidence substantiate the preservation of all of the words of the original documents of Scripture? The advocates of the King James-Only theory argue that it does. Therefore, they attempt to base their argument upon the empirical evidence.

All of the authors of this book agree with King James Version advocates that the text of Scripture has been preserved and that it has been preserved with a very high degree of accuracy. Enough evidence is available in the manuscripts, the ancient versions, and the citations of the church fathers to place the vast majority of the text beyond question. So the question is *not* whether the words of the originals have been preserved with a high degree of accuracy but whether *all* of the words of the originals, and *only* the words of the originals, have been preserved with absolute and perfect precision. To establish this claim, these pages will challenge the King James-Only advocates to present compelling evidence that shows where a particular manuscript, edited text, or translation of the Bible contains all of the words, and only the words, that were in the original documents.

Sometimes the King James-Only proponents act as if they can make their case by attacking certain manuscripts or texts. They try to cast doubt upon the usefulness of Codex Sinaiticus, Codex Vaticanus, the Ben-Asher Hebrew text, or the Greek text of Westcott and Hort. Even if they are right in rejecting all of these authorities, however, that point still does not prove their conclusions. They must go further. They must show us evidence that will help us to know where we can find all of God's words and only God's words. By their own standards, this source must be publicly accessible. It must have been in continuous use by the people of God. The questions that we will pose are these: how will we know that source when we see it, and what evidence exists to compel acknowledgement of that hypothetical source?

Later chapters in this book will examine some of the proposed evidence in detail. They will generally suggest two lines of reasoning for evaluating the evidence. First, if the standard is *perfect* preservation (*all* of the words and *only* the words of the originals), then all true copies of the originals must contain *exactly* the same words. It will not be enough that two sources are similar. If they differ at all, even in a single word, then they both cannot preserve the words of God perfectly; at least one of them must be corrupted. Therefore, in any instance in which two or more proposed sources differ, only one of them can count as evidence.

Second, given differing sources (whether manuscripts, edited texts, or translations), the King James-Only advocates must provide a convincing method for determining which source is the perfectly preserved source. The criterion of public accessibility is not a sufficient test, for many sources that are publicly accessible disagree with each other in some particular. The King James-Only theory suggests that it was pointless for God to inspire the words if He did not intend to preserve them. We suggest that it was pointless for God to preserve the words if we cannot know—with the assurance of explicit scriptural, logical, or empirical authority—in which specific source God's very words are preserved.

Again—this point cannot be overemphasized—perfect preservation demands that *all* of the words and *only* the words that were in the originals be present. If the King James-Only controversialists begin to equivocate on this point, they have really given away the debate. If they can admit that a legitimate margin of error exists within their sources, then they do not really believe in perfect preservation at all; they do not really believe that all of the very words of God *must be preserved* to have *the Word of God.* If they are willing to recognize two dependable sources that differ on even a single word, then, in principle, they agree with our position. They ought to drop the theological, doctrinal judgments that attend their view and admit that the whole controversy is simply an academic debate over acceptable percentages. Our discussion should turn from theologizing to the doing of textual criticism.

These are the key questions to be addressed in the following pages. Must we have all of the exact words of God to have the Word of God? Does God promise in the Bible that He will perfectly preserve all of the words from the original documents in one particular text, family of texts, edition, or translation? Is it reasonable to insist that He must have done so? Does the evidence indicate that He actually did? To these questions we now turn.

Chapter Notes

1. See Appendix B, "Fundamentalism and the King James-Only Position," for evidence that historic fundamentalism did not espouse a King James-Only position.

Chapter 1

The Background and Origin of the Version Debate

Douglas K. Kutilek

AT PRESENT, THERE IS A WIDESPREAD and enthusiastic movement among conservative Christians, especially among Baptists, that claims that the King James Version (KJV) of the Bible is the only legitimate translation of the Bible in English. Many of these enthusiasts further affirm that the KJV is an infallible, error-free translation, the equal of the Bible in the original languages. Some of them even suggest that the KJV is superior to the Greek and Hebrew texts. A few of them go so far as to assert that no one can be saved unless the KJV is used to show them the way of salvation. These claims must be examined in light of the teachings of Scripture.

In analyzing any movement that has substantially challenged historical, biblical doctrine, some knowledge of the history of that movement, of the "leading lights" involved, and of the events that brought it to its current condition is usually instructive. The fact that the origin of the current King James-Only movement is not obscured by the passage of years but can be distinctly set forth is to our advantage. The principal figures involved at each step in its development can be named and their contribution to the movement pinpointed.

Psychologically, the King James-Only movement has its origin in the quest for certainty.[1] We do not criticize this desire for certainty. Indeed, the Scriptures themselves give us firm ground for certainty about many

27

truths regarding God and His relationship to the world in general and to ourselves in particular. We can be certain, from Scripture, that God has revealed Himself to man, that His self-revelation was recorded inerrantly and infallibly in the Scriptures, that God became incarnate in the person of Jesus Christ, that Christ voluntarily offered Himself on the cross as an all-sufficient sacrifice in payment for our sins, and that all who come to God by Him will not perish but will have everlasting life. These and many related truths we can know with full assurance, for God explicitly states them in His Word.

However, in demanding of God more than an infallible Bible as originally given (2 Peter 1:20–21; 2 Tim. 3:16), some people have "gone beyond that which is written" and have begun to require of God something that He never promised, that is, the infallible and perfect preservation of Scripture in the copying and translating processes. Strangely enough, Dean John W. Burgon (1813–1888), who on one hand is the champion of many people in the King James-Only movement, expressly and emphatically *denied* what this movement affirms: that God ever made any promise in Scripture of the inerrant and infallible transmission of the Bible from the originals. Burgon wrote, ". . . That by a perpetual miracle, Sacred Manuscripts would be protected all down the ages against depraving influences of whatever sort, was not to have been expected; certainly, was never promised."[2]

In spite of Burgon's strong denial, King James-Only proponents demand and expect that God must have given them an infallible Bible, preserving perfect copies of the Greek and Hebrew text. Some of them go further, demanding a perfect translation in English. It is strange indeed, and culturally myopic at best, that those who insist that God *must* have given an infallible Bible translation to them in English nevertheless deny that God has given to anyone such a Bible in any other language. Consistency would lead us to expect that, if He *must* have given a perfect translation to us in English, He *must* have also done the same in Latin, German, French, Spanish, Dutch, Swahili, and Japanese for those who spoke or speak those tongues.

This demand for an absolutely error-free Bible translation did not originate in the twentieth century with the King James-Only movement. It has appeared repeatedly ever since the Bible began to be translated into foreign tongues. We shall survey this phenomenon in general before considering the history of the King James-Only movement in particular.

The Septuagint

The Septuagint (commonly abbreviated LXX) is a translation of the Hebrew Old Testament into Greek. It was made about two centuries before the birth of Christ, probably in Alexandria, Egypt.[3] The chief written source of information about the date and origin of the LXX is the "Letter of Aristeas." This letter, written in Greek about 100 B.C., is a mixture of fact and fable.[4] The letter claims to have been written by an adviser of King Ptolemy Philadelphus of Egypt (r. 285–246 B.C.). According to this letter, Ptolemy solicited for his library a translation of the Jewish Law from Hebrew into Greek. The Jewish high priest sent six scholars from each of the twelve tribes to Alexandria. With them he sent an accurate copy of the Law, written in gold letters on the finest parchment. The seventy-two translators, after feasting with the king and impressing him with their wise answers over a series of days, set about the work of translation.

The work of translating, described very briefly at the end of the letter, reportedly took precisely seventy-two days. Aristeas reports, "They set to completing their several tasks, reaching agreement among themselves on each by comparing versions. The result of their agreement thus was made into a fair copy by Demetrius [the agent of the king]."[5] Later writers interpreted this admittedly obscure statement as a declaration of the precise (and miraculous) verbal agreement of all of the independently made translations by each of the seventy-two translators.

The letter continues with a description of the publication, reception, and preservation of this version.

> The outcome was such that in seventy-two days the business of translation was completed, just as if such result were achieved by some deliberate design. When it was completed, Demetrius assembled the company of the Jews in the place where the task of translation had been finished, and read it to all, in the presence of the translators, who received a great ovation from the crowded audience for being responsible for great blessings. Likewise also they gave an ovation to Demetrius and asked him, now that he had transcribed the whole Law, to give a copy to their leaders. As the books were read, the priests stood up, with the elders of the people, and said, "Since this version has been made rightly and reverently, and in every respect accurately, it is good that this should remain exactly so, and that there should be no revision."

There was general approval of what they said, and they commanded that a curse should be laid, as was their custom, on anyone who should alter the version by any addition or change to
any part of the written text, or any deletion either. This was a
good step taken, to ensure that the words were preserved completely and permanently in perpetuity.[6]

Thus, we see that an aura of unalterable perfection had already begun to
gather around the LXX by 100 B.C. or so.

Philo of Alexandria

The Jewish author Philo of Alexandria (ca. 20 B.C.–ca. A.D. 45) wrote
extensively in Greek, chiefly seeking to harmonize the teachings of
the Old Testament with Greek philosophy. This harmonization was
accomplished primarily by allegorizing the Scriptures. In his extensive
works, Philo quotes from the Bible in Greek translation and shows unmistakable familiarity with the Letter of Aristeas. Philo summarizes
Aristeas' account of the origin and work of making the Greek translation
of the Law of Moses, apparently accepting the supernatural inspiration of
the Greek translation. First, he notes the seriousness with which the translators undertook their task.

Considering among themselves how important the affair was to
translate laws which had been divinely given by direct inspiration, since they were not able either to take away anything, or to
add anything, or to alter anything, but were bound to preserve
the original form and character of the whole composition, they
looked out for the most completely purified place of all the spots
on the outside of the city.[7]

Philo here echoes the desired inalterability of the LXX described in
Aristeas, but he applies it instead to the original Scriptures. Philo then
relates the actual work of translation.

They, like men inspired, prophesied, not one saying one thing
and another, but every one of them employing the self-same
nouns and verbs, as if some unseen prompter had suggested all
their language to them.[8]

The result is thus described:

> If the Chaldeans were to learn the Greek language, and if the
> Greeks were to learn Chaldean [i.e., Hebrew], and if each were
> to meet with those scriptures in both languages, namely, the
> Chaldaic and the translated version, they would admire and rev-
> erence them both as sisters, or rather as one and the same both in
> their facts and in their language; considering these translators
> were not mere interpreters but hierophants and prophets to
> whom it had been granted [to] their honest and guileless minds
> to go along with the most pure spirit of Moses.[9]

Thus, Philo, a resident of Alexandria where the translation work reportedly took place, uncritically accepts the account of Aristeas and goes
beyond Aristeas in interpreting him to say that each of the translators,
working independently, produced verbally identical translations. Philo
finds an explanation for this phenomenon in ascribing to the translators
more than mere human labors. He credits them with having the aid of
the Spirit who originally moved Moses to write the Law. Note also that
Philo limits the work of translation to the Law of Moses.

Josephus

Flavius Josephus (A.D. 37–ca. A.D. 100), like Philo, was aware of the
account of Aristeas. Indeed, Josephus closely paraphrases nearly one
third of the Letter of Aristeas, mentioning Aristeas by name.[10] Because
Josephus's account follows Aristeas closely, it does not, like Philo,
make extravagant claims of perfection or inspiration of the Greek translation, although he does note the provision for the preservation of the
translation from any and all corruption.[11]

Justin Martyr

Born of pagan parents in Samaria about A.D. 100, Justin Martyr became a Christian in his early thirties, and thereafter he spent his life as a
propagator of and an apologist for Christianity until he was martyred for
his faith in A.D. 165.[12] In an apologetic commonly ascribed to him,[13] Justin shows full familiarity with the Aristeas legend of the origin of the
LXX, including Philo's embellishment regarding the precise verbal agreement of all seventy translators. Justin notes that Ptolemy "was struck with

amazement and believed that the translation had been written by divine power."[14] According to Justin, Ptolemy had reportedly required that there be no collusion between the translators so that he could be assured of the accuracy of their version. Justin further notes that he had personally been to Alexandria, had seen the place of translation, and had spoken with local inhabitants about the events surrounding the making of the LXX. He appeals to the accounts of these things in the writings of Philo of Alexandria and Josephus as proof that he has given an accurate account.[15] Justin also declares, "[the fact] that the books relating to our religion [viz., the Old Testament] are to this day preserved among the Jews, has been a work of Divine Providence on our behalf."[16]

Irenaeus

A native of Smyrna in Asia Minor, but having Lyons in Southern Gaul (France) as the chief scene of his ministerial labors, Irenaeus was among the most prominent of Christian leaders in the second half of the second century A.D. He defends the accuracy of the Septuagint translation of Isaiah 7:14, particularly the translation of the Hebrew word *almah* by the Greek word *parthenos,* which means "virgin." He supports the LXX and opposes the revisions made in the verse (namely, making the Hebrew word mean "young woman") by Theodotion and Aquila, Jewish proselytes, and by the Ebionites (that is, the translation of Symmachus).[17]

Irenaeus defends the LXX on several grounds. He cites its pre-Christian Jewish origin, which precludes any pro-Christian bias on the part of the translators. At this point, he relates the Aristeas legend but with certain expansions. First, he asserts that the LXX is the whole Hebrew Old Testament, not just the Law as Aristeas says. (This point is a necessity for Irenaeus because Isaiah, which is under discussion, is not a part of the Law). Second, he inserts into the account, as did Justin, that Ptolemy compelled the translators to work separately:

> But he, wishing to test them individually, and fearing lest they might perchance, by taking counsel together, conceal the truth in the Scriptures, by their interpretation, separated them from each other, and commanded them all to write the same translation. He did this with respect to all the books.[18]

He then notes the amazing result of their separate labors:

> But when they came together in the same place before Ptolemy,
> and each of them compared his own interpretation with that of
> every other, God was indeed glorified, and the Scriptures were
> acknowledged as truly divine. For all of them read out the com-
> mon translation [which they had prepared] in the very same words
> and the very same names, from beginning to end, so that even
> the Gentiles present perceived that the Scriptures had been
> interpreted by the inspiration of God.[19]

Irenaeus defends the ability of God to inspire a translation by appeal to
an event which occurred after the Babylonian exile (as reported in the
apocryphal 2 Esdras 14), when God purportedly "inspired Esdras the priest
of the tribe of Levi, to recast all the words of the former prophets."[20]

Irenaeus continues with claims of the inalterability of the LXX:

> Since, therefore, the Scriptures have been interpreted with such
> fidelity, and by the grace of God, since from these God has
> prepared and formed again our faith towards His Son, and has
> preserved to us the unadulterated Scriptures in Egypt, . . . truly
> these men are proved to be impudent and presumptuous, who
> would now show a desire to make different translations, when
> we refute them out of these Scriptures, . . .[21]

At this point, we must ask, In what particulars does the view of Irenaeus
regarding the LXX differ from the claims of some people today regarding the KJV? Both views claim that the translators were particularly and
specially used by God in the translation process even to the point of claim-
ing a "second inspiration," that God has specifically and distinctly
preserved His unadulterated Word in this translation, and that any who
would dare to revise or alter it in any regard are impudent and presump-
tuous. Both views also go far beyond the original claims regarding the
translation. In the case of the LXX, the Aristean account nowhere claims
unalterable perfection for the LXX. In the case of the KJV, the introduc-
tory "Translators to the Reader," written by translator Miles Smith on
behalf of all of the translators, expressly denies any infallibility or perfection to their work.[22]

Cyril of Jerusalem

Cyril of Jerusalem (ca. A.D. 310–A.D. 386) conveys the same account of the origin of the LXX as presented by Justin Martyr and Irenaeus. He views the whole Old Testament (not just the Law) as the object of the translator's labors, he asserts the separate and isolated labors of each translator, and he espouses belief in the resultant seventy-two identical copies. Cyril instructs the reader of his catechism: "read the Divine Scriptures, the twenty-two books of the Old Testament, these that have been translated by the Seventy-two interpreters . . ." he explains, "for the process was no word-craft, nor contrivance of human devices; but the translation of the Divine Scriptures, spoken by the Holy Ghost, was of the Holy Ghost accomplished."[23]

Augustine and After

Augustine of Hippo (A.D. 354–A.D. 430), the most influential of the Latin "fathers," mentions the subject of the LXX in his *magnum opus, The City of God*. After relating the Aristean account in the form known to Irenaeus and others, he notes that although other, more recent Greek versions of the OT exist (he expressly mentions four), "nevertheless the church has received this Septuagint as if it were the only translation, and the Christian peoples of the Greek world use it, most of them being quite unaware whether there is any other."[24] Those Greek Christians were, then, "LXX Only."

Augustine mentions the Latin translation of the Septuagint, a translation of a translation that was then in common use among Latin-speaking Christians, and he also mentions the work of Jerome, who translated the Old Testament into Latin from the Hebrew original. Augustine declares that, in spite of Jerome's abilities, the work of this one man should not be preferred over the combined labors of many men, that is, the seventy Septuagint translators.

> The churches of Christ have passed judgment that no man is to be set above the authority of such a number, who were chosen for this great task by Eleazar, who was then high priest. For even supposing that there had not appeared among them one Spirit that was beyond doubt divine, and that the seventy learned men had like ordinary men compared the words of their translations so that what proved acceptable to all should stand approved, even

so no one translator should be preferred to them. But since so great a sign of divinity was manifested in their case, it is certain that any other faithful translator of these Scriptures from the Hebrew into any other language either agrees with the Septuagint translators, or else, if he is seen not to agree with them, we must believe that the greater prophetic depth is found in the other version.[25]

Of course, the *a priori* assumption of the divine inspiration of the LXX creates problems, especially when on good authority (namely, Jerome and Jews who were knowledgeable in Hebrew) it is pointed out that differences exist between the Hebrew text and the LXX translation. What was Augustine's solution to the problem of discrepancies? Both, he said, are the work of the Holy Spirit!

For the same Spirit that was in the prophets when they delivered those messages was present in person in the seventy men also; and he surely had it in his power to say something else, just as if the prophet had said both, because it was the same Spirit that said both. And the Spirit could say the very thing in different ways, so that though the words were not the same, yet, when they should be properly understood, the same meaning should shed its light through them; and he could omit or add something, so as to show in this way too that the work was not accomplished by a man enslaved to a literal rule of thumb, but by the power of God flooding and guiding the intelligence of the translator.[26]

What about discrepancies between the Hebrew original and the LXX Greek version? Should corrections be made?

Some, to be sure, have supposed that the Greek manuscripts of the Septuagint translation should be corrected by the Hebrew manuscripts; yet they have not dared to expunge what the Hebrew lacks and the Septuagint set down, but only added what was found in the Hebrew, though lacking in the Septuagint.[27]

What is the proper course to follow when the Hebrew original and "inspired" Greek translation are at odds?

If, then we see, as it behooves us to see, in these Scriptures no
words that the Spirit of God did not speak through men, it follows that whatever is in the Hebrew text but not in that of the
seventy translators is something that the Spirit of God did not
choose to say through the latter, but only through the prophets.
On the other hand, where anything that is in the Septuagint is
not in the Hebrew text, the same Spirit must have preferred to
say it through the former rather than through the prophets, thus
showing that these as well as those were prophets.[28]

Thus, according to Augustine, both the original Hebrew and the
Greek translation were deemed inspired (the former opinion based on
the self-testimony of the Scriptures and the latter view based solely on
legend and human embellishments). Where the Greek translation has
information new or different from the original Hebrew, it is, in effect,
a new revelation from the Spirit. This is precisely parallel to the claim
by some people that the KJV has new revelations in advance of the inspired
original texts.

Both the Eastern Orthodox Church and the Roman Catholic Church
recognize the tradition of the church fathers as having authority equal to
or even greater than that of written Scripture. As a consequence of the
excessive, even superstitious, view of the Septuagint first propagated in
the "Letter of Aristeas," then accepted by Philo and Josephus, and finally
adopted and exaggerated by several of the early church fathers, these
groups, especially the Eastern Orthodox Church, to this day accept the
Septuagint as divinely inspired. Timothy Ware wrote,

> As the authoritative text of the Old Testament, [the Orthodox
> Church] uses the ancient Greek translation known as the
> Septuagint. When this differs from the original Hebrew [which
> happens quite often], Orthodox believe the changes in the
> Septuagint were made under the inspiration of the Holy Spirit,
> and are to be accepted as part of God's continuing revelation.[29]

Unfortunately, Ware cites no official church documents, decrees, or
councils to support his affirmation. Yet, the expressed affirmations of several church fathers who assert their belief in the inspiration of the LXX
seem sufficient authority for the Orthodox Church to adopt this view.

Poorly founded belief in the perfect rendition of a single translation is nothing new to religious thought.

The Targum Onkelos

Many of the Jews of the New Testament and post-New Testament era did not know Greek and therefore were unable to use the Septuagint. Their native language was Aramaic. Therefore, they felt the need for a translation of the Law into that tongue. Ultimately, an officially approved and sanctioned Aramaic translation of the Law was produced. That translation is known as the Targum Onkelos, *targum* meaning "translation" or "interpretation," and Onkelos being the name of the man to whom the translation is traditionally credited. This translation achieved "canonical" status among the Jews, as expert in Rabbinic literature John Gill relates:

> His [i.e., Onkelos's] targum is in great esteem with the Jews, as appears from its being inserted after the text of Moses, verse for verse, in the ancient manuscripts of the Pentateuch, and is in continual use with them. Elias Levitas says, we are obliged, every week, to read a section [of the law] twice, once in the Scripture, and once in the Targum of Onkelos. Indeed, they too much magnify this version, and make it equal with the sacred Scripture; the sense of it they represent as traditionally handed down from Mount Sinai, which being delivered from one to another, he [Onkelos] received it from the mouth of R. Eliezer and R. Joshua; and they say, that when he added any thing, it was not from his own judgment, but was given him from Sinai.[30]

Such claims, especially the explanation of the origin of additions to the original text, are reminiscent of Augustine's explanation of the origins of expansions in the LXX. The only difference is that what Augustine ascribed to a second act of inspiration by the Spirit, the Jews ascribed to an unbroken chain of oral tradition from Sinai to Onkelos.

The Peshitta Syriac

In places more remote from the Greek-speaking regions of the Orthodox Church, other "vernacular" versions attained an authoritative status similar to that of the LXX in the Greek Church. Among the Syrian

Orthodox, the Peshitta Syriac version is invested with virtually absolute authority. The Peshitta has been the sole Syriac version in ecclesiastical use in the Syrian Church since the middle of the fifth century.[31] George Lamsa, from a Syrian Orthodox background, made an English translation of the Peshitta. In the preface to that version, he quotes Mar Eshai Shimun, Patriarch of the Church of the East, as saying that "the Peshitta is the text of the Church of the East which has come down from the Biblical times without any change or revision." Lamsa, in his "Introduction," claims that there are no variations in the manuscripts, and both Christians and Muslims universally accept and revere the Peshitta as authoritative.[32]

The Latin Vulgate

The Council of Trent in 1546 issued a decree in which the absolute authority of the Latin Vulgate translation of Jerome was expressly adopted as official Church doctrine.

> Moreover, the same sacred and holy Synod,—considering that no small utility may accrue to the Church of God, if it be made known which out of all the Latin editions [i.e., translations], now in circulation, of the sacred books, is to be held as authentic,—ordains and declares, that the said old and vulgate edition, which by the lengthened usage of so many ages, has been approved of in the Church, be, in public lectures, disputations, sermons, and expositions, held as authentic; and that no one is to dare, or presume to reject it under any pretext whatever.[33]

This decree of the Council of Trent was not an innovation but merely a formal, official statement of the view generally held in the Roman Catholic Church. The doctrine was made official as a reaction to the proliferation of various Latin translations of the Bible made in the Reformation era. To a lesser degree, this pronouncement was also a response to both the appeals by Protestants to the authority of the original language texts, and the production of vernacular translations in the various languages of Western Europe.

Even Erasmus (1466–1536), a Roman Catholic priest and the editor of the first published Greek New Testament, published a revised Latin translation of the New Testament in parallel with the Greek text, which he issued in 1516. The reaction to Erasmus' new Latin translation w:

swift and hostile. Roland Bainton gives some account of the vehemence of Erasmus' adversaries, in a quotation valuable not only because it sets forth the common Roman Catholic view of the Vulgate but also because it gives Erasmus' masterful refutation of this error:

[Martin] Dorp was shocked and outraged to hear that Erasmus proposed to publish the New Testament in Greek and accompanied by a new translation. To be sure, Ambrose and Augustine had not depended on Jerome's translation, but after he had castigated all of the errors his rendering had become standard as the basis for the decrees of councils. "What councils?" demanded Erasmus, "There were Greek councils which did not know Latin at all." "Don't listen to the Greeks," said Dorp. "They were heretics." "But," rejoined Erasmus, "Aristotle was even a pagan. Will you not read him? If you claim that the Vulgate is inspired equally with the original Greek and Hebrew and that to touch it is heresy and blasphemy what will you say of Bede, Rhabanus, Thomas Aquinas, and Nicolas of Lyra, not to mention others who undertook to make improvements? You must distinguish between Scripture, the translation of Scripture, and the transmission of both. What will you do with errors of copyists?" Dorp was later persuaded and Erasmus was thereby confirmed in his judgment that courtesy rather than invective is the better way to win over an opponent. A sharper antagonist was Sutor, once of the Sorbonne, later a Carthusian who asserted that "if in one point the Vulgate were in error the entire authority of Holy Scripture would collapse, love and faith would be extinguished, heresies and schisms would abound, blasphemy would be committed against the Holy Spirit, the authority of theologians would be shaken, and indeed the Catholic Church would collapse from the foundations." Erasmus pointed out that prior to Jerome the early Church had not used the Vulgate and had not collapsed. To all who cried, "Jerome is good enough for me," he replied, "You cry out that it is a crime to correct the gospels. This is a speech worthier of a coachman than of a theologian. You think it is all very well if a clumsy scribe makes a mistake in transcription and then you deem it a crime to put it right. The only way to determine the true text is to examine the early codices."[34]

J. A. Froude also notes both the common Catholic view of the Vulgate's inspiration and the extreme hostility shown toward Erasmus by individuals prejudiced against his revised Latin version:

> Pious, ignorant men had regarded the text of the Vulgate as sacred, and probably inspired. Read it intelligently they could not, but they had made the language into an idol, and they were filled with horrified amazement when they found in page after page that Erasmus had anticipated modern criticism, correcting the text, introducing various readings and retranslating passages from the Greek into a new version. He had altered a word in the Lord's prayer. Horror of horrors! he had changed the translation of the mystic LogoV from *Verbum* into *Sermo,* to make people understand what LogoV meant.[35]

Of course, the Roman Catholic Church was long plagued with trying to produce an "infallible" edition of the Vulgate. In 1590, Pope Sixtus V produced an official edition that was set forth as *the* standard Vulgate text, and dire threats were made toward anyone who would dare to presume to revise or alter the text in any way. Two years and four popes later, Pope Clement VIII issued a revision of Sixtine's text, differing from it in nearly five thousand places. It is conceded today that neither of these is an accurate presentation of the Vulgate as originally written.[36]

Perhaps the finest single statement made in refuting the notion of an infallible Vulgate translation (or any other Bible version) is that made more than two hundred years ago by renowned London Baptist preacher and scholar John Gill (1697–1771). In delimiting to what the quality of inspiration does (and does not) apply, he wrote,

> This [i.e., inspiration] is to be understood of the Scriptures, as in the original languages in which they were written, and not of translations; unless it could be thought, that the translators of the Bible into the several languages of the nations into which it has been translated, were under divine inspiration also in translating, and were directed of God in the use of words they have rendered the original by; but this is not reasonable to suppose. The books of the Old Testament were written chiefly in the Hebrew language, unless some few passages in Jeremiah, Daniel,

Ezra, and Esther in the Chaldee language; and the New Testament in Greek: in which languages they can only be reckoned canonical and authentic; for this is like the charters and diplomas of princes; the wills or testaments of men; or any deeds made by them; only the exemplar is authentic; and not translations, and transcriptions, and copies of them, though ever so perfect: and to the Bible, in its original languages, is every translation to be brought, and judged, and to be corrected and amended; and if this was not the case, we should have no certain and infallible rule to go by; for it must be either all the translations together, or some one of them; not all of them, because they agree not in all things: not one; for then the contest would be between one nation and another which it should be, whether English, Dutch, French, &c. and could one be agreed upon, it could not be read and understood by all: so the papists, they plead for their vulgate Latin version; which has been decreed authentic by the council of Trent; though it abounds with innumerable errors and mistakes; nay, so far do they carry this affair, that they even assert that the Scriptures, in their originals, ought to submit to, and be corrected by their version; which is absurd and ridiculous.[37]

Virtually every argument used in the sixteenth century to defend the Vulgate against any revision is employed today by King James-Only advocates in their rejection of modern English translations: its long use by the churches, the blessing of God upon it over many years, the danger of abandoning a single standard, and other similar arguments. The refutation made of these fallacious arguments by Erasmus and Gill applies with equal force to the arguments set forth to defend the perfection of the KJV.

Luther's German Bible

No book had a greater impact on the Reformation in Germany than Luther's own translation of the Hebrew and Greek Scriptures into German. Although numerous German translations had been made and printed before Luther's work, all had been based on the Latin Vulgate and were rather meager productions.[38] When Luther's New Testament first appeared in September 1522, "some indiscreet friends of the reformer, impressed by the beauty of the translation, imagined they could recognize in it a second inspiration."[39] Luther himself never entertained such extravagant notions but continued to revise and correct his translation as long as he lived.[40] Nevertheless, some people seem to have persisted even into the nineteenth century in seeing Luther's version as "inspired."[41]

Claims of an Inspired KJV Before the Modern King James-Only Movement

Some people might wonder why, in a study of the King James-Only movement, so much attention has been given to claims made centuries earlier of the inspiration and infallibility of translations of the Bible into Greek, Aramaic, Syriac, Latin, and German. The answer is simple: philosophically, psychologically, and theologically, these earlier claims are all of a piece with the King James-Only movement. The line of argument is the same in each case: God had His hand in a special way on the translators, the translation has proved its superiority (indeed, inspiration) by its long use and the manifest blessing of God upon it, any revision would undermine the authority of the Bible, revisers have sinister and dangerous motives, and so on. The fact that zealous but misguided men of the past have ascribed inspiration and infallibility—a quality possessed by only the original Scriptures—to translations in Greek, Aramaic, Latin, Syriac, and German would lead us to suspect that some people might be inclined to make similar unfounded claims regarding some English Bible version. Indeed, not surprisingly, we do find evidence of the same, not only in the modern King James-Only movement but also before it and indeed separate and unconnected with it.

Henry Alford (1810–1871), noted English New Testament scholar and a member of the English Revised Version translation committee, mentions, in passing, the belief of some people whom he knew that the KJV was infallible. In his comments on Hebrews 10:23, he remarks,

We have here an extraordinary example of the persistence of a blunder through the centuries. The word *"faith,"* given here by the A.V., instead of **hope**—breaking up the beautiful triad of vv. 22, 23, 24,—faith, hope, love,—was a *mere mistake,* **hope** being the original, without any variety of reading, and **hope** being accordingly the rendering of all the English versions previously to 1611. And yet this is the version which some would have us regard as infallible, and receive as the written word of God![42]

Spencer Cone (1785–1855) was one of the eminent Baptist pastors and leaders in the first half of the nineteenth century in America. He served by turns in the leadership of the American Bible Society, the American and Foreign Bible Society, and the American Bible Union. He was center stage in the controversy that raged among Baptists of that era over the question of sponsoring a revision of the KJV, an idea that Cone favored. His biography, written by his sons, gives an extended account of this controversy and mentions the extreme position adopted by some of Cone's adversaries:

> A great deal had been said in regard to the translation and translators of the Scriptures. He [Cone] had heard his brethren here utter the most singular remarks in relation to the forty-nine translators appointed by King James; and some had gone so far as to pronounce the Bible as translated by the distinguished forty-nine, *a perfect work!*[43]

Baptist pastor and historian Thomas Armitage (1819–1896) was closely associated with Spencer Cone in his leadership of the American Bible Union and was his successor as president of that organization. In his famous Baptist history, Armitage also notes some of the excessive claims made by some of the Baptist brethren at a particularly acrimonious meeting during the Bible revision controversy: "Many others also talked as much at random, as if they feared that the book which they hinted *had come down from heaven in about the present shape, printed and bound,* was now to be taken from them by force."[44]

Basil Manly Jr. (1825–1892) was one of the founding professors of Southern Baptist Theological Seminary. In his book on the biblical doctrine of inspiration, he addresses and refutes some faulty views of the subject:

> We do not deny that there have been some wild and unfounded assertions on the subject, just as there is now, with some ignorant persons, an assumption of the infallibility and equality with the original of some particular translation, as the Vulgate, or King James's, or Luther's. But we are not responsible for such statements.[45]

These citations are sufficient to show that the modern King James-Only movement is not without precedent, although no traceable connection exists between those of the nineteenth century who held such a view with those of the latter part of the twentieth century. That they are of the same mindset, no one need doubt, just as they are philosophically one with those who claim inspiration for the Septuagint, Vulgate, Targum Onkelos, Peshitta Syriac, and Luther's German version.

The Modern "King James–Only" Movement

Having surveyed the enduring concept of "perfect" and "inspired" translations of Scripture in general, we now turn to the modern King James-Only movement in particular. How did the twentieth-century King James-Only movement begin? Who were the principals in bringing this movement to its current state?

Benjamin G. Wilkinson

The beginning of the modern movement that asserts the essential inspiration and inerrancy of the King James Version of the Bible in English can certainly be traced to the publication of a book in 1930.[46] That book, *Our Authorized Bible Vindicated,* was written by Seventh-Day Adventist missionary, educator, and theologian Benjamin G. Wilkinson (1872–1968). That Wilkinson was an Adventist was not widely known (and was not announced by those who did know it). The book was little noticed when it was first released and for good reason. It was full of misinformation, inaccuracies, defective reasoning, and distortion.[47] Wilkinson, for example, was the first person to assert that the Old Latin version, instead of the Vulgate, was the Bible of the medieval Waldensians and that the Old Latin corresponds textually with the Greek Textus Receptus, both of which assertions are demonstrably false.[48] He was the first person to demonize Westcott and Hort, making them the "bogey men" in the text and translation debate often by distorting their words.[49] Wilkinson was also the first person to misapply Psalm 12:6–7 as though it were a promise of the preservation of the KJV.[50] Apparently, one of the reasons for his strong disliking of the English Revised Version was that it robbed him of several favorite Adventist proof texts. For example, in Acts 13:42 a change in the Greek text deprived Wilkinson of evidence that Gentiles observed the Sabbath, and in Hebrews 9:27 a translation more literal than the KJV took away a proof text for soul sleep. Note that Wilkinson did not go so far as to affirm either the perfect preservation or inspiration of the KJV but only maintained its superiority over the English Revised Version in both its underlying Greek text and the English translation.

James Jasper Ray

Wilkinson's book lay largely unnoticed and without influence for a quarter of a century until it came to the attention of James Jasper Ray, a Baptist Bible teacher in the Pacific Northwest. Ray apparently was so poorly acquainted with the topics found in Wilkinson's book that he was unable to detect the vast quantity of misinformation it contained. Heavily dependent on and extensively copying verbatim from the work of Wilkinson, Ray published the book *God Wrote Only One Bible* (1955), which, in spite of its lack of merit, has been repeatedly reprinted to this day.[51] Among other errors, Ray adopts Wilkinson's misinterpretation and misapplication of Psalm 12:6–7 as though it were a promise of the preservation of the KJV. Ray was apparently the first to suggest that no one can be saved through use of a Bible based on any other text than the Textus Receptus.[52] Notably, he did not claim that the KJV was unalterably perfect, and he even acknowledged that the KJV does contain translation errors and needs revision.[53]

David Otis Fuller

Ray's book kept alive the errors of Wilkinson and transmitted them to later writers and editors. Chief among the subsequent propagators of Wilkinson's views was David Otis Fuller. Fuller, who died in the late 1980s, was a long-time Regular Baptist pastor in Michigan. According to Fuller's own words in his book *Counterfeit or Genuine?* he was "moved to begin this fascinating faith-inspiring study" by Ray's book *God Wrote Only One Bible.*[54] Ray and his book are also repeatedly mentioned in Fuller's 1970 volume *Which Bible?*[55]

Fuller's book *Which Bible?* has perhaps been most responsible for fanning the flames of the King James-Only controversy in recent years.[56] Nearly one-half of *Which Bible?* is an edited reprint of much of Wilkinson's *Our Authorized Bible Vindicated.* Curiously, *Which Bible?* was not published until just *after* Wilkinson's death in 1968.

In reproducing Wilkinson's material in *Which Bible?* Fuller carefully concealed Wilkinson's theological orientation by deleting footnote references to the writings of Adventist prophetess Ellen G. White, although

he left the quotes themselves in the text. Fuller also deleted other statements in Wilkinson's book that would have immediately disclosed
Wilkinson's Adventism.[57] Fuller did attempt, via footnotes, to correct
some of Wilkinson's grosser errors, but by no means did he correct all of
the errors in the material he reprinted. Fuller praised Wilkinson as a great
scholar and a reliable author in spite of the gross blunders that Fuller
himself had discovered in the book. Fuller never informed the reader
that the text had been edited, or that some of the footnotes were his own
and not Wilkinson's.

Fuller distorted the views of other great Christian men of the past,
men whom he professed to admire, especially Charles Spurgeon and
Robert Dick Wilson. Fuller compiled and widely distributed a single
page of excerpted "quotations" from Spurgeon's last address to the Pastors' College Conference, "The Greatest Fight in the World," also commonly known as "Spurgeon's Final Manifesto."[58] As edited and assembled
by Fuller, the quotations seem to present Spurgeon as a strong "King
James-Only/Textus Receptus-Only" advocate who vigorously denounced both the Greek text of Westcott and Hort and the English Revised Version. But when read in context and in full, Spurgeon's remarks
make clear that he was not even addressing these subjects and in fact
contradicts what Fuller wanted the reader to think that Spurgeon
believed.[59]

As for Robert Dick Wilson, one of Fuller's professors at Princeton
Seminary, Fuller claimed that his views and those of Wilson were exactly
alike. In a letter by Fuller published in 1980, Fuller wrote,

> In more than fifty years of my ministry I have taught and preached
> the FACT that the King James Version is my final and absolute
> authority. I take the identical stand my Hebrew professor at
> Princeton Seminary took, the renowned Robert Dick Wilson
> B. F. [before the foul flood of apostasy inundated those sacred
> walls]. I well remember him in Hebrew class saying, "Gentle-
> men, the things I do not understand in the Bible [and he had
> clear reference to the King James Version] I put down to my
> own ignorance."[60]

Anyone familiar with the published writings of Wilson knows assur-
edly that the view that Fuller imputes to Wilson was *not,* in fact, what

Wilson believed. Wilson expressly looked to the original language text and not any translation as his final authority, and he expressly stated that in some cases even the Masoretic Hebrew text of the Old Testament required correction and emendation on the basis of ancient translations to restore the text to its original condition.[61]

In 1978, Fuller became a founder and the first president of "The Dean Burgon Society," an organization dedicated to King James-Only views. The appropriation of Burgon's name (and hence his fame and reputation) to this society seems highly incongruous. Although Burgon was indeed a vigorous opponent of the Greek text of Westcott and Hort, he never seems to have attacked them personally as do Fuller and others. Also, while Burgon strongly denounced the English Revised Version as a whole, he nevertheless recognized that the Textus Receptus needed to be corrected on the basis of manuscript evidence.[62] Burgon further acknowledged that the KJV is in need of revision, even admitting that in some places the English Revised Version is an improvement over the KJV.[63] Gary Hudson, on these and other bases, asserted that, were Dean Burgon alive today, he would not be a member of The Dean Burgon Society.[64]

Peter S. Ruckman

A second writer who came under the direct influence of J. J. Ray is Peter S. Ruckman. Ruckman has pastored a small congregation in Pensacola, Florida, for four decades. Ruckman is without any doubt the most caustic and abusive among King James-Only partisans, typically denouncing conservative Bible scholars such as B. B. Warfield and A.T. Robertson, lumping them together in the same vituperation with Julius Wellhausen, Harry Fosdick, and Adolf Hitler. He is also the most singularly inaccurate writer in the fray, neither presenting the truth nor apparently caring enough to discover the truth. Even many of those who advocate a King James-Only position disassociate themselves from Peter Ruckman.

Ruckman's first book on the Bible translation controversy, *The Bible Babel,* issued in 1964, shows unmistakable dependence on Ray's book.[65] In a published review of Ruckman's literary firstborn, Zane Hodges warned the reader, "So distorted indeed is so much of the material presented that any reader would be well-advised to trust nothing which he cannot verify."[66] Unfortunately, too few readers have heeded Hodges' advice.

Since his first literary effort, Ruckman has continued a steady stream of vitriol in his monthly magazine, *The Bible Believer's Bulletin,* as well as in a growing series of books. Besides his coarse and often profane language and vicious style, Ruckman has done the disservice to his readers of exposing them to vast quantities of misinformation. He is the person who fabricated the false view that the Septuagint originated in the third century A.D.[67] He has also claimed that no Protestant scholar has ever seen the Vaticanus manuscript.[68] He has falsely asserted that the KJV is not copyrighted.[69] He claims that the KJV has genuine advanced revelations, containing new information not found in the original Scriptures.[70] He dogmatically and erroneously asserts that Luther's German Bible contained 1 John 5:7.[71] He was the person who first claimed that the KJV has won more souls than the original manuscripts.[72] A horde of other errors of fact crowd Ruckman's every work.

Wilkinson, then, forms the first generation in the rise of the King James–Only movement, with Ray in the second generation, and Fuller and Ruckman in the third generation. These latter two men have generated an immense following, including such notables as Jack Chick, D. A. Waite, E. L. Bynum, Jack Hyles, David W. Cloud, and Gail Riplinger. Links can be traced back to Fuller or Ruckman or both from all modern King James–Only advocates and, from them, back through Ray to Wilkinson.

Edward F. Hills

Another individual who made a sizable contribution to the King James–Only movement, although not drawing directly from the works of Wilkinson and Ray, is Edward F. Hills (1912–1981). Hills actually possessed genuine academic credentials in New Testament textual criticism. His chief contribution to the King James–Only controversy was in the development and elaboration of a view that asserted that the Textus Receptus, as followed by the KJV, contained the precise form of the preserved Word of God.[73] In reality, Hills's view is not one of Divine *preservation,* but rather one of Divine *restoration,* since he frankly admits that a number of readings in the Textus Receptus are not found in Greek manuscripts but were ostensibly lost in antiquity, only to be *restored* to the Greek text on the basis of the Latin Vulgate at the time of the Reformation.

Unfortunately, Hills's writings must be characterized as highly suppositional. He assumes, *a priori,* that the Greek text followed by the KJV is *the* correct text and must be maintained at all costs, regardless of the evidence, even in the absence of supporting evidence and the presence of strong contradictory evidence.

Hills expressly rejects many characteristic King James-Only lines of argument. For example, he recognizes a pre-Christian date for the Septuagint and admits that numerous readings in the Textus Receptus were inserted by Erasmus solely on the authority of the Latin Vulgate. Nevertheless, those who espouse a King James-Only position often appeal to Hills, apparently because he gives scholarly "credentials" to the movement, which otherwise looks askance at scholars. Hills's argument provides some antecedents for the King James-Only movement's unique doctrine of the perfect preservation of Scripture in the Textus Receptus.

The Impact of the King James-Only Movement

The influence of the King James-Only viewpoint has become widespread and strong. Unfortunately, the effects of this movement have often been highly destructive. Beside the strife and dissension that many organizations have faced, some groups have actually split over this issue. Many local churches have faced similar, unfortunate conflict and division. The King James-Only movement has spilled over onto mission fields, causing distress in national churches and alienating missionaries from each other. It has led some American missionaries to denounce reliable foreign language translations simply because those translations were not based on or did not always agree with the KJV. What is most unfortunate is that all of this schism is grounded in a belief that has no biblical basis: that the original autographs of Scripture have been perfectly preserved in a particular text, text family, or English translation.[74]

Accepting the tenets of the King James-Only movement has become a standard of orthodoxy for many people. Unfortunately, belief in this one standard, the King James Only, often seems to excuse unorthodoxy in other areas. If a man or woman believes in adherence to only the KJV, he or she often overlooks other doctrinal, ethical, or moral errors. Sometimes, little else really seems to matter.

The King James-Only movement has been more destructive and distractive among Baptists than any controversy since the Campbellite heresy of the nineteenth century. This modern movement may well exceed the Campbellites in its overall evil effects. The modern King James-Only movement began small. It found its roots in an obscure, Seventh-Day

Adventist book that lay neglected for a quarter of a century. A subsequent author accepted much of this information (or misinformation). Then these theories were spread to others who, in turn, propagated them to still others. Few voices were raised against the growing error of the King James-Only movement in its first two decades, the 1950s and 1960s. A few people began to resist it in the 1970s, but many others accommodated the error and placated its adherents for the sake of harmony and unity, not fully understanding its long-term consequences. The battle was fully joined only in the 1980s and 1990s, when a few Bible teachers, pastors, churches, and schools began to call one another to reaffirm the true, historic, and biblically consistent doctrine of inspiration, inerrancy, and providential preservation of Scripture.

In truth, the King James-Only movement has not created any new doctrines. Claims of divinely assisted translators and infallible versions, perfect providential preservation, new revelations in translations, and corrections to original language texts based on later translations are old errors. All of these ideas were espoused in the past for Bible versions in Greek, Aramaic, Syriac, Latin, and German. Applying these old errors to an English translation today does not make them any less erroneous. In the past, belief in the perfect preservation, inspiration, inerrancy, or infalliblity of any one particular Bible translation was roundly and deservedly rejected by Christian leaders such as Gill, Spurgeon, and many others who took the Scriptures as their sole guide for faith and practice. We, like they, are bound to defend what the Scriptures clearly teach, just as we are bound to speak out against that which errs from the clear teachings of Scripture.

Chapter Notes

1. The subject of this movement's "quest for certainty" is addressed in detail in chapter 4, "The Preservation of Scripture and the Version Debate."

2. John W. Burgon, *The Revision Revised* (1883; reprint, Paradise, Pa.: Conservative Classics, n.d.), 335.

3. One of the unsupported assumptions of some in the modern King James-Only movement is the claim that the LXX dates from *after* the time of Christ and is the work of Origen of Alexandria (ca. A.D. 185–ca. A.D. 254). This peculiar view originated with Peter S. Ruckman and was espoused, apparently, to avoid the fact that Christ and the apostles in the New Testament frequently quote from the LXX, a translation that those in the Kin

James-Only movement admit to be imperfect. The logical corollary of Jesus' and the NT writers' use of a less-than-perfect translation (the LXX) is that we today can also use a translation effectively, even though it falls short of the perfection of the inspired original. This conclusion, however, destroys the very foundation of the King James-Only movement. For a refutation of the claim of a post-New Testament origin of the LXX, see Doug Kutilek, "The Septuagint: Riplinger's Blunders, Believe It or Not," *Baptist Biblical Heritage* 5, no. 2 (3d quarter 1994): 3–4, 12.

4. The "Letter" was certainly written before the death of Philo of Alexandria, ca. A.D. 50, because Philo displays knowledge of the contents of the letter. The complete text of the Letter of Aristeas in English translation by R. J. H. Shutt may be found in James H. Charlesworth, ed., *The Old Testament Pseudepigrapha*, vol. 2 (Garden City, N.Y.: Doubleday, 1985), 12–34. The complete Greek text may be found in Henry Barclay Swete, *An Introduction to the Old Testament in Greek*, rev. Richard Rusden Ottley (1914; reprint, New York: Ktav, 1968), 533–606.

5. Paragraph 302 of the Letter of Aristeas according to Shutt's translation as found in Charlesworth, *Old Testament Pseudepigrapha*, 2:32–33.

6. Ibid., pars. 307b–311, 2:33.

7. Philo, *The Life of Moses*, 2.5–7, in C. D. Yonge, *The Works of Philo*, updated ed. (Peabody, Mass.: Hendrickson, 1993), 493–94.

8. Ibid.

9. Ibid.

10. *Antiquities of the Jews*, bk. 12, chap. 2, as found in Ralph Marcus, trans., *Josephus*, vol. 7 (Cambridge, Mass.: Harvard University Press, 1986), 8–9 note b. An older translation of Josephus's whole account can be found in William Whiston, trans., *The Works of Josephus*, vol. 3 (reprint, Grand Rapids: Baker, 1979), 149–63.

11. Marcus, *Josephus*, 55. Both Philo and Josephus, *not later than the first century a.d.*, are aware of and do not dispute the account of the origin of a Greek translation of the Law as related in the Letter of Aristeas. This awareness is unchallengable proof that the Greek version of the Old Testament known as the Septuagint existed in their day and would certainly have been available to the writers of the New Testament. Those who claim a third century A.D. origin for the Septuagint not only have no basis in fact for their claim but also contradict this clear and irrefutable evidence of their error.

12. G. L. Carey, "Justin Martyr," in *The New International Dictionary of the Christian Church*, ed. J. D. Douglas, 2d ed. (Grand Rapids: Zondervan, 1978), 558.

13. Marcus Dods, trans., "Justin's Hortatory Address to the Greeks," in *The Apostolic Fathers with Justin Martyr and Irenaeus,* ed. Alexander Roberts and James Donaldson (reprint, Grand Rapids: Eerdmans, 1979), 278–79. Some people, including Johannes Quasten, *Patrology,* vol. 1 (Utrecht, Holland: Spectrum, n.d.), 205, believe this work to be pseudonymous and, therefore, falsely ascribed to Justin. The alleged third century date of writing, if pseudonymous, still makes it an early testimony regarding the view of the LXX current among early Christians.

14. Dods, "Justin's Hortatory Address to the Greeks," 278–79.

15. Ibid., 279.

16. Ibid.

17. See chapter 21 of "Irenaeus against Heresies," in *Apostolic Fathers with Justin Martyr and Irenaeus,* ed. Roberts and Donaldson, 451.

18. Ibid.

19. Ibid., 451–52.

20. Ibid., 452.

21. Ibid.

22. See F. H. A. Scrivener, "The Translators to the Reader: Preface to the King James Version," in *The Authorized Edition of the English Bible (1611), Its Subsequent Reprints and Modern Representatives* (Cambridge: At the University Press, 1884), 267–304. A complete copy of "The Translators to the Reader" may be found in appendix C of this book. This document is essential reading for everyone interested in this debate. In it, the KJV translators themselves clearly disavow the very elements upon which King James-Only advocates attempt to build their case. The "Translators to the Reader" is discussed in more detail in chapter 2, "The Old Testament Text and the Version Debate."

23. "Catechetical Lectures," lecture 4, pars. 33–34, in Edward Hamilton Gifford, trans., "The Catechetical Lectures of S. Cyril," in *A Select Library of the Nicene and Post-Nicene Fathers of the Christian Church,* ed. Philip Schaff and Henry Wace, 2d series, vol. 7 (reprint, Grand Rapids: Eerdmans, 1989), 26–27.

24. W. C. Greene, trans., *Saint Augustine: The City of God against the Pagans,* vol. 6 (London: William Heinemann, 1969), bk. 18, chaps. 42–43, p. 31.

25. Ibid.

26. Ibid., 31, 33.

27. Ibid., 33.

28. Ibid., 33, 35.

29. Timothy Ware, *The Orthodox Church* (New York: Penguin Books, 1964), 208.

30. John Gill, *An Exposition of the New Testament,* vol. 1 (1852–1854; reprint, Grand Rapids: Baker, 1980), vi–viii.

31. T. H. Darlow and H. F. Moule, comps., *Historical Catalogue of the Printed Editions of the Holy Scripture in the Library of the British and Foreign Bible Society,* vol. 2, part 3 (London: British and Foreign Bible Society, 1903–1911), 1527.

32. George M. Lamsa, *The Holy Bible from Ancient Eastern Manuscripts* (Philadelphia: A. J. Holman, 1957), i, ii, v, vi, viii, xii. The subtitle calls the Peshitta "The Authorized Bible of the East."

33. Philip Schaff, ed., *The Creeds of Christendom,* vol. 2, rev. David S. Schaff, 6th ed. (reprint, Grand Rapids: Baker, 1983), 82.

34. Roland Bainton, *Erasmus of Christendom* (New York: Charles Scribner's Sons, 1969), 135.

35. J. A. Froude, *Life and Letters of Erasmus* (London: Longmans, Green, and Co., 1900), 234.

36. A detailed accounting of the particulars surrounding both the Sixtine and the Clementine Vulgate editions may be found in Darlow and Moule, *Historical Catalogue of the Printed Editions of the Holy Scripture,* vol. 2, part 2, 958–63. A similar problem faces King James–Only advocates when they are pressed as to which *one* of the many differing KJV editions is their infallible standard.

37. John Gill, *A Complete Body of Doctrinal and Practical Divinity: Or, a System of Evangelical Truths* (London: Mathews & Leigh, 1839), 13. Gill is incorrect with regard to Esther, which is written entirely in Hebrew and not at all in Aramaic.

38. See Ll. J. M. Bebb, "Continental Versions," in *A Dictionary of the Bible,* vol. 5, ed. James Hastings (Edinburgh: T & T Clark, 1904), 411–14.

39. J. H. Merle D'Aubigne, *History of the Reformation of the Sixteenth Century* (1846; reprint, Grand Rapids: Baker, 1976), 337.

40. Philip Schaff, *History of the Christian Church,* vol. 7 (reprint, Grand Rapids: Eerdmans, 1974), 348.

41. See the following quotation from Basil Manly Jr. Even Philip Schaff drifts into this view. He wrote, "Luther's version of the Bible is a wonderful monument of genius, learning, and piety, and may be regarded in a secondary sense as inspired" (*History of the Christian Church,* 354). Such a belief can be affirmed only by debasing the meaning of the word *inspired* to mean less than Scripture means by that term (2 Tim. 3:16).

42. Henry Alford, *The New Testament for English Readers,* vol. 4 (reprint, Grand Rapids: Baker, 1983), 1546. All emphases is in the original.

43. Edward Winfield Cone, *The Life of Spencer H. Cone* (New York: Sheldon, Blakeman, & Co., 1857), 355–56. Italics is in the original. A brief sketch of Cone's life and labors by Doug Kutilek was recently published in *Frontline* 10, no. 1 (January–February 2000): 39.

44. Thomas Armitage, *History of the Baptists,* vol. 2 (reprint, Minneapolis: James & Klock, 1977), 901. Emphasis is added. See appendix D for an address regarding Bible translations that Armitage delivered at the founding of the American Bible Union.

45. Basil Manly Jr., *The Bible Doctrine of Inspiration* (reprint, Harrisonburg, Va.: Gano Books, 1985), 83–84.

46. For a concise survey of the rise and development of the modern King James-Only movement, see Doug Kutilek, "The Unlearned Men: The True Genealogy and Genesis of King-James-Onlyism," *Baptist Biblical Heritage* 5, no. 4 (1st quarter 1995): 2–5.

47. The whole spectrum of Wilkinson's manifold errors are examined in the article titled "Wilkinson's Incredible Errors" by Doug Kutilek in *Our Authorized Bible Vindicated, Baptist Biblical Heritage* 1, no. 3 (fall 1990): 1, 4–7.

48. Wilkinson's error on both counts are documented in Doug Kutilek, "The Truth About the Waldensian Bible and the Old Latin Version," *Baptist Biblical Heritage* 2, no. 2 (summer 1991): 1, 7–8.

49. See Doug Kutilek, "Erasmus and His Greek Text," *The Biblical Evangelist* 19, no. 19 (1 October 1985), 3–4; and idem, "Erasmus and His Theology," *The Biblical Evangelist* 19, no. 20 (16 October 1985), 3–4. Both articles were later republished in slightly revised form as *Erasmus, His Greek Text, and His Theology* (Hatfield, Pa.: Interdisciplinary Biblical Research Institute, 1986).

50. See Doug Kutilek, "A Careful Investigation of Psalm 12:6, 7," *The Biblical Evangelist* 17, no. 21 (14 October 1983), 1, 7–8. Psalm 12:6–7 is also discussed more extensively in chapter 4, "The Preservation of Scripture and the Version Debate."

51. See, for example, James Jasper Ray, *God Wrote Only One Bible,* rev. ed. (Junction City, Ore.: Eye Opener, 1970). Gary Hudson carefully demonstrated that Ray knew and heavily plagiarized Wilkinson's book in "The Real Eye Opener," *Baptist Biblical Heritage* 2, no. 1 (spring 1991): 1–4.

52. Ray, *God Wrote Only One Bible,* 122

53. Ibid., 30–31, 102.

54. David Otis Fuller, ed., dedication to *Counterfeit or Genuine?* (Grand Rapids: Grand Rapids International Publications, 1975).

55. David Otis Fuller, *Which Bible?* 5th ed. (Grand Rapids: Grand Rapids International Publications, 1975), 2–4.

56. Ibid. The book was in its fifth edition by 1975 and its twelfth printing as of 1987.

57. Gary Hudson and Doug Kutilek, "The Great 'Which Bible?' Fraud," *Baptist Biblical Heritage* 1, no. 2 (summer 1990): 1, 3–6.

58. Charles Haddon Spurgeon, *The Greatest Fight in the World* (reprint, Pasadena, Tex.: Pilgrim, 1990).

59. See Doug Kutilek, *An Answer to David Otis Fuller* (Pasadena, Tex.: Pilgrim, n.d.), which documents from Spurgeon's own writings exactly what Spurgeon did believe and teach.

60. The letter was published in *The Plains Baptist Challenger* 34, no. 6 (June 1980): 3–4.

61. See Robert Dick Wilson, *Studies in the Book of Daniel,* vol. 1(reprint, Grand Rapids: Baker, 1972), 84–85; and idem, *A Scientific Investigation of the Old Testament* (Chicago: Moody, 1959), 61.

62. Burgon proposed more than one hundred fifty changes in the Greek text of the first fourteen chapters of Matthew alone.

63. These views of Burgon are documented directly from Burgon's *The Revision Revised,* in Doug Kutilek, *As I See It* 1, no. 6 (June 1998).

64. See Gary Hudson, "Why Dean Burgon Would Not Join the Dean Burgon Society." A pamphlet printed by *The Pilgrim* magazine.

65. See Kutilek, "The Unlearned Men."

66. Zane Hodges, "Review of *The Bible Babel,*" *Bibliotheca Sacra* (October 1967), 362.

67. As discussed above. See also Kutilek, "The Septuagint: Riplinger's Blunders, Believe It or Not," 3–4, 12.

68. See Doug Kutilek, "Ruckmanism: A Refuge of Lies," *Baptist Biblical Heritage* 4, no. 4 (January 1994): 5–6.

69. See Doug Kutilek, "The KJV Is a Copyrighted Translation," *Baptist Biblical Heritage* 4, no. 3 (October 1993): 5–8.

70. See Doug Kutilek, "Ruckman's Phony 'Advanced Revelations,'" *The Biblical Evangelist* 24, no. 5 (May 1990): 1, 4–6.

71. Doug Kutilek, "Ruckman on Luther and I John 5:7" (unpublished article).

72. This assertion is addressed and answered by Doug Kutilek, *J. Frank Norris*

and His Heirs: The Bible Translation Controversy (Pasadena, Tex.: Pilgrim, 1999), 90–95.

73. Edward F. Hills's views are embodied in two books, *Believing Bible Study* (Des Moines: Christian Research, 1967); and *The King James Version Defended,* 4th ed. (Des Moines: Christian Research, 1984). James A. Price, in chapter 2 of his unpublished Th.D. dissertation, pp. 41–82, addresses the "King James Only Views of Edward F. Hills." An abbreviated form of this chapter was published as "King James Only View of Edward F. Hills," *Baptist Biblical Heritage* 1, no. 4 (winter 1990–1991): 1, 4–7.

74. The ensuing chapters present a detailed discussion regarding the incorrect basis and unbiblical nature of belief in the perfect preservation of the Scriptures in one particular edition, translation, or family of texts.

Chapter 2

The Old Testament Text and the Version Debate

Roy E. Beacham

A GREAT DEAL OF THE DEBATE about Bible versions centers on the text of the New Testament (NT). Volumes have been written regarding the question of which NT Greek text or family of manuscripts best represents or, as some would say, "perfectly preserves" the original documents of NT Scripture. Not much is said about the Old Testament (OT) text. This neglect of the OT is unfortunate because many issues that attend OT textual analysis also affect NT textual analysis. This chapter will focus on the development of the OT text and the effect of that development on our English versions, particularly the King James Version.

Arguments against Perfect Preservation in the Masoretic Text

Frequently, the question regarding which OT text best represents or "perfectly preserves" the original documents is answered by "the Masoretic Text." A number of problems attend this simplistic answer, particularly if someone suggests that the Masoretic Text needs no critical analysis or somehow "perfectly preserves" all of the original words of the OT Scriptures.

A Brief History of the Masoretic Text

The "Masoretic Text" is the product of the work of the Masoretes, who labored over the text of the OT between approximately A.D. 500 and 1000.[1] During the span of some two thousand years before the Masoretes (1500 B.C.–A.D. 500), as well as during their own time, numerous factors were at work in the development of the text of the OT Scriptures.

Linguistic Developments

When Moses, David, Isaiah, and the other human authors of Scripture wrote their original works, those original texts or autographs were produced under the direct influence of the Holy Spirit and, as inscripturated, were both inspired and inerrant (2 Tim. 3:16; 2 Peter 1:20–21). When those texts of Scripture were later copied by other men, apart from the direct supervision of the Holy Spirit (for the Bible never speaks of Spirit supervision apart from the original authors and autographs), various influences affected the text. For example, the alphabet, script, and spelling of the Hebrew language changed over the centuries during which these texts were being copied. Furthermore, grammatical constructions changed and were updated, and vocalization of the consonants gradually evolved.[2] Scribes were extremely careful in preserving the text of Scripture as they made their copies; however, they also were concerned that the Scriptures be updated in script, spelling, grammatical forms, and pronunciation. The Scriptures would be meaningless if the populace of the copyist's day could not read them. Developments in the writing and style of the Hebrew language over those thousands of years of copying the Scriptures were similar to, although not as pronounced as, the developments in English between the time of the epic poem *Beowulf* (Old English—ca. eighth century A.D.), Chaucer's *Canterbury Tales* (Middle English—ca. fourteenth century A.D.), and contemporary English. Attempting today to read those ancient English works in their original forms is equivalent to reading a foreign language.

Scribal Changes

Along with the fact that the inscriptional, orthographic, grammatical, and phonetic (vocalization) styles of biblical Hebrew evolved as the Scriptures were copied, other, more significant developments affected the text. No matter how careful the scribes attempted to be in their copying of sacred texts, various scribal errors inevitably were made. Words or letters were miscopied or transposed; words or entire phrases were accidentally left out or inserted. Mistakes were made in the process of hand-copying that are normal to that medium. Along with unconscious mistakes, specific evidence confirms that both early and later scribes occasionally made intentional changes to correct the text, protect their theological biases, or substitute euphemisms.[3] The texts of OT Scripture unquestionably underwent changes and alterations as they were copied over and over again.

Providential Preservation

All of these factors did not hopelessly pollute the text of Scripture or even significantly alter it. Changes in script, grammar, spelling, and vocalization are minor in terms of words and their meaning. Changes through scribal activity, whether accidental or intentional, are both expected and recognizable. God's Word continued to be available to people in the various, multiple copies that existed, and those copies were dependable and authoritative to the degree that they accurately reflected the autographs. Some modifications, adaptations, and scribal errors were evident in these copies. However, those relatively minor changes and variations that did exist in the copies had no substantial effect on the basic truths or teachings of Scripture.[4] God providentially perpetuated His Word by means of multiple copies. Still, only the original autographs of Scripture were directly inspired and wholly without error (see figure A).

Textual Families

In the sixth century B.C., the Jewish State disintegrated under the strong hand of the Babylonians, and the Jews were scattered in exile throughout the Middle East. Various textual "families" began to develop as scribes in different geographic regions (Babylon, Palestine, and Egypt) could perpetuate only those copies of texts that were available to them. Later, after the Babylonian exile ended and many Jews returned to their homeland, a plurality of text types or "families" continued to be in use. Copies of biblical texts at Qumran, texts that date from the middle of the third century B.C. to A.D. 68,[5] reflect up to five different varieties of textual traditions,[6] all of which present readings that differ from each other in places.

The Standardized Text

After A.D. 68, with the continued decline in the ability of the general populace to speak Hebrew and because of factors such as the fall of

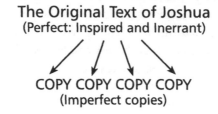

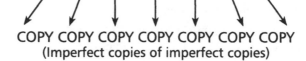

The Original Text of Joshua
(Perfect: Inspired and Inerrant)

COPY COPY COPY COPY
(Imperfect copies)

1. Internal: scribal errors naturally occurred
2. External: copies differed from each other

COPY COPY COPY COPY COPY COPY COPY
(Imperfect copies of imperfect copies)

1. More scribal errors and alterations
2. More variation between copies
3. Some linguistic updating as centuries pass

COPY COPY COPY COPY COPY COPY COPY COPY

Conclusion: Imperfect copies should be compared and evaluated

1. God's Word is preserved in the multiplicity of copies
2. All copies contain minor variations and inaccuracies
3. Yet each copy is reliable and authoritative to the extent
   that it accurately reflects the original

Figure A: The proliferation of hand-copied texts

Jerusalem in A.D. 70, the renewed scattering of the Jews, and the rise of Christianity, Jewish scholars became concerned about the state of the OT text.[7] These scholars, who were precursors to the Masoretes, were not satisfied with the fact that numerous text types were circulating in the Middle East, all of which offered some readings that differed from the readings of other copies. These religious leaders then made a conscious effort to evaluate the various extant texts in order to create a rendition of the entire OT that could become a somewhat standardized version for the Jewish religion. This basic, standardized text type was probably established in Palestine by the end of the first century A.D.[8] This text type became the precursor of the pointed and annotated Masoretic texts (A.D. 500–1440) as we know them today (see figure B).

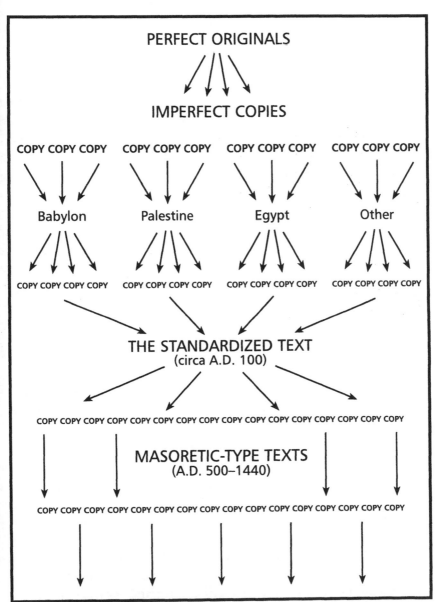

Figure B: Regional, Standardized, and Masoretic texts

Reasons Why the Masoretic Text Is Not a Perfect Text

Two major objections can be raised against the assertion that the Masoretic text is a flawless, pristine copy of the original autographs of Scripture from which a flawless translation can be made.

The Masoretic Text Is a Late Recension

First, the Masoretic text should not be perceived as a perfect copy of the originals because it is a late recension (i.e., a conscious revision based upon earlier, divergent texts). This recension took place when Jewish scholars attempted to standardize the text of the entire OT in the first century A.D. These scholars had to compare and analyze various updated and imperfect copies of the texts of OT books. The updated and imperfect copies presented variant readings when they were compared one with another. Religious scholars, then, were forced to choose from among those various texts and textual traditions a single reading, text, or tradition that they deemed to be acceptable in accordance with their particular criteria at that particular time. The autographs themselves no longer existed, and so far as anyone knew (much less suggested), no continuous line of perfect copies of the OT autographs existed that could be brought together to establish a perfect text of the entire OT. The process of seeking to produce a standardized text certainly did not produce a pristine text. The scholars involved in the process did not follow any single textual tradition but incorporated elements from a plurality of the different textual families in circulation at that time.[9] The texts that these particular scholars preferred, for whatever reasons, were not necessarily always the best available texts.[10] Furthermore, this process failed to eliminate all of the variant texts and the variant readings, even within the standardized family.[11]

Because of the evidence of evolution in script, spelling, and vocalization, and because of the evidence of the updating and smoothing of the text grammatically, as well as the detectable signs of scribal errors and intentional alterations, it is impossible to suppose that Jewish scholars in the first century A.D. restored all of the very words of the original writings exactly as they were originally written. These scholars certainly did not revert to the ancient scripts of the originals or to all of the old grammatical constructions and spellings of the autographs. They clearly did not eliminate every scribal error and they occasionally altered the text intentionally. Furthermore, they did not view one exclusive family of texts to be perfect, nor did they always select the best text as the standard, and they did not eliminate textual variants. God nowhere in Scripture assures us that the Jewish scholars of the first century A.D. produced a corpus of Scripture that perfectly mirrored the originals. Thus, the Masoretic text should not be considered a flawless reproduction of the autographs. Rather, the Masoretic text evolved from a late, standardized recension of variant, imperfect, and updated copies made by imperfect men.

Many Different Masoretic-Type Texts Exist

Second, the Masoretic text should not be perceived as a perfect copy of the originals because no such thing as *the* Masoretic text or *one* Masoretic text actually exists. Although Jewish scholars in the first century A.D. apparently sought to standardize the OT text, experts debate whether these scholars actually ever created one, single "master copy" of the entire corpus of OT Scriptures.[12] Certainly no such "master copy" exists today. Even if these scribes did produce a "master copy" in the first century A.D., no evidence exists that such a text was ever accepted, much less ever portrayed, as a perfect replica of the originals. The standardized text simply reflected a textual tradition that was accepted by a central party of scribes at a certain time in history.[13] Furthermore, although this emerging Masoretic type of text became accepted as the preferred type of text in Palestine around A.D. 100, variant readings continued to exist even within this family. The medieval Masoretic-type texts that exist today perpetuate well over a thousand variant readings internally, where the consonantal text (called the *Kethiv*—"what is written") differs from what the Masoretes suggest is the text as it should be read (the *Qere*—"what is read").[14] Furthermore, when one compares all of the poststandardization Masoretic-type texts to each other, he still finds variant readings.[15] Thus, *"the"* Masoretic text cannot be a perfect copy of the originals because no singular Masoretic text exists, but many extant Masoretic-type texts exist, all of which include internal variants and many of which differ when compared with each other (see figure C).

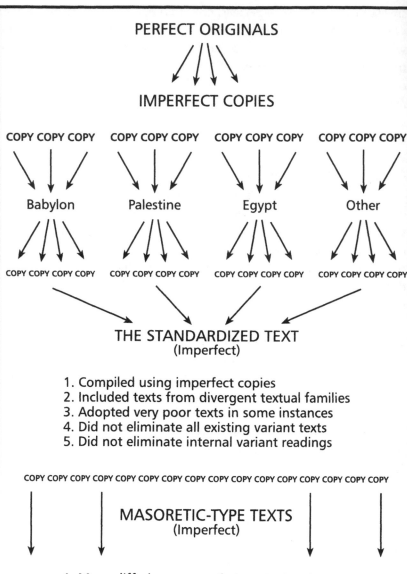

Figure C: Imperfections in the Standard and Masoretic Texts

Summary

One must remember that the Masoretic family of texts, that family associated with the standardization of the OT around A.D. 100, is a later, recensional, and diverse family. It is a later family because all of the original autographs were written hundreds of years before standardization and had gone through an evolution of hand-copying that included the updating of script, spelling, grammar, and vocalization as well as the phenomena of scribal errors and alterations. It is a recensional family because it was formulated by comparing variant texts and selecting one reading, manuscript, or tradition over other possible readings, manuscripts, or traditions. It is a diverse family because the copies that grew out of the standardization process still contained hundreds of internal variants as well as, or along with, readings that differed from other copies in the same family. These facts force the student of textual transmission to conclude that, although Masoretic-type texts as a whole are highly reliable witnesses of the original autographs, they reflect only one textual tradition among many, and they do not perfectly replicate the originals. They fail to offer a wholly unaltered and thoroughly univocal facsimile of the autographs of Scripture.

Arguments Against Perfect Preservation in One Edition or One Translation of the Masoretic Text

What if someone were to suggest that he or she believes, "by faith," that God perfectly preserved His Word in one specific edition of the Masoretic text or in one particular translation? Such a person might assert, for example, that God enabled the Jewish scholars of A.D. 100 to bring together all of the right copies and make all of the right critical decisions to restore perfectly the words of the original autographs. Such a view would face a number of problems, the most obvious being the fact that no "master copy" from A.D. 100 exists today, and all of the currently known manuscripts of Masoretic-type texts contain variant readings. In other words, if the assumed standardized text of A.D. 100 were a perfect reproduction of the originals, it, like the autographs, has been lost. Some people might suggest, then, that God allowed a *later* editor of a *specific* Masoretic-type text to bring together all of the right copies and to make all of the right critical decisions regarding variant readings so that a perfect restoration of the originals was accomplished. Some staunch defenders of the King James Version, for example, suggest that the Second

Rabbinic Bible, edited by Jacob Ben-Chayyim and published by Daniel Bomberg in Venice in 1524–25, was a "perfect" Masoretic text. Some people assert that they believe "by faith" that this Second Rabbinic Bible is a pristine reproduction of the original manuscripts. Furthermore, some people suggest that they believe "by faith" that the King James Version is a pure translation of this pristine Masoretic text (see figure D). Such views suffer from a number of serious problems.

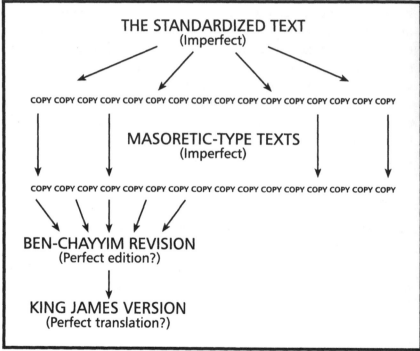

Figure D: One perfect Masoretic text or English translation?

The Rabbinic Bible Was an Eclectic Recension

First, Jacob Ben-Chayyim's edition was an eclectic recension, a conscious revision based upon a mixture of sources. This printed edition was based upon late, medieval manuscripts (twelfth century A.D. or later) as well as numerous other printed editions then available to the editor, all of which were imperfect updated copies or versions and most of which contained variant readings.[16] Jacob Ben-Chayyim, when confronted with textual variants, chose "from the available sources" whatever reading he deemed "best . . . without regard to its origin," a procedure that resulted in a "mixed [eclectic] text."[17] This edition itself included Aramaic translations, Masoretic notations, Rabbinic comments, personal alterations, and a host of variant readings.[18] That Ben-Chayyim believed his edition to be a perfect replica of the originals is doubtful. How could he be certain that every reading that he chose was, in fact, the "original" reading? Why would he offer variant readings in his edition if he thought it were perfect, and which of the variant readings suggested by Ben-Chayyim were actually the pure readings? No logical or biblical reason exists for asserting that Ben-Chayyim's edition was pristine.

The King James Version Does Not Replicate the Rabbinic Bible

Second, even if the Second Rabbinic Bible were, somehow, a perfect replica of the originals, the King James Version translators did not use the Second Rabbinic Bible of Jacob Ben-Chayyim exclusively in their translation of the OT. By their own testimony the King James Version translators used multiple older and current editions, versions, translations, and even commentaries to evaluate, correct, and stylize their translation.[19] In fact, the King James Version does not consistently follow the readings of the Second Rabbinic Bible.[20] How could the King James Version be a perfect translation of a perfect edition of the Masoretic text (the Second Rabbinic Bible) if the King James Version does not exclusively and inalterably follow the readings of this supposedly pristine Rabbinic version of the OT text? One or the other must alter the words of the original Scriptures because they do not perfectly agree. Therefore, it is not possible to be correct in the assertion that both the Second Rabbinic Bible and the King James Version are pure representations of the original autographs. At best, one or the other must contain imperfections.

The King James Version Translators Deny Perfection

Third, the King James Version translators disclaimed perfection in any copied text or translation,[21] including their own.[22] In fact, these translators ascribed perfection to only the original autographs, "The original thereof being from heaven, not from earth; the author being God, not man; the inditer, the Holy Spirit, not the wit of the Apostles or Prophets; the penmen, such as were sanctified from the womb, and endued with a principal portion of God's Spirit."[23] Why should one believe the King

James Version to be a perfect translation of a pristine Hebrew text if the translators themselves did not believe either the Hebrew text or their own translation to be inerrant (see figure E)?[24]

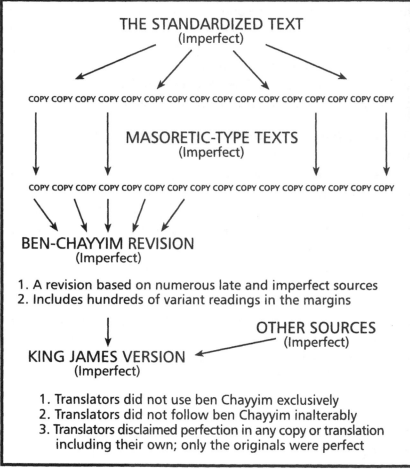

Figure E: Imperfections in the Ben Chayyim revision and in the KJV

Biblical Faith Must Be Grounded in Biblical Revelation

Fourth, is it biblical "faith" to believe *a priori* that some particular edition of the Masoretic text perfectly reproduced all of the original words of the OT or that some particular English version perfectly translates the autographs? Biblical faith is absolute belief in the explicit revelation of God. It is *not* biblical faith to trust in human assumptions that are only peripherally associated with God's explicit revelation. For example, it is biblical faith to believe that Noah built an ark that safely housed his family and numerous animals during a universal deluge. The Scriptures explicitly say that it was so. However, it is not biblical faith to believe that Noah's ark has been perfectly preserved in the ice on top of Mount Ararat. One may believe in the perfect preservation of Noah's ark, but that belief is not biblical faith, for the Bible does not teach it.

People should believe, by biblical faith, that God has spoken inerrantly and authoritatively through the apostles and prophets, for the Bible explicitly teaches that truth. It is incorrect, however, to assert "by faith" that God has inerrantly and authoritatively spoken through later human figures such as the Pope or other religious leaders, textual editors, or Bible translators, for the Bible teaches no such thing. It is biblical faith to believe that God, through the process of inspiration, produced an inerrant corpus of revelation by the hand of the original authors. The Bible explicitly teaches this truth. However, it is not biblical faith to believe that God, through providence or direct superintendence, oversaw the production of one particular copy, edition, or translation of Scripture to replicate the autographs perfectly. The Bible nowhere teaches such a notion. Extending the concept of faith to include secondary, nonbiblical assertions is both cultic and unscriptural.

It is one thing to believe that God *could* providentially or supernaturally propagate His Word; it is another thing to believe that God *did* providentially or supernaturally preserve His word *in a particular edition or translation*. The Bible does teach about God's providential and supernatural power. However, the Bible does not explicitly teach or even tenuously imply that God providentially or supernaturally preserved His Word perfectly in the supposed standardized text of A.D. 100, the Second Rabbinic Bible of Jacob Ben-Chayyim, or any particular English translation, be it the King James Version or some other translation. For a person to assert that he or she believes, "by biblical faith," such specific preservation of the autographs of Scripture in one particular copy or version is itself grossly unbiblical, for the Bible does not teach any such thing. God may just as well have chosen to propagate His Word providentially through *multiple* copies and versions as through any *one* particular copy or version. The Bible nowhere promises perfection in relation to any specific edition or translation of Scripture. We cannot believe by *biblical* faith that which God has not revealed in Scripture.

Conclusion

God, by the process of inspiration, produced through human agents a wholly inerrant and completely authoritative corpus of truth: the autographs of Scripture. The words of those inspired, inerrant OT documents were propagated for millennia through multiple copies and, eventually, through multiple translations of some of those copies, all of which can be compared and evaluated as witnesses to the autographs of Scripture. So far as God has told us, no single copy or translation ever perfectly preserved all of the exact words of the originals with pristine accuracy. Yet, through all of the passing centuries of human history, God expected men to study copies and translations of Scripture in order to know Him and His will. Such copies and translations, although not unquestionable facsimiles of the originals, were reliable enough to be both authoritative and instructive; they were "the Word of God." People were held accountable for believing in and living by their content. A person did not need to possess a text or translation with every last one of all of the exact words of the autographs precisely as they were inscribed, spelled, grammatically constructed, and vocalized by the original authors to know what God said, what God meant, and what God expected. In fact, people did not have access to perfect replicas of the originals.

Jesus and the apostles, when quoting the OT, did so with obvious variety. Sometimes they quoted a Greek version of the OT. Other times they quoted a text similar to the emerging Masoretic text. Occasionally their citations reflected a mixture of textual traditions or were free renditions of an OT passage.[25] If Jesus, the apostles, and multiplied thousands of other Bible students throughout the millennia of human history have depended on multiple copies, versions, and translations as authoritative records of God's Word insofar as they accurately reflected the autographs, should believers today (since A.D. 1611, for example) expect God to give them a perfectly restored copy or translation of the autographs? The King James Version translators, by their own testimony, did not believe that God preserved His sacred Word by means of perfect copies and translations. To agree with them on this point is most biblical. Like the vast majority of Bible students who have preceded them, today's students of Scripture gladly accept the grand privilege and the great responsibility to study, analyze, and evaluate God's authoritative Word as He has chosen to propagate it through multiple copies and translations. Here again is wholehearted agreement with the King James Version translators: "We do not deny, nay, we affirm and avow, that the very meanest translation of the Bible in *English* set forth by men of our profession . . . containeth the word of God, nay, is the word of God."[26]

Chapter Notes

1. E. Brotzman, *Old Testament Textual Criticism* (Grand Rapids: Baker, 1994), 47. Other authors suggest different dates that closely approximate those suggested by Brotzman.

2. B. Waltke and M. O'Connor, *An Introduction to Biblical Hebrew Syntax* (Winona Lake, Ind.: Eisenbrauns, 1990), 15–19; and F. Deist, *Towards the Text of the Old Testament,* trans. W. K. Winckler (Pretoria, S. Africa: N. G. Kerkboekhandel Transvaal, 1978), 70–73.

3. In their Masoretic notations (most of which are confirmed by Talmudic sources), the scribes themselves mention eighteen "emendations" or "corrections" *(tiqqune)* where changes were made in the text to avoid what they considered to be irreverence. Rabbi Johanan ben Zacchai said, "It is always better to take out a letter from the Torah rather than to be in danger of profaning the Name of God during public reading." The Talmud also mentions some seventeen scribal "omissions" *(itture)* where certain conjunctions or words were omitted from the text. For a discussion and complete listings of these alterations see Deist, *Towards the Text of the Old Testament,* 59–61; Brotzman, *Old Testament Textual Criticism,* 116–21; and E. Wurthwein, *The Text of the Old Testament,* trans. Erroll F. Rhodes (Grand Rapids: Eerdmans, 1979), 17–19, 105–10.

4. C. Armerding, *The Old Testament and Criticism* (Grand Rapids: Eerdmans, 1983), 107.

5. E. Tov, *Textual Criticism of the Hebrew Bible* (Minneapolis: Fortress, 1992), 106.

6. Ibid., 114–17. Other authors following F. M. Cross suggest a base of only three textual families.

7. Deist, *Towards the Text of the Old Testament,* 50–51.

8. Wurthwein, *The Text of the Old Testament,* 15–16.

9. The precise method that the Jewish scholars of the first century A.D. used to formulate a standardized text is unclear and debated. Cross suggests that "in a given biblical book of the Hebrew Bible the rabbis chose exemplars of one textual family or even a single manuscript as a base. They did not collate all the wide variety of text types available. . . ." (F. M. Cross, "The Text Behind the Text of the Hebrew Bible," in *Understanding the Dead Sea*

Scrolls, ed. Hershel Shanks [New York: Random House, 1992], 150). Even if their standardization involved a broad acceptance of specific manuscripts as the base of particular biblical books, "they did not select, in the case of every book, texts having a common origin or local background" (ibid., 150). Some base texts were of the Babylonian tradition (particularly in the Pentateuch and Former Prophets) whereas others reflected the Palestinian tradition (particularly in the Latter Prophets) (ibid., 150–51; see also Brotzman, *Old Testament Textual Criticism,* 44–46; and Armerding, *The Old Testament and Criticism,* 104).

10. A more holistic method of choosing a textual base no doubt made standardization easier, if this method was actually used. However, the wholesale acceptance of one particular manuscript or family would not necessarily always produce the best text (Cross, "The Text Behind the Text of the Hebrew Bible," 151; and Tov, *Textual Criticism of the Hebrew Bible,* 24). Most notorious in the Masoretic tradition for its poorer quality is the book of Samuel (Tov, *Textual Criticism of the Hebrew Bible,* 194, 196; Deist, *Towards the Text of the Old Testament,* 20–21; and F. M. Cross, "Light on the Bible from the Dead Sea Caves," in *Understanding the Dead Sea Scrolls,* 157).

11. Although one particular manuscript might have been chosen in the first century A.D. as the exemplar for a given OT book or series of books, corrections continually had to be made in extant texts within the family of the exemplar to bring those extant texts into conformity with the exemplar (Tov, *Textual Criticism of the Hebrew Bible,* 28–29). That the ideal of complete standardization was ever attained is doubtful (ibid., 29).

12. Waltke, following Lagarde, suggests that one official, master scroll was probably produced (Waltke and O'Connor, *An Introduction to Biblical Hebrew Syntax,* 21). Deist and Tov seriously doubt that such a master scroll ever existed (Deist, *Towards the Text of the Old Testament,* 51; and Tov, *Textual Criticism of the Hebrew Bible,* 25, 28).

13. Deist, *Towards the Text of the Old Testament,* 51; and Tov, *Textual Criticism of the Hebrew Bible,* 23–24.

14. Brotzman, *Old Testament Textual Criticism,* 54; and Wurthwein, *The Text of the Old Testament,* 17–18.

15. Tov, *Textual Criticism of the Hebrew Bible,* 33–39.

16. Wurthwein, *The Text of the Old Testament,* 37; Brotzman, *Old Testament Textual Criticism,* 60; and Tov, *Textual Criticism of the Hebrew Bible,* 78.

17. Yeivin, *Introduction to the Tiberian Masorah,* trans. and ed. E. J. Revell (Missoula, Mont.: Scholars Press, 1980), 31. Yeivin comments further, "The

tradition presented in this edition—both in the Masorah and in the vocalization and accentuation—was good, but it was not uniform. It contains many traces of much older features along with much later ones, that is it represents the sort of mixed tradition described above" (ibid., 31–32).

18. Wurthwein, *The Text of the Old Testament,* 37; and Tov, *Textual Criticism of the Hebrew Bible,* 78.

19. F. H. A. Scrivener, "The Translators to the Reader: Preface to the King James Version," in *The Authorized Edition of the English Bible (1611), Its Subsequent Reprints and Modern Representatives* (Cambridge: At the University Press, 1884), par. 16: "Truly, good Christian Reader, we never thought from the beginning that we should need to make a new translation, nor yet to make of a bad one a good one; . . . but to make a good one better, or out of many good ones one principal good one. . . . Neither did we think much to consult the translators or commentators, *Chaldee, Hebrew, Syrian, Greek,* or *Latin;* no, nor the *Spanish, French, Italian,* or *Dutch;* neither did we disdain to revise that which we had done, and to bring back to the anvil that which we had hammered: but having and using as great helps as were needful . . . we have at the length . . . brought the work to that pass that you see."

It is incumbent upon anyone who takes the version debate seriously to read the entire text of the King James Version "Translators to the Reader." In this document, the translators of the King James Version clearly affirm tenets that King James-Only proponents deny (e.g., the attribute of perfection residing only in the original autographs). The translators also firmly deny tenets that the King James-Only proponents affirm (e.g., perfection in any translation, the use of a single edition for the translation of their version, etc.). There is, perhaps, no better argument against the King James-Only position than the testimony of the King James translators themselves. This document can be read in its entirety in appendix C of this book.

20. James Price writes, "It is generally believed that the King James Version of the Bible faithfully follows the Textus Receptus of the Old and New Testaments without variation. However, there are at least 232 places in the AV where the translators followed some other text tradition, such as the Greek Septuagint (LXX), the Latin Vulgate (Vg), the Syriac Version (Syr), or merely Rabbinic tradition, rather than the Textus Receptus." Price lists "a few examples of where the KJV departs from the Hebrew Textus Receptus of the OT [Second Bomberg Edition of Ben-Chayyim] and follows the LXX against all other authorities (2 Chron. 17:4; 33:19; Job 1:19; 15:11;

Song 4:1; 6:5; Isa. 57:8; Hos. 13:16)," and "a few examples of where the KJV follows the LXX and the Vg against the Hebrew Textus Receptus (Gen. 7:22; Num. 10:29; 13:6, 8, 24; Deut. 2:27; 1 Sam. 5:9, 12; 6:4, 5; Pss. 39:13; 68:23; Prov. 24:28; Jer. 50:11; 52:12; Lam. 1:8; Ezek. 21:16)." James D. Price, e-mail to R. E. Beacham, 1 May 1996.

21. "The King's speech which he uttered in Parliament, being translated into *French, Dutch, Italian,* and *Latin,* is still the King's speech, though it be not interpreted by every translator with the like grace, nor peradventure so fitly for phrase, nor so expressly for sense. . . . No cause therefore why the word translated should be denied to be the word, or forbidden to be current, notwithstanding that some imperfections and blemishes may be noted in the setting forth of it. For whatever was perfect under the sun, where Apostles or apostolick men, that is, men endued with an extraordinary measure of God's Spirit, and privileged with the privilege of infallibility, had not their hand? . . . The like we are to think of translations. The translation of the *Seventy* dissenteth from the Original in many places, neither doth it come near it for perspicuity, gravity, majesty; yet which of the Apostles did condemn it? Condemn it? Nay, they used it, (as it is apparent, and as Saint *Hierome* and most learned men do confess) which they would not have done . . . if it had been unworthy the appellation and name of the word of God. . . . But we weary the unlearned, who need not know so much; and trouble the learned, who know it already" (Scrivener, "The Translators to the Reader," pars. 13–14). See appendix C.

22. See the King James Version translators' discussion on variant readings, which readings they themselves included in the margin of their translation (Scrivener, "The Translators to the Reader," par. 17). Regarding variant readings, they say, "Some peradventure would have no variety of senses to be set in the margin, lest the authority of the Scriptures for deciding of controversies by that show of uncertainty should somewhat be shaken. But we hold their judgment not to be so sound in this point. . . . It hath pleased God in his Divine Providence here and there to scatter words and sentences of that difficulty and doubtfulness, not in doctrinal points that concern salvation, . . . but in matters of less moment, that fearfulness would better beseem us than confidence. . . . Now in such a case doth not a margin do well to admonish the Reader to seek further, and not to conclude or dogmatize upon this or that peremptorily? For as it is a fault of incredulity, to doubt of those things that are evident; so to determine of such things as the Spirit of God hath left (even in the judgment of the

judicious) questionable, can be no less than presumption. Therefore as S. *Augustine* saith, that variety of translations is profitable for the finding out of the sense of the Scriptures: so diversity of signification and sense in the margin, where the text is not so clear, must needs do good; yea, is necessary, as we are persuaded. . . . They that are wise had rather have their judgments at liberty in differences of readings, than to be captivated to one, when it may be the other" (Scrivener, "The Translators to the Reader," par. 17). See appendix C.

23. Scrivener, "The Translators to the Reader," par. 5. See appendix C.

24. Closely associated with the question of "perfect" translation is the question of consistent verbal equivalence. Interestingly, the King James Version translators insisted on some degree of freedom of sense in translation. "Another thing we think good to admonish thee of, gentle Reader, that we have not tied ourselves to an uniformity of phrasing, or to an identity of words, as some peradventure would wish that we had done, because they observe, that some learned men somewhere have been as exact as they could that way. . . . For is the kingdom of God become words or syllables? Why should we be in bondage to them, if we may be free? use one precisely, when we may use another no less fit . . . ? we cannot follow a better pattern for elocution than God himself; therefore he using divers words in his holy writ, and indifferently for one thing in nature; we, if we will not be superstitious, may use the same liberty in our *English* versions. . . . We desire that the Scripture may speak like itself, as in the language of *Canaan,* that *it* may be understood even of the very vulgar" (Scrivener, "The Translators to the Reader," par. 18). See appendix C.

25. For a comparison of NT quotations with the German Bible Society's editions of the Septuagint and Masoretic text, see Gleason L. Archer and G. C. Chirichigno, *Old Testament Quotations in the New Testament: A Complete Survey* (Chicago: Moody, 1983).

26. Scrivener, "The Translators to the Reader," par. 13. See appendix C.

Chapter 3

The New Testament Text and the Version Debate

W. Edward Glenny

ONE OF THE REASONS FOR THE confusion concerning Bible translations is a failure to define and explain precisely some of the significant terms used in the discussion. The goal of this chapter is to address that problem by summarizing some of the most important aspects of New Testament (NT) textual criticism and defining key terms such as Eclectic Text, Majority Text, and Textus Receptus (TR). To define and explain these key terms precisely will require describing the contents and characteristics of these various NT texts and showing how they relate to the KJV.

Textual Criticism

Textual criticism sounds like a negative and destructive field of study, but it need not be so. It is the study of the copies and translations of any written composition of which the autograph (the original) is unknown for the purpose of determining as closely as possible the original text.[1] It is necessary to apply textual criticism to the text of the NT for two reasons. First, none of the original copies of Scripture is extant; second, no two of the extant manuscripts are exactly alike. In fact, the most similar manuscripts disagree six to ten times per chapter.[2]

Manuscripts

In comparison with other books of the ancient world, we have an abundance of manuscripts of the NT (5,656 in Greek, more than 10,000 in Latin, and more than 1,000 in other languages).[3] Of the extant Greek manuscripts, fifty-nine have the complete text of the NT; most have a few verses, chapters, or books of the NT. The Greek manuscripts come to us in four main forms: papyri, uncials, minuscules, and lectionaries.

Papyri refers to manuscripts made of the papyrus plant (rather than animal skin, called vellum); they are in uncial (capital) script. Because papyrus does not stand up as well as vellum, only about one hundred of these manuscripts have survived, most of them from Egypt. These manuscripts are early (second to eighth centuries A.D.) and most of them have been discovered in the past one hundred years. Only nine of the papyri were discovered before the year 1900.

Uncials are manuscripts made of animal skins and are written in capital letter script. Of the about three hundred uncials that we have, only one of them has the complete text of the NT. They date from about the third to the tenth century A.D.

Minuscules are written in a cursive script that has smaller, connected letters. This script began to be used in the ninth century to save time and because the letters take less space than do uncial letters. These manuscripts (about 2,850 of them) are primarily from the Majority (or Byzantine) text type. More than 2,400 *lectionaries* also exist. These service books of Scripture for church meetings are the least important of the Greek manuscripts. The text of the lectionaries is "basically Byzantine."[4]

In working with all of these manuscripts, the first step is to classify them according to "text types." Although no two of these manuscripts are precisely identical, the manuscripts that belong to a particular text type generally reflect the same or similar readings in passages that have variant readings.[5] A manuscript that reflects more than one text type is said to have a mixed text.

Classification of Text Types

Modern textual critics classify manuscripts in at least three text types: Majority, Alexandrian, and Western.

Majority Text Type

The Majority (or Byzantine) text type is the basis of the recently published Majority Text and the text type from which the Textus

Receptus comes.[6] As the various names for this text type suggest, it contains the great majority of manuscripts of the Greek NT, and most of them come from the Byzantine Empire, where Greek was the native or primary language. About 80 percent of the manuscripts of the Greek NT belong to this tradition. This text type is generally judged to be inferior to the other two text types because all manuscripts containing this text type are from the fourth century or later. Most of the manuscripts in this family are minuscules and lectionaries, and the great majority of them are a thousand years or more removed from the autographa. Other reasons why this text type is considered to be inferior to the other two main text types are because of its smoothness, conflation (combining two variant readings to form a new reading not exactly identical with either of the two source readings), harmonization of the text (making parallel passages agree), and its liturgically motivated readings.

This text type enjoyed widespread use in Eastern Christendom and apparently came to be the majority about the ninth century.[7] Its main strength is the number of manuscripts containing this text type. The main arguments used against this text type are its scarcity in early manuscripts and versions, its absence in the papyri before the fourth century and in the Ante-Nicene Fathers,[8] and the inferior style and content of this text type.[9] The fact that no Greek manuscript with this text type is known from before the fourth century makes it questionable whether it existed before that time.

Western Text Type

The Western text type is the least clearly defined of the three types. Evidence of this text type existed as early as A.D. 200, and it is the text type reflected in the earliest Christian writers in Palestine and Asia Minor. It comes primarily from texts found in the Western Mediterranean area and is similar in characteristics to the Old Latin (the Latin version used before Jerome's Vulgate).[10] The Western text type tends to be a full text and is especially important where it agrees with one of the other two text types.[11]

Alexandrian Text Type

The Alexandrian is the text type that is generally found in the earliest manuscripts, including most of the papyri. Some papyri with this text type date as early as the second century.[12] This text type is generally judged to be superior on the basis of internal evidence: its readings tend to be more difficult (thus best accounting for the existence of the variants in the other text types) and shorter.[13] Most textual critics believe that this text type, as represented in the early uncials Vaticanus and Sinaiticus and the early papyri, is the best text type now extant.[14]

Major Greek Texts

Since the invention of the printing press in the middle of the fifteenth century, hundreds of different texts of the Greek NT have been published. Three of them are at the center of the discussion of translations and texts today: (1) the Eclectic Text (United Bible Societies [UBS]/Nestle-Aland [NA]), (2) the Majority Text, and (3) the Textus Receptus (TR).

The Eclectic Text

This text is called eclectic (or sometimes the "critical text") because it is based on and uses all of the manuscripts and text types, and all important textual variants are displayed in the textual apparatus.[15] It reflects a broader textual base than the Majority Text or the Textus Receptus and is based on the theory that the date and quality of manuscripts is more important than the number of manuscripts. This means that sometimes, because of the early date and perceived superiority of their text, the readings adopted in the Eclectic Text are based on only a few manuscripts. Both the fourth revised edition of the United Bible Societies' *Greek New Testament* (1993) and the twenty-seventh edition of the Nestle-Aland *Novum Testamentum Graece* (1993) contain this text.[16] These two Greek texts differ, however, in the textual apparatuses at the bottom of the pages. The United Bible Societies' text (UBS) lists fewer textual variants but gives a fuller treatment of the variants it does discuss.

The committees that compiled this Greek text used a method called reasoned eclecticism to choose the best readings among the variants. Reasoned eclectics use both internal and external evidence to choose the preferred reading in any given situation.[17] External evidence includes the following:

1. the date and character of manuscripts supporting a variant and the text type they embody,
2. the geographical distribution of the manuscripts supporting a variant,

3. the genealogical relationship of manuscripts and families of manuscripts, and
4. the genealogical solidarity of manuscripts supporting a variant.

Internal evidence is based on (1) transcriptional probabilities, which concern the habits of scribes and the resulting changes they sometimes made in the texts, and (2) intrinsic probabilities, which concern the style and theology of the original author and what he was most likely to have written in the context under consideration. The most important criterion for internal and external considerations is that the preferred reading is that which best explains the existence of the other variants.

The Eclectic Text tends to favor the earlier manuscripts that are found in the Alexandrian text type; thus, it follows, in large part, the text (1881) of the famous Cambridge text critics, Westcott and Hort. Many conclusions of Westcott and Hort have been confirmed by the subsequent discovery of papyri. The fact that the critical or Eclectic Text favors the earlier manuscripts and in many regards agrees with the text of Westcott and Hort is not because the editors of these texts have simply followed the methodology of Westcott and Hort. In fact, the reasoned eclecticism that best characterizes the methodology of these editors is different from the methodology of Westcott and Hort. This difference in methodology accounts for most of the differences in the texts, especially the tendency in the most current editions of the Eclectic Text not to depend as exclusively on the Alexandrian text type and, thus, to give more weight to the readings found in the other text types. The Eclectic Text is the basis of several translations, including the NASB and the NIV.

The Majority Text

In 1982, the first Greek New Testament based on the Majority (or Byzantine) text type was published. *The Greek New Testament according to the Majority Text,* edited by Zane C. Hodges and Arthur L. Farstad,[18] is based exclusively on the Majority text type and represents all the manuscripts of that text type (well over 4,000).[19] The editors of the Majority Text state that their method of determining the text of the NT is based on the following two principles:

(1) Any reading overwhelmingly attested by the manuscript tradition is more likely to be original than its rival(s). . . . (2) Final

decisions about readings ought to be made on the basis of a reconstruction of their history in the manuscript tradition.[20]

What this means is that all readings in this Greek text are from the Majority text type, which is, according to their first principle, considered most likely to represent the original. However, the Majority text type is not always united. In fact, there are five distinct strands of manuscripts in this text type, and the manuscripts of this text type often differ on individual readings.[21] Therefore, Hodges and Farstad theorize that the best way to find the correct reading within the Majority text type, where it is divided, is by constructing a genealogy of the manuscripts (principle 2). They constructed such a genealogy for only John 7:53–8:11 and the book of Revelation, and the ironic result of this construction is that the reading that their genealogy (stemma) of manuscripts indicates to be the correct reading, is not the majority reading 153 times in Revelation and half of the time in John 7:53–8:11 (15 of 30).[22] Therefore, their two principles contradict, and their results demonstrate that to find the correct reading the textual critic must do more than just count the number of manuscripts supporting each reading.[23]

No translation is based on the Majority Text. Although it is sometimes wrongly assumed that the New King James Version is based on the Majority Text, it is actually based on the same text as the KJV the Textus Receptus (TR). However, some editions of the NKJV give translations of the Majority Text in the margin where the Majority Text differs from the TR.

The Majority Text, which represents the Byzantine manuscripts, is quite different from the Eclectic Text, differing from it in more than 6,500 places.[24] Two major differences between the Majority Text and Eclectic Text are their treatment of Mark 16:9–20 and John 7:53–8:11. These passages are in double brackets in the Eclectic Text,[25] but they are included in the text in the Majority Text. However, the Majority Text differs not only from the Eclectic Text but also the TR in about 1,800 places, and the difference between these two texts is often blurred or not realized, especially in the arguments of King James-Only advocates.[26]

The Textus Receptus

The Textus Receptus (TR) is the title given to the 1633 version of the Greek text edited and first published by Erasmus in 1516.[27] Erasmus was a Roman Catholic priest and humanist who came to Basel in 1514 to publish his annotations on the New Testament with a text of the Latin Vulgate. His publisher, Froben, pressured him to include the Greek NT in his work. Consequently, in eight months Erasmus edited his Greek NT based on the seven manuscripts available to him at Basel. Erasmus described his text as "thrown together rather than edited."[28] It had many typographical errors, and with regard to these errors, F. H. A. Scrivener said it is "the most faulty book I know."[29]

Of the seven manuscripts that Erasmus used, none contained the whole NT. One was complete except for Revelation, and all of the rest had various parts of the NT (one had only Revelation, except for the last six verses; two had only the Gospels; two had only Acts and the Epistles; and one had only the Pauline Epistles). All of them date from the eleventh to the fifteenth centuries.

As a result of his editing of these seven manuscripts, Erasmus produced in 1516 a new Greek text that had never before existed. Remember, the closest manuscripts differ from each other six to ten times per chapter. He took the manuscripts that he had available from different parts of the NT and edited them to make a new text. He used two main manuscripts and wrote his corrections and changes on them, and the printer then used these to make the printed text. A comparison of Erasmus' notes and the 1516 edition of the TR shows that at times the printer did not accept Erasmus' corrections, and at other times he made revisions that Erasmus had not made.

Because Erasmus possessed only one manuscript (and that in a commentary) for the book of Revelation, he had a fresh copy of the text of Revelation made. In copying the text of Revelation, the copyist made several errors that are still found in the TR text published today. Some of these errors are words unknown elsewhere in Greek literature, and other words are not found in any known Greek manuscripts. Because Erasmus had no Greek manuscript(s) containing the last six verses of Revelation, he translated these verses from the Latin Vulgate into Greek. These verses contain at least twenty errors that have no support whatsoever in any Greek manuscripts and yet are still found in the TR today.[30]

In Acts 9:6, Erasmus added to his Greek text the words "and he trembling and astonished said, Lord, what wilt thou have me to do? and the Lord said unto him." Erasmus admitted that he took these words from the Latin Vulgate. They are not found in any Greek manuscripts at this passage but are still found in the edition of the TR published by the Trinitarian Bible Society.[31]

The *Comma Johanneum,* the trinitarian formula in 1 John 5:7, 8, which is included in the TR, is found in only four late manuscripts. Erasmus did not include these words in his first two editions (1516, 1519) because they were not in any of the Greek manuscripts of 1 John that he had examined. When he received pressure from Catholic officials, he agreed to include these words ("the Father, the Word and the Holy Ghost: and these three are one . . . and there are three that bear witness in earth") if they could be found in one Greek manuscript. Thus, when Erasmus was presented with such a manuscript (Codex Montfortianus or Greg. 61), he was constrained to put these words in his third edition. Metzger suggests that "the Greek manuscript had probably been written in Oxford in 1520 by a Franciscan friar named Froy who took the disputed words from the Latin Vulgate."[32] Metzger notes that the reading has been found in only four Greek manuscripts, the earliest from the fourteenth century, and in the margin of four others. The arguments used for the inclusion of the *Comma Johanneum* in the TR and the KJV are a good example of the thinking and methodology of King James-Only advocates. As White notes, "There are, quite literally, *hundreds* of readings in the New Testament manuscript tradition that have better arguments in their favor that are *rejected* by both Erasmus and the KJV translators. And yet this passage is defended by King James-Only advocates to this day."[33] It is defended, of course, because it was included in the TR.

As was noted earlier, the Majority Text differs from the TR in about 1,800 places; Dan Wallace has counted 1,838 differences.[34] Before the Majority Text was published in 1982, its proponents predicted that it would differ from the TR in more than a thousand places.[35] These facts are important because they demonstrate that proponents of the Majority Text have recognized for many years that it is not the same as the TR; furthermore, they have wanted to distinguish their text from the TR. They realize that several readings in the TR (for example, the passages mentioned earlier as well as Acts 8:37 and phrases in Rev. 1:6, 8; 5:14; 14:1; 15:3) are not in the Majority Text or are different in the Majority Text than they are in the TR (see figure A).[36]

Remember that even though the TR and the Majority Text are similar, they are not the same. Therefore, advocates of the TR and King James-Only position should not use the Majority Text or the Majority

(Byzantine) text type to defend their position. Proponents of the Majority Text generally do not desire to be identified with the TR or King James-Only position. They realize that there are several important differences between the Majority Text and the TR. First, the Majority Text is based on a large textual base (well over four thousand manuscripts); the TR is essentially based on the seven late manuscripts that Erasmus used to prepare his text in 1516. Second, the TR includes several Greek readings that did not exist before 1516 when Erasmus put them in the Bible, whereas all of the readings of the Majority Text have support in known Greek witnesses.[37] Third, the TR differs from the Majority Text more than eighteen hundred times. Most of the TR readings that differentiate it from the Majority Text are also found in the KJV, calling into question any argument for the superiority, let alone the infallibility, of the text of the KJV.

The History of the Textus Receptus

The Textus Receptus published today by the Trinitarian Bible Society had its origin in the five printed editions (1516, 1519, 1522, 1527, and 1535) of the Greek text of Desiderius Erasmus (1469–1536). The Greek text was changed in his second edition. He added the trinitarian formula in 1 John 5:76–8a to his third edition, and in the fourth edition he altered the text of Revelation in about ninety places with changes based on the Complutensian Polyglot. His fourth and definitive edition became the basis of subsequent editions of the TR.

Erasmus' editions of the Greek NT (especially the 1527 and 1535 editions) were the bases of four editions of the Greek text published by Robert Estienne (1503–1559), who is better known by his Latin name Stephanus. Stephanus's third and fourth editions (1550, 1551), which are closer to Erasmus' 1527 and 1535 editions than are Stephanus's other editions, became the standard text of the Greek NT for many people, especially in England. Stephanus included variant readings in his text from about a dozen Greek manuscripts and the Complutensian Polyglot, showing that, like Erasmus, he was not averse to considering variants in the Greek text.

Theodore Beza (1519–1605) is the third key link in the development of the TR. Beza was John Calvin's friend and successor at Geneva. He published eleven editions of the Greek NT, the first in 1564.[38] He used Stephanus's lists of variant readings and added more of his own from other manuscripts. At times, he edited the text based on his own

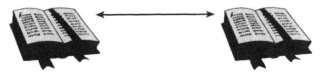

1,838 Differences between them

Textus Receptus	*Majority Text*
• Originally based on seven manuscripts of the Byzantine text type	• Based on all (about four thousand) manuscripts of the Byzantine text type
• Earliest manuscript—eleventh century	• Earliest manuscript—fourth century
• Contains the trinitarian formula in 1 John 5:7–8	• *Does not* contain trinitarian formula in 1 John 5:7–8
• Contains Acts 8:37; Luke 17:36	• *Does not* contain Acts 8:37; Luke 17:36
• Contains a large portion of Acts 9:6 and a phrase in 9:5	• *Does not* contain a large portion of Acts 9:6 and a phrase in 9:5
• Contains the questionable section in Acts 24:6b–8a	• *Does not* contain the questionable section in Acts 24:6b–8a
• Contains Acts 15:34	• *Does not* contain Acts 15:34
• Eph. 1:18—"the eyes of your *understanding*"	• Eph. 1:18—"the eyes of your *heart*"
• Eph. 3:9—"the *fellowship* of the mystery"	• Eph. 3:9—"the *administration* of the mystery"
• Second Timothy 2:19— "everyone that nameth the name of *Christ*"	• Second Timothy 2:19— "everyone that nameth the name of *the Lord*"
• Rev. 22:19—"*book* of life"	• Rev. 22:19—"*tree* of life"

Figure A: Differences between the Textus Receptus and the Majority Text

conjecture, such as in Revelation 16:5, where he changed "who art and who wast, *O Holy One*" to "which art and wast *and shalt be,*" a reading found in the KJV that has no Greek manuscript supporting it.[39] Beza's Greek text hardly differs from Stephanus's fourth edition (1551), and the KJV translators used Beza's editions extensively in completing their translation in 1611. Zane Hodges rightly warns, "It is important to keep in mind that in speaking of the Textus Receptus, we are talking about an entity which to this day retains a certain fluidity. There are more than 25 early editions of the Received Text, all varying slightly from one another. No absolutely definitive edition of it as yet exists."[40] This also is a good time to point out that the translators of the KJV used several sources (mainly Erasmus', Stephanus's, and Beza's texts), and when these texts differed, the translators chose between the various readings.[41]

Note that the name Textus Receptus was first applied to this textual tradition in 1633, two decades after the publication of the KJV. At that time, the Elzevirs published the second edition of their Greek NT with the publisher's blurb in the preface that this is the "text . . . now received by all." In Latin, the words "text" and "received" are *textum* and *receptum,* from which is derived the phrase "Textus Receptus," or "Received Text." This 1633 edition mainly followed Beza's text but also used Stephanus's and other sources (see figure B).[42]

The development in the TR from Erasmus to Stephanus to Beza to the Elzevirs makes inadmissible the claim of inspiration or perfect preservation for the TR (or KJV) that some King James-Only advocates make today. Furthermore, the standard edition of the TR used today (published by the Trinitarian Bible Society) is not identical to any of the editions of the TR that we have been discussing but is an "eclectic" text that draws its readings from different sources. The modern TR could be called a "made up" text, which in the case of variants determines what readings to include by following the English KJV.[43] The history of the TR leaves no doubt that its text has changed many times. This is a major problem for those who would claim that it exactly represents the originals. Yet D. A. Waite declares in fact, *"It is my own personal conviction and belief, after studying this subject since 1971, that the WORDS of the Received Greek and Masoretic Hebrew text that underlie the KING JAMES BIBLE are the very WORDS which God has PRESERVED down through the centuries, being the exact WORDS of the ORIGINALS themselves"* (emphasis Waite's).[44]

In the light of the historical evidence such a statement has no

1516	Erasmus' first edition	
1519	Erasmus' second edition	More than four hundred changes in the Greek text (chiefly corrections of misprints)
1522	Erasmus' third edition	More than one hundred changes from his second edition; addition of trinitarian formula in 1 John 5:7–8
1527	Erasmus' fourth edition	More than one hundred alterations of the third edition, ninety of them in Revelation
1546	Stephanus's first edition	
1549	Stephanus's second edition	More than sixty changes from Stephanus's first edition
1550	Stephanus's third edition	Includes variant readings in the margins
1551	Stephanus's fourth edition	The first time the text is divided into numbered verses
1565–1604	Beza's eleven editions	Minor changes in Stephanus's text. All of Beza's editions vary somewhat from Stephanus's and from each other.
1633	Elziver's second edition	First called the Textus Receptus (twenty-two years after the publication of the KJV)
1650	Elziver's third edition	Differs from the second edition in about 287 places

These are a few of the more than twenty-five revisions of the TR.

Figure B: The fluid history of the Textus Receptus (TR)

foundation. About which edition or revision of the TR is Waite talking? Which could measure up to his claim? How does he explain the reading in his edition of the TR that cannot be found in any Greek manuscript? Did God somehow reinspire His Word when the authoritative version of the TR was made (whenever that was)? Waite's view espouses belief in a miracle that is nowhere claimed or prophesied in Scripture. Furthermore, his theory contradicts the history of the TR. There is no objective, historical evidence that God's Word has been exactly preserved in the TR that underlies the KJV. Therefore, Waite must say that his otherwise unfounded assertion is, *a priori,* his "own personal conviction and belief." False claims such as this, even though they are meant to give certainty to God's people, lead only to larger problems.[45]

The Text of the King James Version

The translation from the TR and the Hebrew to the KJV was not as simple and direct as some people might imagine. Ira M. Price explains that the KJV

> was really a revision based on the Bishops' Bible, with free use made of the Genevan, the Rheims New Testament, and the material of Tremellius (1579), Beza (1556, 1565, and 1598), and other Latin versions. . . . King James's translators had no standard, or "received" Hebrew text, hence they were compelled to use the four current Hebrew Bibles and the Complutensian and Antwerp Polyglots. For the Greek New Testament they had Beza's improvements on Erasmus and Stephanus (see figure C).[46]

The original translators' manuscript that was given to the printer has been lost (like the autographa). We have only copies of it, all of which differ from not only each other but also the original because all of the editions have printers' errors in them.

Geisler and Nix state that "Many hundreds of editions and revisions of the King James Version (Authorized Version) were made between 1611 and 1881. . . ."[47] Therefore, another question that King James-Only advocates must answer is "Which edition of the KJV are you using?" The 1611 edition of the KJV is very different from the KJV Bibles printed today. The original 1611 edition had more than eight thousand notes in the outer margins giving more literal translations, alternative textual readings, and

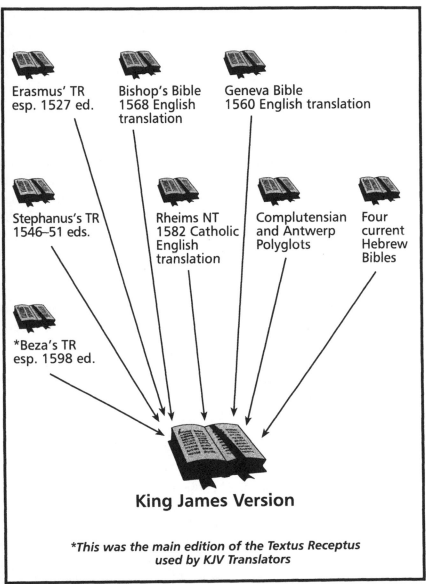

Erasmus' TR
esp. 1527 ed.

Bishop's Bible
1568 English
translation

Geneva Bible
1560 English translation

Stephanus's TR
1546–51 eds.

Rheims NT
1582 Catholic
English
translation

Complutensian
and Antwerp
Polyglots

Four
current
Hebrew
Bibles

*Beza's TR
esp. 1598 ed.

King James Version

****This was the main edition of the Textus Receptus
used by KJV Translators***

Figure C: Some of the texts used by the King James Version translators

explanatory notes.[48] Several of these textual notes suggested readings now employed by some of the more modern translations. The original KJV was also printed in the English of its time, in which many words were spelled differently than they are in modern editions of the KJV.

An edition of the KJV with changes from the original was published in 1611 and others followed in 1612, 1613, 1616, 1629 and 1638. "By 1659 William Kilburne, in a tract titled *Dangerous Errors in Several Late Printed Bibles to the Great Scandal and Corruption of Sound and True Religion* could claim that 20,000 errors had crept into six different editions printed in the 1650s."[49] Most modern KJV's are based on the 1769 revision made by Benjamin Blayney. Blayney's edition is estimated to differ from the original 1611 version in at least 75,000 details.[50] It is interesting to note that the first edition of the KJV to exclude the Apocrypha was printed in 1629, and the Apocrypha was not generally omitted until the nineteenth century.[51]

Most changes that have taken place in the various editions of the KJV involve small matters such as spelling and punctuation and are not a problem to people who realize that the KJV is not a perfectly preserved representation of the autographs. However, if the KJV is supposed to be a perfect representation of the autographs, as many King James-Only advocates claim, then these changes are a major problem. F. H. A. Scrivener lists several changes that have taken place in the KJV over the years, including the following:

- Josh. 13:29   "Manasseh" to "the children of Manasseh";
- Deut. 26:1   "the LORD" to "the LORD thy God";
- Ps. 69:32   "seek good" to "seek God"
- Jer. 49:1   "inherit God" to "inherit Gad";
- Matt. 16:16   "Thou art Christ" to "Thou art the Christ"
- Mark 10:18   "there is no man good, but one" to *"there is* none good but one"
- 1 Cor. 4:9   "approved unto death" to "appointed unto death"; and
- 1 John 5:12   "hath not the Son" to "Hath not the Son of God."[52]

Interestingly, the American Bible Society found twenty-four thousand variants in the text and punctuation of six nineteenth-century editions of the KJV.[53] One uncorrected misprint in the KJV is the phrase "strain at a gnat" in Matthew 23:24, which should read "strain out a gnat." In this context, Jesus is condemning the Pharisees for scrupulous observance of minor details (strain a gnat out of your drinking water) and neglect of other more major details (swallow a camel).[54] Most believers realize that people can make mistakes in copying and printing the Bible; furthermore, they believe that only the original autographs were inspired, not the KJV, the TR, or any other translation or edition. However, for the King James-Only advocate, such differences are more than an embarrassment; they are a contradiction of the King James-Only position. How can the KJV be inspired and yet have errors in it that should be changed? If it has been changed, which edition is the inspired edition (see figure D)?

Conclusion

This summary of information on textual criticism, Greek texts, and the KJV is intended to help answer some of the questions that honest readers have about the King James-Only position. The goal is not to attack the King James Version. Many of us have grown up using this Bible and still use it. In fact, it is unfortunate that time must be spent pointing out the weaknesses of a translation that has been used greatly for God's glory. However, the excesses of some of its defenders make this necessary.

One purpose of this chapter was to help the reader understand the difference between the Majority Text and the TR. Proponents of the TR cannot claim that their text is the same as the Majority Text or that it is always supported by the majority of manuscripts. The TR is based essentially on a few manuscripts from the Majority or Byzantine text type and differs in about eighteen hundred places from the Majority Text, which most accurately represents that text type. Neither the TR nor the KJV is a fixed phenomenon; both were revised and edited numerous times, and the present editions differ markedly from the original editions.

Another purpose of this chapter was to help those who are seeking the truth on this issue to see the false claims of anyone who says that the KJV or the TR is inspired or who would argue that one of these texts is always superior to all others and therefore must always be the closest to the original. Such claims are obviously false, and people who make them are, perhaps unwittingly, using arguments that are historically inaccurate to defend what they think is a biblical position.

These are some of the thousands of changes in the KJV since 1611. The original translators' manuscript that was given to the printer is lost (like the autographa). We have only copies, all of which differ from each other. Also, all of them differ from the original because all of them have printers' errors.

1611 original edition	More than eight thousand notes in the outer margins giving more literal translations, alternative textual readings, and explanatory notes; the translators put variant Greek readings in the margins of the NT
1613 edition	More than four hundred variations from the first edition
1616 edition	Changed "approved to death" to "appointed to death" (1 Cor. 4:9)
1629 edition	Major revision of the KJV (printed at Cambridge)
1629 edition	First time the KJV excludes the Apocrypha (not generally omitted until the nineteenth century); printed at London
1631 edition	Called the "Wicked Bible"—the word *not* is omitted from the seventh commandment
1638	Further revisions
1717 printing	Called the "Vinegar Bible"; Jesus gives a parable of the *vinegar* in Luke 20
1745 printing	Called the "Murderer's Bible"; Mark 7:27 reads, "Let the little children first be killed" instead of "filled"
1762 Thomas Paris edition	Extensive revisions, published at Cambridge
1769 Blayney edition	Basis of most modern KJV Bibles; differs from the 1611 edition in at least seventy-five thousand details
1873 Cambridge Paragraph Bible	Contained sixteen closely printed pages of differences from the original 1611 edition

Figure D: The fluid history of the King James Version

Chapter Notes

1. A secondary purpose, that is sometimes also mentioned is "to establish the history of transmission." See Maurice A. Robinson and William G. Pierpont, eds., *The New Testament in the Original Greek According to the Byzantine/Majority Textform* (Atlanta: Original Word Publishers, 1991), ix. Good introductions to New Testament textual criticism are Bruce Metzger, *The Text of the New Testament: Its Transmission, Corruption, and Restoration,* 3d ed. (New York: Oxford University Press, 1992); and Kurt and Barbara Aland, *The Text of the New Testament: An Introduction to the Critical Editions and to the Theory and Practice of Modern Textual Criticism,* trans. Erroll F. Rhodes, 2d ed. (Grand Rapids: Eerdmans, 1989). A more concise introduction can be found in J. H. Greenlee, *Introduction to New Testament Textual Criticism,* rev. ed. (Peabody, Mass.: Hendrickson, 1995).

2. Daniel B. Wallace, "Some Second Thoughts on the Majority Text," *Bibliotheca Sacra* 146, no. 583 (July–September 1989): 281, n. 50.

3. See Aland, *Text of the New Testament,* 72–84, for a description of the manuscripts of the New Testament. One of the most recent tabulations of NT manuscripts is in Kurt and Barbara Aland, eds., *Kurzgefasste Liste der griechen Handschriften des Neuen Testaments* (Hawthorne, N.Y.: Walter de Gruyter, 1994). This source lists the extant Greek manuscripts of the NT as 99 papyri, 306 uncials, 2,855 minuscule, and 2,396 lectionaries for the total given in this paper.

4. Carroll D. Osburn, "The Greek Lectionaries of the New Testament," in *The Text of the New Testament in Contemporary Research: Essays on the Status Quaestionis,* ed. Bart Ehrman and Michael Holmes (Grand Rapids: Eerdmans, 1995), 61–74, especially 67. Studies in the text of the lectionaries indicate significant influence on the text of the lectionaries by what some people call the Caesarean text type, and some portions of the lectionaries are actually more allied to that type of text than they are to any form of the Byzantine text. On the Caesarean text type, see Gordon D. Fee, "Textual Criticism of the New Testament," in *Textual Criticism of the New Testament,* ed. Eldon J. Epp and Gordon D. Fee (Grand Rapids: Eerdmans, 1993), 3–16, especially 8.

5. Robinson and Pierpont define a text type as "a specific pattern of variant readings shared among a fairly distinct group of manuscripts" (*New Testament in the Original Greek According to the Byzantine/Majority Textform,* xvi, n. 6).

6. In this essay, Majority text type refers to the text found in the majority of

extant Greek witnesses; this text type is often also called the Byzantine text type. Majority Text refers to the published text (Zane C. Hodges and Arthur L. Farstad, eds., *The Greek New Testament According to the Majority Text,* 2d ed. [Nashville: Nelson, 1985]). A slightly different edition of the Majority Text was published by Robinson and Pierpont in 1991 *(New Testament in the Original Greek According to the Byzantine/Majority Textform).* The Textus Receptus (TR) refers to any edition of the Greek New Testament based primarily on Erasmus' text (which is described later in this chapter). The form of text found in both the TR and the Majority Text, though different, is similar, and both of them, or a text that is in proximity to either, could be called the "traditional text." They are all some form of the Byzantine or Majority text type, and proponents of the traditional text could include proponents of the TR or Majority Text. It should be noted that proponents of the Majority Text do not like to be lumped together with proponents of the TR because of the differences in their texts and their theories of textual criticism. Proponents of the TR, however, often incorrectly use arguments that support only the Majority Text to defend the TR. The classifications used here are based on those of Daniel B. Wallace, "The Majority Text Theory: History, Methods, and Critique," in *The Text of the New Testament in Contemporary Research: Essays on the Status Quaestionis,* 297–320.

7. Daniel B. Wallace, "Inspiration, Preservation, and New Testament Textual Criticism," *Grace Theological Journal* 12, no. 1 (spring 1992): 30. The 80 percent figure appears to be a reasonable estimate. See Wallace, "The Majority Text Theory," 311. In 1975, Hodges said that 80 percent was a "safe estimate" of the number of Greek MSS agreeing with the Majority text type (which "closely resembles the kind of text which was the basis of the King James Version"). See Zane Hodges, "The Greek Text of the King James Version," in *Which Bible?* ed. David Otis Fuller, 5th ed. (Grand Rapids: Grand Rapids International Publications, 1975), 26, n. 3.

8. See Daniel B. Wallace, "The Majority Text and the Original Text: Are They Identical?" *Bibliotheca Sacra* 148, no. 590 (April–June 1991): 158–66, on the lack of early evidence for the Majority text type. It is important to remember that there is a difference between a Majority/Byzantine reading in a text and a text that can be classified as a Majority/Byzantine text type. For example, Harry Sturz argues that Majority/Byzantine readings are found in the papyri, but he does not suggest that any early papyri (before the fourth century) could be classified as Majority/Byzantine text-type manu-

scripts. See Harry Sturz, *The Byzantine Text Type and New Testament Textual Criticism* (Nashville: Nelson, 1984). Scattered readings do not make a text. No manuscript evidence exists for the Majority *text type* before the fourth century.

9. See Gordon D. Fee, "Modern Textual Criticism and the Revival of the Textus Receptus," *Journal of the Evangelical Theological Society* 21 (1978): 19–33, for a discussion of some of the weaknesses of the Majority text type. Another good source is H. A. Sturz, *The Byzantine Text Type and New Testament Textual Criticism* (Nashville: Nelson, 1984). Sturz gives both the weaknesses and the strengths of the Majority text type. Probably the most thorough defense of the Majority text type is Wilbur N. Pickering, *The Identity of the New Testament Text* (Nashville: Nelson, 1977). Fee writes concerning the Majority text type, "Most of the readings peculiar to this text are generally recognized to be of a secondary nature. A great number of them smooth out grammar; remove ambiguity in word order; add nouns, pronouns, and prepositional phrases; and harmonize one passage with another. Its many conflate readings (e.g., Mark 9:49), where the Byzantine text type combines the alternative variants of the Egyptian and Western texts, also reflect this secondary process" ("Textual Criticism of the New Testament," 8).

10. Fee, "Textual Criticism of the New Testament," 7–8. One of the main arguments of the King James-Only advocates is that the Old Latin favors the Majority text type in some places. Even if that were true, the affinity of the Old Latin for the Western text type is well established. In fact, however, the King James-Only advocates tend to base this claim upon a minimum of hard evidence.

11. Although the variants peculiar to this text type are firmly established in manuscripts coming from the western Mediterranean countries, the early evidence of this text in the east suggests that it might have actually originated there (Fee, "Textual Criticism of the New Testament," 7–8). Fee characterizes this text type as follows: ". . . 'Western' describes a group of manuscripts headed by Codex D, obviously related by hundreds of unusual readings, sometimes found in one or several, sometimes in others, but apparently reflecting an uncontrolled, sometimes 'wild,' tradition of copying and translating. This text type is particularly marked by some long paraphrases and long additions, as well as by harmonistic tendencies and substitutions of synonyms. In fact, the Western text of Acts is about ten percent longer than other texts and almost certainly reflects an early revision" (ibid., 7).

12. For a classification of all of the papyri, see Aland, *Text of the New Testament,* 95–102, 106. According to Aland, all of the papyri that were produced before the fourth century agree with the Alexandrian text type. Only three of eighty-eight papyri can be classed as purely or even predominantly Byzantine, and these papyri are from the fourth through the seventh centuries (ibid., 7, 25, 73).

13. The basic guideline concerning internal evidence is that the variant that best accounts for the existence of the others is most likely to be the original reading. Because scribes would not try to make a text harder to understand but would rather attempt to improve it, the most difficult variant is often preferred on the basis of internal evidence. Fee writes concerning the Alexandrian text type, "Although this text type has occasional 'sophisticated' variants, it commonly contains readings that are terse, somewhat rough, less harmonized, and generally 'more difficult' than those of other text types, though on closer study they regularly commend themselves as original. Furthermore, it is consistently so across all the NT books, with a minimal tendency to harmonize an author's idiosyncrasies with more common Greek patterns. All these facts give the impression that this text type is the product of a carefully preserved transmission" ("Textual Criticism of the New Testament," 7).

14. To give a thorough comparison of the various text types in this paper is impossible. For a discussion and evaluation of the various text types, see Metzger, *Text of the New Testament: Its Transmission, Corruption, and Restoration,* 211–9. Aland suggests that the Greek manuscripts of the NT be classified according to a more precise system involving five categories. This system is based upon systematic testing and collection of more manuscripts than have ever before been studied, but because of its recent publication it has not had much impact yet in popular literature. Furthermore, his categories are not based on text types; two of his categories contain manuscripts from the Alexandrian text type, and another category contains manuscripts from various text types (Aland, *The Text of the New Testament,* 159).

15. By "important textual variants" I mean those judged to be so by the committee that edited the text. In the case of the United Bible Societies' apparatus, some variants that would be considered important by proponents of the "traditional text" are not included.

16. Today the Nestle-Aland, *Novum Testamentum Graece,* 27th ed. (Stuttgart: Deutsche Bibelgesellschaft, 1993), and the United Bible Societies, *Greek*

New Testament, 4th ed. (New York: American Bible Society, 1993), share the same text, as they did in their previous editions. See the introduction to the Nestle-Aland, *Novum Testamentum Graece,* 27th ed., 44–46.

17. "Reasoned Eclecticism holds that the text of the New Testament is to be based on both internal and external evidence, without a preference for any particular manuscript or text type" (David Alan Black, *New Testament Textual Criticism: A Concise Guide* [Grand Rapids: Baker, 1994], 37).

18. Zane C. Hodges and Arthur L. Farstad, eds., *The Greek New Testament According to the Majority Text* (Nashville: Nelson, 1982). Technically speaking, proponents of the Majority Text do not call the Byzantine or Majority manuscripts a text type. To them, the Majority Text (sometimes majority text when referring to the manuscripts rather than the published text) is the majority of manuscripts, not a text type per se.

19. A more recent edition of the Majority Text is by Robinson and Pierpont, eds., *The New Testament in the Original Greek According to the Byzantine/Majority Textform.* Robinson and Pierpont followed different principles in constructing their edition of the Majority Text than Hodges and Farstad did; therefore, the texts are not identical. Robinson and Pierpont explain, "Textual distinctions from Hodges-Farstad are due either to their particular interpretation of identical data, their use or rejection of additional data, or because some items in the difficult-to-read Von Soden apparatus were neglected or misinterpreted by them. Minor differences are most noticeable where closely divided Byzantine readings appear sporadically from Matthew through Jude (marked "M^{pt}" in the Hodges-Farstad apparatus). Many of these divided readings appear in brackets [ ] in this edition when simple omission or inclusion is indicated. . . ." Furthermore, major differences from the Hodges-Farstad text occur in their text in John 7:53–8:11 and in Revelation because Hodges and Farstad used a stemmatic (genealogical) approach in those passages. Robinson and Pierpont do not use stemmatics anywhere in constructing their text.

20. Hodges and Farstad, *Greek New Testament According to the Majority Text,* xi–xii.

21. An excellent example of this division is the famous textual problem in Romans 5:1 'exomen/'exwmen. Wallace, "The Majority Text and the Original Text," 168, discusses the splits. Hodges and Farstad describe the five strands of the Majority text type in their introduction (*Greek New Testament According to the Majority Text,* ix–xliv). On the strands in the Majority text see also Sturz, *The Byzantine Text Type and New Testament Textual Criticism,* 94.

22. Wallace, "Some Second Thoughts on the Majority Text," 283–84.

23. A major reason why Robinson and Pierpont *(The New Testament in the Original Greek According to the Byzantine/Majority Textform)* published their text in 1991 was their disagreement with the genealogical principle of Hodges and Farstad *(Greek New Testament According to the Majority Text).*

24. Wallace, "Some Second Thoughts on the Majority Text," 277, states that he has counted 6,577 differences between these two texts.

25. Both recent editions of the Eclectic Text explain the meaning of the double brackets in their introductions. The double brackets indicate that the enclosed words are known not to be a part of the original text, but they are included because they derive from a very early stage of the tradition and have often played a significant role in the history of the church. James R. White gives summaries of why good reason exists to doubt the authenticity of these two passages *(The King James Only Controversy* [Minneapolis: Bethany House, 1995], 255–57, 262).

26. These statistics are from Wallace, "Some Second Thoughts on the Majority Text," 276–77. Before the Majority Text was published, Pickering, a strong proponent of the Majority or Byzantine text type, predicted that "the *Textus Receptus* will be found to differ from the original [by this he meant the Majority Text] in something over a thousand places, most of them being very minor differences, whereas the critical texts will be found to differ from the original in some five thousand places, many of them being serious differences" *(The Identity of the New Testament Text,* 177).

27. This summary of the TR follows Metzger, *Text of the New Testament: Its Transmission, Corruption, and Restoration,* 95–106; White, *King James-Only Controversy,* 53–89; and William W. Combs, "Erasmus and the Textus Receptus," *Detroit Baptist Seminary Journal* 1, no. 1 (spring 1996): 35–53.

28. Metzger, *Text of the New Testament: Its Transmission, Corruption, and Restoration,* 99; Combs, "Erasmus and the Textus Receptus," 42.

29. F. H. A. Scrivener, *A Plain Introduction to the Criticism of the New Testament,* 4th ed. (London: George Bell and Sons, 1894), 185.

30. See the discussion in Combs, "Erasmus and the Textus Receptus," 47, and Metzger, *Text of the New Testament: Its Transmission, Corruption, and Restoration,* 100.

31. White, *The New Testament: The Greek Text Underlying the English Authorized Version of 1611* (London: The Trinitarian Bible Society, 1977). White discusses the weaknesses of the TR in the book of Revelation *(King James-Only Controversy,* 64–66). Some words in the TR, such as in Revelation

17:4, are new Greek words that were never seen before. Other readings in Revelation 15:3 and 22:19 have no Greek manuscripts as support. See White for discussion of other verses.

32. Metzger, *Text of the New Testament: Its Transmission, Corruption, and Restoration,* 101.

33. White, *King James-Only Controversy,* 61. The old *Scofield Reference Bible* (1325) states that the phrase in 1 John 5:7–8 "has no real authority, and has been inserted."

34. Wallace; "The Majority Text Theory," 302, n. 28.

35. In 1968, Wilbur N. Pickering predicted that the Majority Text would have between five hundred and one thousand differences from the TR ("An Evaluation of Contribution of John William Burgon to New Testament Textual Criticism" [Th.M. thesis, Dallas Theological Seminary, 1968], 120). In 1977, he predicted that the Majority Text would differ from the TR in "something over a thousand places" (idem, *The Identity of the New Testament Text,* 177).

36. See n. 21. The differences between the Majority Text and the TR are accented by the fact that different societies have been established to support them. The Majority Text Society was established in Dallas in 1988. Members sign the creed "I believe that the best approach to the original wording of the New Testament is through the Majority Text, or I wish to cooperate in testing that hypothesis." The Trinitarian Bible Society in Great Britain has been in existence since 1831 and since 1958 has vigorously supported the TR. The Dean Burgon Society in the USA was founded in 1978 and also strongly defends the TR, even against the Majority Text. For an example of the emphatic manner in which Majority Text proponents stress their distinction from TR proponents, see Robinson and Pierpont, *The New Testament in the Original Greek According to the Byzantine/Majority Textform,* xli–xliii.

37. Metzger states concerning the TR, "And in a dozen passages its reading is supported by no known Greek witnesses" (*Text of the New Testament: Its Transmission, Corruption, and Restoration,* 2d ed. [New York: Oxford University Press, 1968], 106).

38. Metzger says that he published no fewer than nine editions from 1565 to 1604 and one edition appeared posthumously in 1611 (*Text of the New Testament: Its Transmission, Corruption, and Restoration,* 2d ed., 105). Dan Wallace has personally related his finding that Beza's real first edition was in 1564 and that Beza published eleven editions of the Greek NT. Wallace's findings are followed here.

39. White, *King James-Only Controversy,* 63.

40. Zane C. Hodges, *A Defense of the Majority Text* (Dallas: Dallas Seminary, n.d.), 1.

41. Beza's 1598 edition was the main source used by the translators (Combs, "Erasmus and the Textus Receptus," 53).

42. F. H. A. Scrivener, *A Plain Introduction to the Criticism of the New Testament*, 2d ed. (London: Deighton, Bell and Co., 1874), 392, suggests that this 1633 edition differs from Stephanus's 1550 edition in 287 places.

43. White, *King James-Only Controversy*, 86, n. 37, reminds us that variants existed between the texts of Erasmus, Stephanus, and Beza, and the KJV translators chose between them. He also says, "[T]he modern TR is a 'made up' text that follows the English KJV in determining which readings to include." The following statement is found on page 2 of the preface in the TR printed by the Trinitarian Bible Society in London: "The present edition of the *Textus Receptus* underlying the English Authorized Version of 1611 follows the text of Beza's 1598 edition as the primary authority, and corresponds with 'The New Testament in the Original Greek according to the text followed in the Authorized Version,' edited by F. H. A. Scrivener, M.A., D.C.L., LL.D., and published by Cambridge University Press in 1894 and 1902."

44. D. A. Waite, *Defending the King James Bible* (Collingswood, N.J.: Bible for Today Press, 1992), 48–49. This is one of the many unbelievable claims in Waite's book, a volume that Wallace ("The Majority Text Theory: History, Methods, and Critique," 305, n. 42) describes as "339 pages of anecdotes, guilt-by-association arguments, and theological invective." Similarly, Thomas Strousse claims, ". . . the TR is essentially equivalent to the *autographa*. . . ." Thomas M. Strousse, "Fundamentalism and the Authorized Version" (paper presented at the National Leadership Conference, Landsdale, Pa., February 1996), 4. The italics are Strousse's.

45. The preservation of Scripture will be addressed in the next chapter.

46. Ira Maurice Price, *The Ancestry of Our English Bible*, 2d rev. ed. by William A. Irwin and Allen P. Wikgren (New York: Harper and Brothers, 1949), 273–74.

47. Norman L. Geisler and William E. Nix, *A General Introduction to the Bible*, rev. and expanded ed. (Chicago: Moody, 1986), 610, n. 5.

48. These notes must be an embarrassment to modern King James-Only advocates who are upset about the variant readings printed in the NKJV.

49. Jack Lewis, *The English Bible: From kjv to niv*, 2d ed. (Grand Rapids: Baker, 1991), 38–39.

50. Edgar J. Goodspeed, "The Versions of the New Testament," in *Tools for Bible Study,* ed. Balmer H. Kelly and Donald G. Miller (Richmond: John Knox, 1956): 119–20. For a wealth of information about the KJV, see Ron Minton, "The Making and Preservation of the Bible," an unpublished notebook. A current draft of this notebook is available from the author at Piedmont Baptist College Graduate Division, 716 Franklin Street, Winston-Salem, N.C. 27101.

51. Lewis, *The English Bible,* 38.

52. F. H. A. Scrivener, *The Authorized Edition of the English Bible (1611)* (Cambridge: 1884), 147–202.

53. Lewis, *The English Bible,* 39.

54. This misprint is most interesting because the 1611 edition had it correct ("strain out a gnat"), and the error that was introduced at a subsequent date has still not been corrected (Lewis, *The English Bible,* 38). For a critique of the problems in the KJV that goes far beyond the limits of this chapter, consult Lewis (ibid., 35–68).

Chapter 4

The Preservation of Scripture and the Version Debate

W. Edward Glenny

The Bible alone, and the Bible in its entirety, is the Word of God written and is therefore inerrant in the autographs.

—Evangelical Theological Society

We believe that all "Scripture is given by inspiration of God," by which we understand the whole Bible is inspired in the sense that holy men of God "were moved by the Holy Spirit" to write the very words of Scripture. We believe that this divine inspiration extends equally and fully to all parts of the writings—historical, poetical, doctrinal, and prophetical—as appeared in the original manuscripts. We believe that the whole Bible in the originals is therefore without error.

—Dallas Seminary,
Dallas, Texas

We believe the Holy Scriptures of the Old and New Testaments to be the verbally and plenarily inspired Word of God and inerrant in the original writings. The sixty-six books of the Old and

New Testaments are the complete and divine revelation of God to man, and therefore, are the final authority for faith and life.

—Calvary Baptist Theological Seminary,
Lansdale, Pennsylvania

We believe in the verbal, plenary inspiration of the Bible, the sixty-six books of the Old and New Testament canon which, being inerrant in the original manuscripts, is the final authority on all matters of faith and practice and any other subject on which it touches.

—Detroit Baptist Theological Seminary,
Detroit, Michigan

We believe that the Bible, sixty-six books in the Old and New Testaments, is without error in its original writing, and the sole authority for faith and practice.

—Central Baptist Theological Seminary of
Minneapolis, Minnesota

THESE CONFESSIONAL STATEMENTS, ranging from the evangelical mainstream to the conservative wing of fundamentalism, share certain perspectives. First, they acknowledge that the canon of Scripture consists of the sixty-six books contained in the Old and New Testaments recognized by Protestant churches. Furthermore, they imply or take for granted the fact that God has preserved His Word in these sixty-six books. Fundamentalists and other evangelicals join together in gladly affirming God's providential control over the events of history so that His Word has been preserved by natural processes in the many extant manuscripts, versions, and other copies of Scripture. What these statements do *not* affirm or imply is that God has perfectly preserved His Word by miraculous, supernatural means in any one manuscript, version, or text type. The Scriptures teach inspiration and inerrancy in relation to only the original autographs.

The reason we must so clarify our position is because of the divergent position of two groups. First, some people support the superiority of the KJV and Textus Receptus (TR). Their main argument is based on the *a priori* assumption of God's supernatural, perfect preservation of Scripture in the KJV or the TR. Second, proponents of the Majority Text do not go as far as supporters of the KJV or TR in assuming the perfect preservation of Scripture, but they do engage the doctrine of preservation in their attempts to prove the superiority of the Majority Text.

The argument of these two groups is developed in two steps. The first step involves the idea that "the doctrine of verbal-plenary inspiration necessitates the doctrine of providential preservation of the text."[1] This argument from reason posits that it would do no good for God to give mankind His Word if He did not preserve it. The second step entails the belief that the doctrine of providential preservation necessarily implies that the Majority Text or the TR is *the* faithful replica of the autographs because it has been preserved in large numbers and used greatly by God, especially in the Western world.

Usually, this argument is further developed along two other lines. First, an inerrant New Testament can be found only in these texts. Second, "if any portion of the New Testament is lost [no matter how small, even if only one word], then verbal-plenary inspiration is thereby falsified."[2]

Some of the more extreme King James–Only advocates actually argue that the KJV is inspired and we should correct the Greek and Hebrew texts by the KJV.[3] This view involves a miraculous preservation and reinspiration of the text at the time the KJV was produced. A much more common position is that of TR and Majority Text advocates for whom inspiration and preservation are linked first to each other and then to the superiority of the TR or Majority Text. Some in the latter group, especially supporters of the TR, are very clear in these connections. One such proponent writes,

> It is my own personal conviction and belief, after studying this subject since 1971, that the words of the Received Greek and Masoretic Hebrew texts that underlie the King James Bible are the very words which God has preserved down through the centuries, being the exact words of the originals themselves. As such, I believe they are inspired words.[4]

Others, especially supporters of the Majority Text, are more subtle in linking together inspiration, preservation, and the superiority of the Majority Text.[5]

In the following discussion, please remember that the form of text found in both the TR and the Majority Text is similar, and both the TR and the Majority Text, or any text that is in proximity to them, could be called the "traditional text." All of these texts offer some form of the Majority (or Byzantine) text type. Therefore, any reference herein to the "traditional text" is a reference to the Majority (or Byzantine) text type, which includes the TR.[6]

The point of this chapter is that the preservation of God's Word, which the facts of history surely confirm, does not imply that the KJV is the only true Bible; nor does it imply that the KJV, TR, or Majority Text is superior to other translations or texts. In addition, the arguments based on the preservation of God's Word that are used to assert the superiority of the KJV, TR, and Majority Text are not credible or consistent. These arguments have at least three types of problems: historical, logical, and biblical.

Historical Problems

The proponents of the TR/Majority Text make the doctrine of preservation a necessary corollary of inspiration, and they seek to establish textual purity and public accessibility as necessary corollaries of preservation. In other words, preservation does not mean anything if the text is not accessible, and inspiration does not mean anything if the text is not purely preserved accessibly. For example, Wilbur Pickering writes that "the doctrine of Divine Preservation of the New Testament Text depends upon the interpretation of the evidence which recognizes the traditional text to be the continuation of the autographa." Here Pickering seems to say that to reject the Majority Text position is to reject the doctrine of preservation. He also argues that "God *has* preserved the text of the New Testament in a very pure form and it has been readily available to his followers in every age throughout 1900 years."[7] Thus, Pickering and other TR/Majority Text proponents make textual purity and public accessibility necessary parts of the preservation of Scripture.

The evidence from history, however, does not support their theory. If the TR/Majority Text is God's inspired Word, then according to their theory one would expect that it has been preserved in the majority of manuscripts throughout the history of the church. This, however, is not the case at all. As was noted in the preceding chapter, the TR never existed before 1516, and the TR text used today was not compiled until almost a century after that. To claim God's pure and accessible preservation of the TR is to ignore the facts of history.

To argue that God has preserved His inspired Word through the ages only in the Majority/Byzantine text type (of which the TR is a representative) is more realistic. However, this line of reasoning also has several problems. First, there is no evidence that the Majority/Byzantine text type existed before the fourth century. To date, approximately one hundred papyrus manuscripts have been found. At most, only three of those papyri can be classified as a predominantly Majority/Byzantine text type, and all three of them date from the fourth century or later.[8] On the other hand, about fifty of the papyri (none with the Byzantine/Majority type text) come from before the middle of the fourth century.[9] The first version of Scripture that generally reflects the Majority text type is the Gothic at the end of the fourth century. None of the earlier versions has the Majority text type.[10] Also, in the last eighty years, no study of the text of a church father has found proof of the use of the Majority text type in the first three centuries of this age.[11] Therefore, if God was preserving His Word in the Majority text type, no evidence of it exists in the manuscripts from the first three centuries.

More damaging to their argument is the fact that no Majority text type manuscript exists for the letters of Paul from before the ninth century. This fact is inconceivable if the Majority text type is the only text in which God has preserved the autographs and if every word of the autographa must be preserved perfectly or inspiration is invalidated. Proponents of the view that the Majority text type represents the autographa take an eight hundred-year leap of faith when they propose that God has perfectly preserved the Pauline Epistles in the Majority text type. Beyond all of that, the Majority text type was not even in the majority numerically until the ninth century, and even today it is outnumbered by manuscripts of other text types if we count the Latin manuscripts because we have more than ten thousand of them, and none of them belongs to the Majority text type (see figure A).

There are major gaps of history from which there is no evidence that the Majority text type even existed! The historical evidence does not indicate that God has been supernaturally preserving the traditional text in every age. It is a text type that apparently never existed before the fourth century, and no extant traditional-text manuscript of the Pauline Epistles exists from before the ninth century. In this regard, any historical argument for the superiority of the traditional text is an argument from silence. A historical argument for the superiority of the TR or the

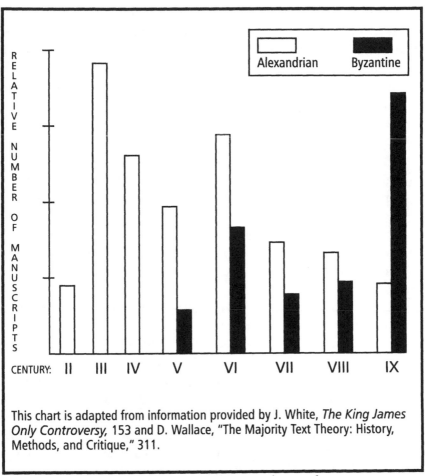

This chart is adapted from information provided by J. White, *The King James Only Controversy,* 153 and D. Wallace, "The Majority Text Theory: History, Methods, and Critique," 311.

**Figure A: Comparative prevalence of
Alexandrian and Byzantine manuscripts**

KJV is even harder to defend than the Majority Text because the TR/KJV texts are not the same text as the Majority text type and they never existed before 1516 and 1611, respectively.

Logical Problems

Proponents of the TR/Majority Text not only have historical problems but also many of them make illogical assumptions. These false assumptions can be summarized as follows.

Perfect Preservation Is a Necessary Corollary of Inspiration

As was already mentioned, King James-Only advocates assume that preservation is a necessary corollary of inspiration and that for inspiration to be true, God must have perfectly preserved the New Testament (NT) text. The difficulty with this assumption becomes obvious when it is carried to its logical conclusion. Bart Ehrman correctly observed,

> Any claim that God preserved the New Testament text intact, giving His church actual, not theoretical, possession of it, must mean one of three things—either 1) God preserved it in all the extant manuscripts so that none of them contain[s] any textual corruptions, or 2) He preserved it in a group of manuscripts, none of which contain[s] any corruptions, or 3) He preserved it in a solitary manuscript which alone contains no corruptions.[12]

The first option certainly and obviously is not true; God did not preserve the NT without any corruption in all of the manuscripts. The closest manuscripts disagree an average of six to ten times per chapter. The second option is also impossible; the New Testament text was not preserved intact in a group of manuscripts of which none contain any error. The Majority text type, which is the most unified of all text types, has five different strands in it, not to mention the disagreements between individual manuscripts. Then, could the third option possibly be true? Has God perfectly preserved His Word in a single manuscript? This option is also impossible because it is easy to demonstrate "that every manuscript has scribal errors in it."[13]

Of course, TR advocates would quickly respond to this objection by saying that the TR, a printed edition of the NT text, can satisfy this requirement; it can preserve the New Testament text intact. However, their theory has some major flaws in it, too. First, in which edition of the TR is God's Word perfectly preserved? The TR has gone through more than twenty-five editions and numerous changes as was detailed in the preceding chapter.[14] Second, as was also noted in the preceding chapter, the TR never existed before 1516, and scores of readings in it were nonexistent before Erasmus created them. Third, the text of the TR was based originally on seven differing manuscripts. How could the TR perfectly preserve the NT text if it was based on seven manuscripts, all of which contained errors? How could it be perfect if it was a compilation of these seven manuscripts along with readings created by Erasmus? Did it become perfect at some point in its editing? Anyone who believes that God has preserved the NT text intact in the TR, if they wish to be consistent, must also argue for reinspiration of Scripture through the person who compiled the edition of the TR that perfectly preserves God's Word (whatever edition that is).

Because most TR advocates want to identify the text of Erasmus with the original text of the NT, these TR supporters make Erasmus, a Roman Catholic priest and the man against whom Luther wrote his famous book *Bondage of the Will,* to be a writer of inspired Scripture. Erasmus was a "lifelong devoted Catholic" who by his own quotations demonstrated that he had an "absolute and undying loyalty to Roman Catholicism, its doctrine and its pope."[15] What is worse, they extend inspiration from the original documents (as the NT teaches in 2 Timothy 3:16–17 and 2 Peter 1:20–21) to the sixteenth century. Such teaching is clearly unscriptural and twists the fundamental doctrine of the inspiration of Scripture in an attempt to support the TR. The obvious alternative is to admit that the TR/KJV text does not perfectly preserve the original NT text.

None of the three options that might be used to argue that God has preserved the New Testament text intact supports that position. He has not preserved the NT text intact in all of the manuscripts or in a group of manuscripts, none of which contains corruption, or in a solitary manuscript which contains no corruption. Therefore, instead of saying that God has preserved His Word in any one text or edition, as the TR/Majority Text advocates argue, it is better to say that He has preserved His Word in and through the thousands of extant manuscripts, and that those who seek truth must compare those manuscripts to determine the correct readings when the manuscripts differ.[16]

God Has Preserved His Word in the Majority of Manuscripts

A second faulty logical assumption made by TR/Majority Text advocates is the assumption that preservation must be through majority rule.[17] The first difficulty with this assumption is that the Bible nowhere tells us how God will preserve His Word. Those who presume that it must be preserved in a certain text or type of text, excluding all other texts, have no scriptural basis for their presumption. A second difficulty is posed by the realization that God often works through a minority rather than through the majority to accomplish His purposes in history and in the world. To argue that a numerical majority is an indication of God's providential blessing would imply that the Roman Catholic church must be correct, and we should all become Roman Catholics.

This argument presumes that we know what God is doing in history. In an article on the canonicity of the New Testament, M. James Sawyer demonstrates where such thinking can lead.

> One's place in history can radically affect his interpretation of an event or process. A chilling example of this phenomenon is seen in the "German Christians'" response to the rise of Adolf Hitler. The "German Christians" spoke of the "Lord of History" who was at that moment in Germany's history speaking in a clear voice. It led a group of theologians at Württemberg to declare in 1934: We are full of thanks to God that He, as Lord of history, has given us Adolf Hitler, our leader and savior from our difficult lot. We acknowledge that we, with body and soul, are bound and dedicated to the German state and to its Führer. This bondage and duty contains for us, as evangelical Christians, its deepest and most holy significance in its obedience to the command of God.[18]

Few today, if any, would claim that God gave Adolf Hitler to the German churches to be their leader and savior. We look at Hitler from a much different perspective. This fact should remind us that the only objective criterion we have by which we can determine God's purposes and will is His interpretation of the events of this world in His Word. Because God has not told His people that He will preserve His Word in the majority of manuscripts or in a certain text type, it is sheer presumption and pride for us to insist that He must do so.

Perceptual Certainty Is Identical to Absolute Truth

Another unsupported assumption of TR/Majority Text advocates is that the pursuit of "certainty" is identical to the pursuit of "truth." Many TR/Majority Text advocates have given up hope of finding absolute textual certainty by means of the standard methods of textual criticism; therefore, they have opted for a simplistic methodology that will give them a settled and certain text, the TR/Majority Text. The methodology that they use to determine the correct text rests upon the *a priori* assumption of God's perfect, providential preservation of His Word in the majority of manuscripts. For example, Theodore Letis argues,

> Without a methodology that has for its agenda the determination of a continuous, obviously providentially preserved text . . . we are, in principle, left with maximum uncertainty . . . versus the maximum certainty afforded by the methodology that seeks a providentially preserved text.[19]

Wilbur Pickering maintains:

> If the Scriptures have not been preserved then the doctrine of Inspiration is a purely academic matter with no relevance for us today. If we do not have the inspired Words or do not know precisely which they be, then the doctrine of Inspiration is inapplicable.[20]

This argument has several problems, and several of the facts mentioned already in this chapter contradict it. First, if they are talking about the TR, then what edition is inspired? Second, how can it be the perfectly preserved Word of God if even a few of the readings in it never existed before 1516? If they are talking about the Majority text type, how can they explain the hundreds of splits in the Byzantine tradition where there is no clear majority? For example, Kurt Aland recently found fifty-two variants in the Majority text type in two verses (2 Cor. 1:6–7).[21] How do we determine what is the original in such situations?

Some proponents of the traditional text claim its superiority and the satanic character of all other text types by ignoring much of the evidence concerning the text of the New Testament. They are cultic in this regard. More important to them than honesty and dealing fairly with all of the evidence is the necessity of a "certainty," which can only come from a one-sided treatment of the question. The temptation for some people is to seek certainty by opting for a simplistic answer that does not have to face the complex facts involved in the issue. Wallace explains clearly the difference between the pursuit of certainty and the pursuit of truth:

> [T]he quest for certainty is not the same as a quest for truth. There is a subtle but important distinction between the two.

Truth is objective reality; certainty is the level of subjective ap-
prehension of something perceived to be true. But in the recognition that truth is objective reality, it is easy to confuse the fact
of this reality with how one knows what it is. Frequently the
most black-and-white, dogmatic method of arriving at truth is
perceived to be truth itself. Indeed, people with deep religious
convictions are very often quite certain about an untruth. For
example, cultists often hold to their positions quite dogmatically
and with a fideistic fervor that shames evangelicals; first-year
Greek students want to speak of the aorist tense as meaning
"once-and-for-all" action; and almost everyone wants simple
answers to the complex questions of life. At [the] bottom [of]
this quest for certainty, though often masquerading as a legitimate epistemological inquiry, is really a presuppositional stance,
rooted in a psychological insecurity.[22]

This psychological insecurity is seen in the *ad hominem* arguments, la-
beling (as "liberal, humanistic, satanic," etc.), question-begging approach,
and guilt-by-association arguments used in many defenses of the traditional text. The lack of legitimate inquiry is seen in the one-sided treatment of the facts so that the issue appears to be simple. The end result of
such teaching will be either to develop people who have no taste for truth
(i.e., "Don't confuse me with the facts; my mind is already made up") or
to deceive people so that they will be devastated if they are someday
confronted with all of the facts and they cannot handle them.

In our defense and propagation of the faith, the key issue is not whether
today we know the precise form of each of the words recorded in the
autographa. To make that our focus moves us away from God to concentrate on the process by which His revelation has come to us. The key
issue is that God has spoken in the autographa, He has spoken with authority and without error, and we are responsible to respond to Him.
Believers should concentrate their efforts on obeying the theology upon
which they can all agree rather than arguing about the texts concerning
which they disagree. The differences of opinion on textual matters makes
very little difference, if any, in the theological beliefs of Christians. Van
Til, after affirming the infallibility of the autographa and denying the
infallibility of any translation, addresses the important issue:

The important point is not whether or not we now possess the autographa but whether they have actually existed. Without them there is no Christ who has spoken anywhere in history. With them we have such a Christ. With them we have many problems of text and translation but no ultimate meaningless mystery, such as we would have without them.[23]

In this same context, van Til suggests two glaring weaknesses that will characterize anyone who claims that a translation is infallible. First, that person's focus is moved away from God and Christ and is redirected toward a supposedly infallible translation. Second, such a person abandons the search for a text or translation that better represents or gives a clearer understanding of the autographa. On the other hand, if a person holds that inspiration applies directly to only the autographa, then he or she will diligently search for the best representation of it. What the world needs to hear is that God has spoken, not that we have only one perfectly preserved text of Scripture and that all others are inferior to it.

Summary

Several logical problems arise in the arguments for the perfect preservation of God's Word in the TR and Majority text type. The first problem is the false assumption that perfect preservation is a necessary corollary of inspiration. A second false assumption is the belief that divine preservation must be found in the majority of manuscripts. Another false assumption is that perceptual certainty is identical with absolute truth. However, these logical fallacies are not the most serious problem with the view that God must flawlessly preserve His Word in the majority of manuscripts. The most serious problem is that some people misuse biblical texts to support the doctrine of perfect, providential preservation.

Biblical Problems

This section outlines two major biblical problems with the view advanced by TR/Majority Text advocates concerning God's perfect, providential preservation of the text of the autographa. These problems stem from the misuse of biblical texts to support their doctrine of perfect, providential preservation of Scripture.

The Text of the Old Testament

A first biblical problem with the position of TR/Majority Text advocates is that their theory does not work for the Old Testament (OT). A study of the text of the OT indicates that God did not perfectly preserve the OT as they claim He must do in the NT. Concerning the NT, E. F. Hills argues that "God must do more than merely preserve the inspired original New Testament text. He must preserve it in a public way . . . through the continuous usage of His church."[24] We have already shown the impossibility of defending this argument for the New Testament text. Even more difficult is arguing that such public preservation is true for the Old Testament text. The Old Testament text was not even preserved publicly throughout Israel's history. King Manasseh must have tried to destroy the Book of the Law, but it was found again in the house of the Lord during the reign of Josiah. Apparently, one of the priests had hidden a copy there when Manasseh tried to destroy it (2 Kings 22:8–20). Thus, for many years (long enough for it to be forgotten), the only extant copy of God's Word was hidden in the Temple and inaccessible to God's people.

Another problem that King James-Only advocates have with the Old Testament text is that it does not meet their criterion of preservation in a majority of manuscripts. The majority of Old Testament textual critics highly regard the Masoretic textual tradition, representing most extant Hebrew manuscripts of the Old Testament, and yet none of them could claim that the Masoretic textual tradition is errorless.[25] Scholars have been forced to emend Hebrew manuscripts on the basis of mere conjecture because of corruption in the text, and many of these conjectures have been vindicated by the discovery of the Dead Sea Scrolls. For example, R. W. Klein says, "Samuel's MT [Masoretic Text] is a poor text, marked by extensive haplography and corruption—only the MT of Hosea and Ezekiel is in worse condition."[26]

The problems in the Old Testament text are easy to demonstrate in the KJV. In 1 Samuel 13:1, the KJV, following the MT, reads, "Saul reigned one year; and when he had reigned two years over Israel. . . ." Apparently at least one of the numbers in this verse has been lost; it makes no sense as it stands in the MT.[27]

In 2 Samuel 8:4, the KJV says, "David took . . . seven hundred horsemen," in contrast to the parallel in 1 Chronicles 18:4 (and the Septuagint [LXX] of 2 Sam. 8:4), which reads "seven thousand horsemen." In

1 Chronicles 8:26, the KJV states that Ahaziah was twenty-two when he began to reign; the parallel in 2 Chronicles 22:2 says that he began to reign at the age of forty-two. In 2 Kings 24:8, Jehoiachin is said to be eighteen years old when he began to reign; in the parallel in 2 Chronicles 36:9, most Hebrew manuscripts and the KJV say that he was eight, which is unlikely because he had wives at that time (2 Kings 24:15).

These obvious discrepancies in the KJV and the Hebrew manuscripts on which it is based show that none of them perfectly preserved the inspired autographa. They also mean that the perfect preservation of God's Word is not a necessary corollary of the inspiration of God's Word. They further demonstrate that the loss of a portion of the original autographa does not make the doctrine of inspiration irrelevant. Many people who acknowledge the preceding discrepancies ardently believe in and defend the doctrine of verbal-plenary inspiration. Proponents of the doctrine of perfect, providential preservation, however, usually do not grapple with these kinds of textual issues. They seem to cover them up or avoid them rather than to deal consistently with all of the biblical evidence. Their theories prove to be untenable in the OT, where the text is sometimes uncertain and the correct reading is not found in the majority of Hebrew manuscripts. To be consistent in their theories for the NT text, they need either to exclude the OT from their Bibles or to admit that their method for determining the NT text is not as certain as they claim. The OT text does not measure up to the criteria that these theorists have established for the NT.

Misinterpreting the Biblical Record

Historical evidence makes biblical preservation abundantly clear. God has preserved His Word. The argument with King James-Only, TR, and Majority Text proponents concerns two subsidiary issues. The first issue is that of God's method of preserving His Word. We have addressed this topic already. The second issue is that of the Bible's own teaching with regard to the preservation of God's Word. We now turn to this subject.

A major weakness with the doctrine of the perfect preservation of Scripture, as taught by KJV, TR, and some Majority Text advocates is that this cornerstone on which their whole system stands is not taught in the verses that they use to support it.[28] The reader is encouraged to take a Bible and examine the verses cited in the following discussion and let the Bible, interpreted in context, be the final judge concerning this doctrine. Note that "the doctrine of preservation was not a doctrine of the ancient church."[29] It first appeared in a church creed in the Westminster Confession of 1647 (I.VIII). Also notable, as was discussed earlier, is the fact that for some passages in the Old Testament the best textual scholars do not know the original reading of the text and must make conjectures in attempting to recreate that reading. Even in the KJV, as was demonstrated earlier, are a few places where words have been lost or are incorrect (especially where parallel passages contradict).

What does the Bible teach about the preservation of Scripture? The following discussion examines the main biblical passages used to support the doctrine of the perfect, providential preservation of Scripture. These passages are grouped according to their content.

Eschatological Fulfillment

The first group of verses used to support the theory of a supernatural and infallible preservation of God's Word, actually, in context, speaks of the eschatological fulfillment of promises, prophecies, and types from the Old Testament (Matt. 5:18; 24:35 [parallel Mark 13:31 and Luke 21:33]; Luke 16:17). Matthew 5:18 is clearly speaking of the fulfillment in Christ of OT ethical (3:15) and prophetic (1:23; 2:15; 4:14; etc.) texts. When Matthew writes in verse 18, "Till heaven and earth pass, one jot or one tittle shall in no wise pass from the law, till all be fulfilled," it must be read in light of its context. Verse 17 says "Think not that I am come to *destroy* the law, or the prophets; I am not come to destroy, but *to fulfill*" (emphasis mine). The point of this verse is that Jesus did not come to destroy (or to perpetuate for that matter) the OT Law. He is the one to whom all of the OT points (Luke 24:25–27, 44–46), and He came to fulfill all that was prophesied about Him in it. Ryrie comments in his study notes, "The Lord's point is that every letter of every word in the O.T. is vital and will be fulfilled."[30] This passage is not speaking about the continual preservation, through written copies, of the exact words found in the autographa; it is declaring that all of the prophecies in the OT that pointed to Christ will be fulfilled down to the smallest detail. In addition, the context makes clear that Jesus is speaking about the fulfillment of every detail in the OT text. Matthew 5:18 does not even refer to the NT text, let alone speak of its perfect, supernatural preservation.

That Matthew 24:35 also refers to fulfillment, not textual preservation, is evident from verse 34. These two verses read, "Verily I say unto you, This generation shall not pass, till all these things be fulfilled. Heaven and earth shall pass away, but my words shall not pass away." Verse 35 itself cannot mean that all of Jesus' words will be perfectly preserved in the text of Scripture because most of His words were not even recorded in the text of Scripture, or anywhere else for that matter (cf. John. 20:30; 21:25). Similarly, Luke 16:17 states that no part of the Law will *fail;* in other words, it will all come to pass. Therefore, when read in their contexts, these passages do not guarantee that every word of the autographs of Scripture will be preserved intact in some text or text type. Instead, they teach that the Word of God is true and that the OT prophecies will all come to pass in every detail; none will fail.

Infallible Decrees

Another group of passages sometimes used to support the doctrine of the perfect preservation of Scripture consists of verses that, in their context, speak of God's infallible decrees and moral laws (Ps. 119:89, 152, 160; Isa. 40:8, quoted in 1 Peter 1:23–25). Psalm 119:89 declares that God's Word is settled forever in heaven. The subsequent verses indicate the point of this verse—that God's Word is infallible. His ordinances are true and they will not fail. The stability of the universe is an evident token of God's faithfulness to His Word (vv. 90–91). This passage says nothing about God's perfectly preserving the written words in the text of Scripture. Even if this verse did teach the perfect preservation of the text of God's Word, it would mean that the text is perfectly preserved in heaven, which is no help to those who want to argue for preservation of the KJV, TR, or Majority Text.

In Psalm 119:152, the psalmist states, "Concerning thy testimonies, I have known of old that Thou hast founded them forever." In the previous verse, he stated that God's Word is truth, and verse 150 teaches that the wicked are far from God's law. In contrast to the wicked, the psalmist is trusting in the veracity of God's Word (vv. 145–149). His confidence is that God's law is not fickle; it is trustworthy and based on God's unchanging moral character. In its context, the focus of verse 152 is the unfailing effectiveness of God's Word, not the preservation of written Scripture.

Psalm 119:160 is in the same type of context as 119:152. The psalmist's hope is not based on the belief that the text of God's Word will remain intact centuries after he dies, nor is he concerned that he has lost part of

God's Word. His confidence is in the fact that God's Word is true and infallible. In contrast with those who do not keep God's Word (v. 158), the psalmist keeps it and is depending upon it to quicken him because it is true (v. 160a). Therefore, when he says, "every one of thy righteous judgments endureth forever," he must be expressing his confidence in the infallibility and absolute trustworthiness of God's Word. Every statement in God's Word is dependable and infallible.

Another verse that belongs in this category is Isaiah 40:8, which in context speaks of the certainty of God's promise to deliver His people from the Babylonian captivity and bring them back to Judah (vv. 9ff.). The grass withers and the flower fades away, but this promise from God "stands forever"; it is infallible. Isaiah 40:6–8 is quoted in 1 Peter 1:23–25, where Peter uses it to support the fact that the Word of God, through which His readers have been born again, is incorruptible (v. 23). Here, Peter's point has nothing to do with every word of Scripture being preserved in a perfect copy of the autographs. Instead, this promise has everything to do with the lasting and life-changing effect of God's Word in the lives of believers (vv. 21–23). God's Word will continue to accomplish its work in those who have received it (2:2–3). It is a seed in believers that is "living" and "enduring" (v. 23).

This passage does not speak of the perfect preservation of the text of God's Word for several reasons. First, Peter knew the OT context from which he was quoting (Isa. 40:6–8). This OT context speaks of the infallibility of God's promises to deliver His people from their captivity in Babylon. Isaiah was saying that God's promises will surely come to pass. Second, as briefly discussed above, the NT context also indicates that it is speaking of the infallibility and incorruptible nature of the Word of God in its designed effect, not of the flawless copying of the original text of Scripture.[31] In his commentary on 1 Peter, Grudem correctly comments regarding this text that ". . . the Isaiah passage is a statement about the character of God's words generally, without reference to any particular form in which they occur."[32] The point of Peter's use of Isaiah 40 is that the Word of God, which has been planted in the hearts of his recipients by the Spirit when they were born again, is alive and incorruptible, and, by means of that implanted Word, they can and should grow to maturity.

Psalm 12:5–8

Another passage used frequently in recent time to support the doctrine of the supernatural, perfect preservation of God's Word is Psalm 12:5–8. The KJV states these truths:

> For the oppression of the poor,
>   for the sighing of the needy,
> now will I arise, saith the LORD;
>   I will set him in safety from him that puffeth at him (v. 5).
> The words of the LORD are pure words,
>   as silver in a furnace of earth purified seven times (v. 6).
> Thou shalt keep them, O LORD,
>   thou shalt preserve them from this generation for ever (v. 7).
> The wicked walk on every side,
>   when the vilest men are exalted (v. 8).

The psalm is an expression of David's confidence in the pure words of God. In verses 1–4, he prays for deliverance from the proud flatterers all around him who cannot be trusted (v. 2b). Verse 5 gives the source of David's confidence; he is assured that the Lord will deliver him from those who are maligning him. In verses 6–8, David declares that his confidence is in God's Word. In this context, David's expression of confidence in God's Word in verse 6 refers to his confidence in God's affirmation that He will deliver the afflicted (v. 5). Then, in verse 7, on the basis of his confidence in God's Word (vv. 5–6), David declares his assurance that God will preserve forever the righteous, who are being afflicted by the wicked of "this generation." The pronoun *them* in verse 7 ("thou shalt keep them") cannot refer to the "words" of verse 6 for grammatical reasons. It refers to the "poor" and the "needy" of verse 5, and the "godly" and "faithful" men of verse 1, whom the Lord will "preserve" (v. 7b). Furthermore, in context the "generation" (v. 7) must be the wicked who are all around the psalmist and dominate his society (vv. 1–4). It would not make sense to say that God will preserve His written Word from the generation of David on throughout eternity. What about the many generations before David? Was God not concerned about His Word then? The point of the psalm is that the godly man will never cease; the faithful will never "fail from among the children of men" (v. 1). The righteous will never disappear from the face of the earth because God will "preserve them from this generation forever" (v. 7). Verse 8 clinches the contextual arguments. It again returns to the topic of the wicked all around from whom David and future generations of the righteous will be delivered.

Hebrew grammar requires that it be the righteous whom God is keeping and preserving in verse 7. In Hebrew, nouns and pronouns have gender and number, and the gender and number of each pronoun normally should be the same as that of its antecedent. The pronoun *them* (v. 7a) is a masculine suffix whereas the noun *words* (v. 6a) is feminine. Furthermore, in the Hebrew text verse 7b reads, "You will preserve *him* from this generation for ever." Delitzsch says that the *him* refers "to the man who yearns for deliverance mentioned in the divine utterance" (v. 5 in Eng.).[33] This connection is clear in the Hebrew because the pronoun on the verb *preserve* (v. 7b) is third person, masculine, and singular.

The textual evidence also supports the contextual and grammatical evidence that Psalm 12:7 does not refer to the doctrine of the preservation of God's Word. There are significant variant readings for the Hebrew pronominal suffixes on the verbs *shalt keep* and *shalt preserve*. As was mentioned earlier, most Hebrew texts record these verbs with third person masculine plural and third person masculine singular suffixes, respectively ("wilt keep *them*" and "wilt preserve *him*," as the NASB translates the verse). There is also some support for *first person plural* suffixes on *both verbs* ("will watch *us*" and "will guard *us*").[34] This support is found in several Hebrew manuscripts, in the Septuagint, and in the Latin Vulgate.[35] These first person plural readings based on textual evidence have better support than the KJV reading ("shalt preserve *them*"), which has no manuscript support at all. None of the textual readings in this verse teaches the doctrine of the preservation of Scripture; all of the possible variant readings of this text indicate that David is speaking of the preservation of the righteous from the wicked people around them.

Other Verses

Two other passages sometimes mentioned to support the doctrine of the preservation of Scripture are Psalm 78:1–8 and Psalm 105:8. Psalm 78 teaches that previous generations were commanded to teach and to pass on God's Word to the generation of the psalmist, and his generation is to do the same for the next generation. This passage does not teach that God will preserve the text of His Word; in fact, it puts the responsibility on men to pass on the content and teaching of God's Word from generation to generation. There is no mention of a doctrine of preservation; instead, the emphasis is on teaching the precepts of God's Word to the next generation, the very place God would have us put the emphasis today.

Psalm 105:8 says that God has commanded His Word to a thousand generations. This context is speaking of God's faithfulness to His covenant with Abraham. The emphasis here is clearly on the infallibility and eternal authority of God's Word. This verse leads to a question that some readers might ask at this point: "How can God's Word be authoritative if we have no Scripture verse to prove that it is perfectly preserved?" That question will be addressed in the next and final section of this chapter. At this point, however, the question is "What do the Scriptures say about the preservation of God's Word?" The Scriptures do not teach that God will perfectly preserve His Word in a certain text or textual tradition. Instead, God commanded through Moses, "Ye shall not add unto the word which I command you, neither shall ye diminish aught from it, that ye may keep the commandments of the LORD your God which I command you" (Deut. 4:2; cf. 12:32; Prov. 30:6). The NT concludes with John's warning in Revelation 22:18–19 not to add to or take away from God's Word. These commands and warnings are important for this discussion because they indicate that it is possible for men to add to or to take away from God's Word, and they teach that it is a serious thing willfully to distort the message of God's Word.[36]

The Doctrine of Preservation

The Scriptures do not teach that God has perfectly preserved every word of the original autographs in one manuscript or text type. A proper understanding of the doctrine of preservation is a belief that God has providentially preserved His Word in and through all of the extant manuscripts, versions, and other copies of Scripture. This conviction is based on the evidence of history. Obviously, God has preserved His Word through the ages for and through His people. Has God perfectly preserved His Word so that no words have been lost? The evidence from the OT text suggests that such is not the case. We might have lost a few words through negligence, but the amount that has been lost is so minimal that it has no effect on overall doctrine and little, if any, on historical or other details. God has wonderfully and providentially preserved His Word in the multiplicity of extant manuscripts. No passage of Scripture states that God has used multiple manuscripts to preserve His Word, but the evidence of history leaves no doubt that such is the case.

The historical evidence for the preservation of God's Word is similar to the evidence we use to determine the limits of the biblical canon. No explicit statement in Scripture details every book that is to be included in the canon, but we hold fast to our conviction concerning the sixty-six books in the canon on the basis of the historical evidence. As Dunbar says, "[T]he shape and limit of the canon are not scriptural affirmations."[37] Instead, it is commonly acknowledged that canon is a theological construct that we use to describe what happened in history. Dunbar goes on to explain, "There is no claim here for ecclesiastical infallibility in the strict sense, yet there is great assurance to be drawn from the widespread judgment of the early Christians that this group of writings comprises the authoritative teachings of the apostles."[38] J. R. McRay rightly states,

> The formation of the NT canon must, therefore, be regarded as a process rather than an event, and a historical rather than a biblical matter. The coming of the Word of God in print is only slightly more capable of explication than the coming of the Word of God incarnate.[39]

The church knows that the issue of which books to include in the canon is primarily a historical matter. It is the same with the issue of the preservation of God's Word. We do not have a promise in God's Word stating that He will flawlessly preserve every word of the autographs, let alone stating details about *how* He might preserve His Word. We do, however, have the historical evidence. Historical evidence demonstrates that God has wonderfully preserved His Word by means of all of the manuscripts, versions, and copies of Scripture available to us. Furthermore, this historical evidence must be the basis for our textual decisions. We must work with all of the manuscript evidence, including the Byzantine and all other text types. Also, we must consider the evidence from all stages of the text's history, including both the earlier and the later centuries.

God has providentially preserved the text of Scripture in multiple manuscripts throughout history so that none of its doctrinal content is lost or affected adversely. However, one must remember that this conclusion is not based on an explicit verse of Scripture; it is based on the evidence of history. Therefore, we need to use all of that historical evidence when we make decisions concerning the text of Scripture.[40]

As Bible believers, we dare not misuse Scripture to support an incorrect understanding of the preservation of God's Word. Let us remember several facts. First, no verse in the Bible tells the reader how God will preserve His Word. Second, the concept of the perfect preservation of Scripture is untenable in the OT text. Third, not only is Scripture without a verse to explain *how* God will preserve His Word, but no statement in Scripture teaches that God *did* preserve perfectly the original text of Scripture in one manuscript, one family of manuscripts, or even in all of the manuscripts.

Are Our Bibles Reliable?

Then how can we be sure that our Bibles are reliable? How can we maintain the authority of God's Holy Word if we do not have a promise from God that He will preserve it perfectly? For several reasons we can have absolute confidence in the Bibles we have today. Let us summarize some of them. First, God has given us 5,656 manuscripts containing all or parts of the Greek NT.[41] It is the most remarkably preserved book in the ancient world. Not only do we have a great number of manuscripts, but some of them are also very close in time to the originals that they represent. Some partial manuscripts of the NT are from the second century A.D., and many of them are within four centuries of the originals. These facts are all the more amazing when they are compared with the preservation of other ancient literature.

No one questions the authenticity of the historical books of antiquity because we do not possess the original copies. Yet, we have far fewer manuscripts of these works than we possess of the NT. Compared with more than fifty-six hundred Greek manuscripts of the NT, the following list demonstrates the poverty of manuscripts of some other ancient documents:[42]

- ten manuscripts of Caesar's *Gallic Wars* (58–50 B.C.)
- eight manuscripts of Thucydides's *Peloponnesian War* (460–400 B.C.)
- eight manuscripts of Herodotus's *History* (ca. 480–425 B.C.)
- two manuscripts of Tacitus's *Histories and Annals* (ca. A.D. 100)

The oldest manuscript of Caesar's *Gallic Wars* is dated nine hundred years after Caesar. The oldest manuscripts of Thucydides and Herodotus date to about A.D. 900. The two manuscripts of Tacitus's work are from the ninth and eleventh centuries. Again, the NT evidence is far superior to these; our earliest manuscript of the NT is only one generation after the originals were written.[43] Therefore, the number and early date of the NT manuscripts give us great confidence that God's Word has been preserved in those documents.

Second, it is important that Christians realize the types of textual variants that exist in NT manuscripts. Somewhat fewer than 150,000 words are in the Greek NT. Among all of the manuscripts of the Greek NT, are an estimated 400,000 variants. There can be more variants than words because variants involve different spellings (of which there could be many for any one word), different word orders (of which there could be several for any word or group of words), omissions, and additions. In a work the size of the NT (which is found in more than fifty-six hundred manuscripts), an enormous number of variations is possible. Of these 400,000 variants, only 1 to 2 percent substantially affect the meaning of the text. About 98 percent are insignificant matters such as spelling, word order, differences in style, or confusion concerning synonyms.[44] Of those variants that significantly affect the meaning of the text, none of them affects the overall doctrinal content of Scripture or touches on any moral commandment or article of faith that is not clear elsewhere in Scripture.

John Grassmick affirms this common belief. He states that "the basic substance of Christian doctrine is not placed in jeopardy by a textual problem. . . ."[45] Although differences of opinion on textual issues might lead to different interpretations of a few verses of Scripture, they will not affect the basic substance of Christian doctrine. In fact, the differences raised by textual problems are far less significant than differences of interpretation where the text is absolutely certain. It is good to remember that no one claims infallibility for every one of his interpretations of Scripture; yet, that fact in no way detracts from the authority of Scripture. Similarly, differences of opinion on textual matters (which are far less significant) do not detract from the Scripture's authority, nor do they alter one's overall doctrinal position.

One last reason that we can have confidence that our Bibles are reliable is the repetition and multidimensional character of God's Word. DeHaan has explained this concept very nicely.

Some Godly friends believe that to have an inerrant Bible, we need more than perfect original MSS [manuscripts]. They insist that divine preservation must extend to every word of our Bibles. They say that if we allow for any error of transmission or translation, the Scriptures cease to be trustworthy.

Their logic suggests that if we allow for any uncertainty, all certainty is lost. A flawed text produces a flawed authority; a flawed authority produces a flawed faith; a flawed faith produces a flawed salvation; a flawed salvation gives false hope; and false hope is not hope at all.

This kind of thinking sounds compelling. But it is misleading. The one-version-only argument is offset by the principle of inspired repetition. By repetition, the Author of the Bible has protected us from the dangers of a miscopied text or an inadequate translation.

The Spirit of inspiration did not limit Himself to one statement about salvation by faith, the distinctions between law and grace, the mission of the church, or the danger of a real lake of fire. He did not limit Himself to one pronouncement about misdirected sexual behavior, the misuse of alcohol, or the importance of prayer. Sacred Scripture repeats its doctrines over and over again through historical narrative, law, poetry, prophecy, parables, and letters.

The 66 books of the Bible reflect a wonderfully orchestrated symphony of testimony. As the Bible itself says, "God, who at various times and in various ways spoke in time past to the fathers by the prophets, has in these last days spoken to us by His Son, whom He has appointed heir of all things, through whom also He made the worlds," Heb. 1:1–2.

Even at the moment of most holy revelation, God committed the words and actions of His Son to multiple pens. He did not give us Matthew only. We might wish He had. Matthew only would have been simpler. Matthew only would have eliminated difficult problems of historical correlation. But Matthew only was not God's plan.

Instead, He also entrusted the record of His Son to the inerrant writings of Mark, Luke, and John. Then He entrusted His inspired story to the letters of Paul, James, Peter, Jude, and John—

not always to provide new information, but to provide a wonderful, jewel-like, multi-faceted revelation of inspired Scripture.

God's Word is wonderful in repetition. It is rich in perspectives. It is deep in complementing parallels which combine their voices to give us the whole counsel of God. It is because of rather than in spite of multiple prophets, multiple apostles, multiple translations, and multiple interpreters that we can say with great confidence that we have in our hands the absolutely reliable Word of God. It is because the Bible was spread throughout the world in many thousands of copies that scholars can assure us that only a small percentage of the original autographs is in question (none of which jeopardize a major doctrine).[46]

Conclusion

Obvious from the evidence of history is the fact that God has providentially preserved His Word for the present generation. However, also obvious from the evidence of history is the fact that God has not miraculously and perfectly preserved every word of the biblical text in any one manuscript or group of manuscripts, or in all of the manuscripts. Therefore, the only honest alternative left for us is to study all of the manuscripts available to us for the purpose of compiling a text better than the best found in any one manuscript or group of manuscripts. Our purpose is, in the words of René Pache, "to reconstruct from all the witnesses available to us the text essentially preserved in all, but perfectly preserved in none."[47]

Chapter Notes

1.   Daniel B. Wallace, "Inspiration, Preservation, and New Testament Textual Criticism," *Grace Theological Journal* 12, no. 1 (spring 1992): 22–23. Wallace's article is the source of much of the material in the first part of this chapter. One goal in this chapter is to summarize his excellent discussion, and in doing that I have (with his permission) used his organization, his sources, and at times his wording. Bart D. Ehrman, "New Testament Textual Criticism: Quest for Methodology" (M.Div. thesis, Princeton Theological Seminary, 1981), 40, concurs with Wallace. He writes concerning advocates of the Majority Text, "One cannot read the literature produced by the various advocates of the Majority text without being impressed by a remarkable theological concurrence. To one degree or another, they all (to my knowledge, without exception) affirm that God's

inspiration of an inerrant Bible required His preservation of its text." Some King James-Only advocates actually affirm that God has supernaturally and perfectly preserved His Word in the KJV.

2. Wallace, "Inspiration, Preservation, and New Testament Textual Criticism," 25.

3. Peter Ruckman, *The Christian's Handbook of Manuscript Evidence* (Pensacola: Pensacola Bible Institute, 1970), 115–38; and idem, *Problem Texts* (Pensacola: Pensacola Bible Institute, 1980), 46–48.

4. Donald A. Waite, *Defending the King James Bible* (Collingswood, N.J.: Bible for Today Press, 1992), 48–49.

5. See Wallace, "Inspiration, Preservation, and New Testament Textual Criticism," 26–29, where he discusses John William Burgon, Wilbur Pickering, and Zane Hodges. Pickering clearly makes the connection between preservation and inspiration in *The Identity of the New Testament Text,* rev. ed. (Nashville: Nelson, 1997), 153–54. Hodges discusses the importance of preservation and faith in *A Defense of the Majority Text* (Dallas: Dallas Seminary, n.d.).

6. See the preceding chapter for more detail on this issue.

7. Wilbur N. Pickering, "An Evaluation of the Contribution of John William Burgon to New Testament Textual Criticism" (Th.M. thesis, Dallas Theological Seminary, 1968), 91, cf. 90. Wallace, "Inspiration, Preservation, and New Testament Textual Criticism," 26–29, gives more details showing how Dean Burgon, Wilbur Pickering, and Zane Hodges connect preservation of Scripture with the superiority of the Majority Text. Theodore Letis, who is a TR advocate, states, "The only reason that the Majority Text proponents even argue for the Byzantine text is because theologically they have both a verbal view of inspiration—and as a hidden agenda an unexpressed [at least as part of their present method] belief in providential preservation" (*The Majority Text: Essays and Reviews in the Continuing Debate,* ed. Theodore Letis [Fort Wayne, Ind.: Institute for Biblical Textual Studies, 1987], 9).

8. See the classification of papyri in Aland, *The Text of the New Testament,* 95–102, 106. Whereas the Alands, in the first edition of their book, classified three out of 88 papyrus manuscripts as purely or predominantly Byzantine (1987), in the second edition (1989) they classified only one out of the 96 papyri listed as purely or predominantly Byzantine. (The 96 papyri listed actually represent 94 different manuscripts, since p. 33=p. 58 and p. 64=p. 67. See chapter 4, footnote 8, for an explanation of the difference

between a reading in a manuscript that could be classified as Majority Byzantine and a manuscript that could be classified as having a predominantly Majority/ Byzantine text type.

9. Eldon Jay Epp, "The Papyrus Manuscripts of the New Testament," in *The Text of the New Testament in Contemporary Research: Essays on the Statu Quaestionis,* ed. Bart Ehrman and Michael Holmes (Grand Rapids Eerdmans, 1995), 5–6, 17.

10. On the versions, see Bruce M. Metzger, *The Early Versions of the New Testament: Their Origin, Transmission, and Limitations* (Oxford: Clarendon Press 1997). Metzger indicates that the Gothic version from the end of the fourth century is "the oldest representative of the . . . Antiochian [Byzantine type of text" (ibid., 385). The earlier Coptic, Ethiopic, Latin, and Syriac versions that antedate the fourth century are all non-Byzantine. See Daniel B. Wallace, "The Majority Text and the Original Text: Are They Identical?" *Bibliotheca Sacra* 148, no. 590 (April–June 1991): 160–62, for a more complete summary of the textual evidence in the early versions.

11. See Wallace, "The Majority Text and the Original Text," 162–66.

12. Ehrman, "New Testament Textual Criticism," 44.

13. Wallace, "Inspiration, Preservation, and New Testament Textual Criticism," 32.

14. It is the same with the KJV; "the NKJV is the fifth major revision of the KJV and the first since 1769" (Jack P. Lewis, *The English Bible from kjv to niv* [Grand Rapids: Baker, 1991], 329).

15. Douglas Kutilek, *Erasmus: His Greek Text and His Theology* (Hatfield, Pa.: Interdisciplinary Biblical Research Institute, 1996), 17. Kutilek's pamphlet nicely summarizes Erasmus' theology. The conclusion to his pamphlet is worth quoting at length:

"Doctrinally there is no question where Erasmus stood. Our perception is not limited to a few hints or suggestions, a deduction here or an inference there. Boldly and repeatedly Erasmus declares himself to be a loyal and devoted Romanist, consenting to all that Rome stood for doctrinally, with its Mary-worship, veneration of the saints, sacrifice of the mass, papal supremacy, ecclesiastical hierarchy, purgatory, sprinkling of infants, monastic vows and orders, and all else. He refused to side with Luther, and vigorously opposed the Protestant Reformation. He sought and got the pope's sanction for his New Testament.

"If theological inclination accredits or discredits a man's work on the text of the New Testament—I do not think there is a *necessary* connection . . .—

if Romish and heretical leanings by Westcott and Hort discredits their Greek text, then the text of Erasmus and all subsequent editions based on it, i.e., *all* textus receptus editions, are blown completely out of the water. I trust advocates of the supremacy of the textus receptus see the corner into which they paint themselves by using this faulty argument. I strongly urge that the merit or demerit of printed Greek Testaments be evaluated on the basis of manuscript evidence, ancient translations, quotations from patristic authors, and principles of textual criticism, and not on the basis of the largely irrelevant issue of the theology of the text-editors" (21).

16. See the discussion in this chapter, "Are Our Bibles Reliable?" Majority Text proponents are not as prone to err as TR proponents in making preservation a necessary corollary of inspiration, but some people such as Wilbur Pickering come very close to the TR proponents in their statements. See the quotations from Pickering on p. 111 of this chapter.

17. This is the strongest argument used for the TR/Majority Text. Hodges and Farstad write, "Any reading overwhelmingly attested by the manuscript tradition is more likely to be original than its rival[s]" (*The Greek New Testament According to the Majority Text,* 2d ed. [Nashville: Nelson, 1985], xi). See Wallace, "The Majority Text Theory: History, Methods, and Critique," in *The Text of the New Testament in Contemporary Research: Essays on the Status Quaestionis,* ed. Bart Ehrman and Michael Holmes (Grand Rapids: Eerdmans, 1995), 310–13, for a discussion of this issue.

18. James M. Sawyer, "Evangelicals and the Canon of the New Testament" *Grace Theological Journal* 11, no. 1 (spring 1991): 45–46. For further development of this idea, see Millard J. Erickson, *Christian Theology* (Grand Rapids: Baker, 1983), 1:404–5.

19. Letis, *The Majority Text: Essays and Reviews in the Continuing Debate,* 200.

20. Pickering, "An Evaluation of the Contribution of John William Burgon to New Testament Textual Criticism," 88.

21. Kurt Aland, "The Text of the Church?" *Trinity Journal* 8 (1987): 136–37.

22. Wallace, "Inspiration, Preservation, and New Testament Textual Criticism," 38.

23. Cornelius van Til, *The Doctrine of Scripture* (Ripon, Calif.: den Dulk Christian Foundation, 1967), 39.

24. E. F. Hills, *The King James Version Defended!* 4th ed. (Des Moines: Christian Research, 1984), 29.

25. See the discussion in Wallace, "Inspiration, Preservation, and New Testament Textual Criticism," 40.

26. R. W. Klein, *Textual Criticism of the Old Testament: The Septuagint after Qumran* (Philadelphia: Fortress, 1974), 70.

27. Charles Ryrie's note in his *Study Bible* suggests various solutions to this problem. He writes, "The original numbers in this verse have apparently been lost in transmission. One way to understand the verse is this: 'Saul was _____ years old when he began to reign, and he reigned _____ and two years over Israel.' Another suggestion renders it 'Saul was one and _____ years old when he began to reign, and when he had reigned two years over Israel then Saul chose for himself 3,000 men of Israel . . .'" (*Ryrie Study Bible* [Chicago: Moody, 1978]). The NIV text reads, "thirty years old" and "Forty two years." The NASB text reads "forty years old" and "thirty-two years."

28. Wilbur Pickering, one of the most prominent defenders of the Majority Text, uses the preservation of Scripture in his defense. After referring to a number of Scripture verses that he believes teach the preservation of Scripture, he states that they ". . . can *reasonably* be taken to *imply* a promise that the Scriptures [to the tittle] will be preserved for man's use . . ." (*The Identity of the New Testament Text,* 153, emphasis mine). In light of his tentativeness concerning this idea, which is so foundational to his theory, it is perplexing that he does not expound and explain the verses to which he refers.

29. Wallace, "Inspiration, Preservation, and New Testament Textual Criticism," 41.

30. *Ryrie Study Bible* (Chicago: Moody, 1978), Matt. 5:18.

31. In the phrase "the Word of the Lord endureth forever" (1 Peter 1:25 KJV), the verb *endureth* is the translation of the Greek verb *menō.* In other translations, it is rendered "abides" (NASB) and "stands" (NIV). W. Bauer, W. F. Arndt, F. W. Gingrich, and F. Danker classify this use of *menō* (and the occurrence in 1:23) under the meaning to "remain, last, persist, continue to live," and suggests "endures" for a translation in 1:23 ("μένω," in *A Greek-English Lexicon,* 4th rev. ed. [Chicago: University of Chicago Press, 1957], 504). The illustration that is used to explain the use of *menō* in 1:23 is 1 Esdras 4:38, which speaks of the fact that "the truth endures." F. Hauck suggests that in 1 Peter 1:23 and 25 *meno* is used of "His Word, which remains as compared with what is human and corruptible" ("μένω," in *Theological Dictionary of the New Testament,* ed. Gerhard Kittel and Gerhard Friedrich [Grand Rapids: Eerdmans, 1967], 4:575). Neither the *Greek-English Lexicon* nor the *Theological Dictionary of the New Testament* understand the idea of 1 Peter 1:23–25 to be that the written Word of God is preserved in a certain place but that God's Word is incorruptible and immutable and will never fail.

32. Wayne Grudem, *1 Peter,* in *Tyndale New Testament Commentaries* (Grand Rapids: Eerdmans, 1988), 90.

33. Franz Delitzsch, *The Psalms,* in *Commentary on the Old Testament* (Grand Rapids: Eerdmans, 1976), 1:197.

34. Part of the confusion is that the suffixes on the verbs *keep* and *preserve* can be read either as first person plural or third masculine singular, depending on the vowel pointing. This explanation accounts for the confusion between the pronouns *us* and *him*. The vowel points, of course, were added long after the Old Testament was originally written and are not part of the inspired text in the studied opinion of most Hebrew scholars.

35. For a summary of the textual evidence for the various readings in this verse, see Peter C. Craigie, *Psalms 1–50* (Waco, Tex.: Word, 1983), 137.

36. The Deuteronomy passages most clearly warn against adding to the covenant stipulations that God is establishing with Israel. Eugene H. Merrill writes concerning Deuteronomy 12:32, ". . . there is a principle of canonization here . . . in that nothing is to be added or subtracted from the word. This testifies to the fact that God himself is the originator of the covenant text and only he is capable of determining its content and extent" (*Deuteronomy* [Nashville: Broadman and Holman, 1994], 229). Revelation 22:18, addressed to "every man that heareth the words of the prophecy of this book," probably has special reference to false teachers or prophets (cf. 2:20) who might attempt to add their teachings or prophecies to those of John or to omit portions from John's prophecies (v. 19). Robert Thomas, who develops these ideas summarizes that "These words of Jesus [vv. 18, 19] head off any attempt to add or subtract from the book's content through deliberate falsification or distortion of its teaching" (*Revelation 8–22: An Exegetical Commentary* [Chicago: Moody, 1995], 517). Cf. pp. 513–19 for his helpful discussion of vv. 18–19. Although the primary application of these verses in Revelation is to false teachers and prophets who might attempt to add to or omit from Revelation, these words also have implications concerning the extent of the NT canon (as Thomas argues), and more than that, concerning scribes who might be tempted to change the text (as I have suggested).

37. David G. Dunbar, "The Biblical Canon," in *Hermeneutics, Authority, and Canon,* ed. D. A. Carson and John D. Woodbridge (Grand Rapids: Zondervan, 1986), 360. Although the NT describes the OT as "the law of Moses . . . the prophets and . . . the psalms" (Luke 24:44), it does not list the books to be included in those three sections of the OT. The Bible

nowhere lists the books that are included in the NT. We also need to re-member that the parallel being made is not between preservation and the doctrine of the canon itself, but rather between the use of historical evidence to recognize that God has preserved His Word and the use of historical evidence to recognize which books are included in the canon. It could be argued that the doctrine of a canon is based on the doctrine of inspiration; that is, the truth of inspiration implies that a canon exists.

It also could be argued that at least some of the criteria by which we recognize what books are in the canon are given to us in Scripture (i.e., 2 Peter 3:15–16), a situation different than preservation. The criteria for determining whether God's Word has been preserved are self-evident (i.e., does it still exist). Our belief in the preservation of God's Word is different from our belief in the canon in that preservation does not follow directly from inspiration nor are we given criteria in Scripture by which we are to determine or prove the preservation of Scripture. But there is a similarity between preservation of Scripture and the doctrine of the canon in that, the recognition of the exact books that are to be included in the canon does not follow directly from the biblical teaching on inspiration or from the criteria given in Scripture to identify them. These criteria must be applied to the historical evidence concerning apostolicity, authorship, authenticity, etc. Based on the historical evidence, we believe that certain books are included in the canon just as we believe on the basis of historical evidence that God has preserved His Word. My point is that just as we use historical evidence to recognize which books meet the criteria necessary to be included in the canon, in the same way we use historical evidence to recognize the fact that God has preserved His Word.

An obvious truth is that a document that is to be included in the canon must be preserved. Therefore, because inspiration implies canonicity, inspiration is indirectly related to the preservation of the *documents* that are included in the canon. However, the preservation addressed and evaluated in this chapter is not the preservation of the *documents* that are in the canon, but rather the perfect preservation of *all of the words of the texts of all of those documents*.

38. Ibid.
39. J. R. McRay, "Canon of Bible," in *Evangelical Dictionary of Theology,* ed. Walter A. Elwell (Grand Rapids: Baker, 1984), 141.
40. When speaking of "all of the evidence," more is intended than merely counting all of the manuscripts at any given period in history. Instead, both external and internal evidence should be examined to choose the

preferred reading in any given situation. See the summary of such a procedure in the preceding chapter.

41. Note the section on "Manuscripts" in the previous chapter.

42. See the discussion in René Pache, *The Inspiration and Authority of Scripture* (Chicago: Moody, 1969), 192; and F. F. Bruce, *The Books and the Parchments,* rev. ed. (Westwood N.J.: Revell, 1963), 180–81.

43. The papyrus fragment p[52] is dated around A.D. 125.

44. John D. Grassmick, *Principles and Practice of Greek Exegesis* (Dallas: Dallas Theological Seminary, 1976), 66. Most of these variants are minor and of little importance. One way to measure the more significant variants is to count the number of variation units that are included in the apparatus of the Nestle-Aland text (ca. ten thousand) and the United Bible Societies text (ca. fifteen hundred). Many of the variation units included in these two Greek texts do not substantially affect the meaning of the text.

45. Ibid., 66. See also Douglas Kutilek, *Westcott and Hort vs. Textus Receptus: Which is Superior?* Research Report number 45 (Hatfield, Pa.: Interdisciplinary Biblical Research Institute, 1996), 12. Kutilek says, "No fundamental point of doctrine rests upon a disputed reading: and the truths of Christianity are as certainly expressed in the text of Westcott and Hort as in that of Stephanus [TR type text]." D. A. Carson demonstrates that non-Byzantine text types are not theologically aberrant (*The King James Version Debate: A Plea for Realism* [Grand Rapids: Baker, 1979], 62–66). However, Carson goes too far when he writes that in spite of the variants in the various Greek manuscripts of the NT, there is "a purity of text of such a substantial nature that nothing we believe to be doctrinally true, and nothing we are commanded to do, is in any way jeopardized by the variants. This is true for any textual tradition. The interpretation of individual passages may well be called in question; but never is a doctrine affected" (ibid., 56). His last statement that no variants affect any doctrine is too strong. Some variants do affect the doctrinal content of individual passages. The point is that disagreements about these individual passages do not change one's overall doctrinal position.

46. This quotation is from a bulletin insert by Mart DeHaan of RBC Ministries. See Mart DeHaan, "Translations," April 1996, <search.gospelcom.net/rbc/td/04-1996/bta.html> (19 December 2000).

47. See René Pache, *The Inspiration and Authority of Scripture* (Chicago: Moody, 1969), 197.

Chapter 5

Translation Theory and Twentieth-Century Versions

Robert W. Milliman

PASTORS AND TEACHERS ARE frequently asked, "What is the best Bible version or translation?" The most appropriate answer to that question, though disappointing to some people, is, "That depends." The search for the "best" Bible is largely conditioned by what the inquirer means by the word *best*. The search for the "best" Bible, then, actually requires a more foundational query: what *criteria* should be used to determine the "best" translation? This question more closely approaches the heart of the issue.

Three major criteria should be examined to determine which Bible is the "best." These, too, might best be stated as questions. First, what underlying Hebrew and Greek texts did the translators employ? Second, to which translation theory did the translators adhere? Finally, to what use does the reader intend to put this translation? For example, is this Bible going to be used primarily for preaching and teaching, for public or personal reading, for family worship, memorization, children's work, or evangelism?

What started out as a simple question has now turned into an extended lecture. Nevertheless, with the multiplicity of Bible translations available and with the constant appearance of new ones, these questions are important to resolve. So, what is the best Bible version or translation?

Better yet, how can one go about making an honest investigation of this subject? The first question to resolve is the matter of the underlying Hebrew and Greek texts.

The Underlying Texts

The question of which version is best may be resolved quickly here, depending on one's preconceptions. The individual books of the Bible were written in Hebrew and Aramaic (Old Testament) and Greek (New Testament). A problem, however, occurs because the original documents penned by the biblical authors no longer exist. Instead, we have a multitude of copies, none of which completely agrees with the other copies. This requires the practice of textual criticism. In places where textual variants occur, the textual critic must gather examples of the textual variation, compare them, evaluate them, explain the variation, and decide which reading, in the examiner's opinion, best reflects the original text.

Little controversy exists over which Old Testament (OT) text translators should use, although even that question is more complex than it might at first appear.[1] Most simply put, the Masoretic Text is, by far, the text of choice in translating the OT. With regard to the New Testament (NT), however, a wide divergence of opinion exists in evangelical and fundamental circles over the appropriate Greek text that should form the basis of a modern Bible translation.[2] The question of which NT text you think is best depends upon the particular theory of textual criticism to which you adhere.

The Textus Receptus as a Textual Base

One position, in reality, rejects any contemporary textual criticism. This view holds, in essence, that the first and last legitimate textual critic was Erasmus, who compiled a Greek text from seven manuscripts in 1516.[3] His text has come down to us today with slight revision and is popularly known as the Textus Receptus (TR).[4] The individual who holds that the TR is the best original language text has two popular English translations from which to choose: the King James Version (KJV) and the New King James Version (NKJV). No other recent English versions are based on the TR. Someone who prefers a version based upon the TR need look no further. This approach to the question, however, ignores the thousands of manuscripts that Erasmus did not consider. Some of those might actually contain the words originally penned by the apostles.

The Majority Text as a Textual Base

Practitioners of the next approach to textual criticism, the "majority text" approach, basically count the number of manuscripts that support the individual variant readings and go with the reading that appears in the majority of manuscripts. While no translation, to date, is based on the majority text, it is one of the features that is highlighted in the marginal notes of the NKJV. Although the NKJV is based on the TR, the marginal notes show the reader where the translation differs from two other major, critical texts. These two texts are (1) the Majority Text, compiled by the NKJV editors, and (2) the Eclectic Text, compiled by editors of the United Bible Societies.[5] Adherents to the Majority Text approach, then, might want to recommend the NKJV, because the "majority" reading is at least noted in the margin. The Majority Text view, however, fails to recognize one of the problems inherent in the repeated copying of manuscripts: copying one particular scribal mistake over and over again may eventually result in a "majority" reading, but it is still a mistake.

The Eclectic Text as a Textual Base

The final approach to textual criticism is the eclectic approach.[6] The eclectic textual critic, using all of the available manuscripts, judges each instance of textual variation. This examiner chooses, for his or her final text, readings that derive from different manuscripts. For each variant reading, the textual critic notes the date, quality, and text type of the manuscript from which it is taken. The geographical distribution of the variant is also noted. In addition, a more subjective factor is considered: Which variant best explains the rise of the others?[7]

The eclectic approach to textual criticism has become the most predominant text-critical method employed in recent history. In the opinion of many people, it is the most reasonable way to reconstruct, with confidence, the original text of the Bible. Beginning with the end of the nineteenth century, virtually all modern translations have been based on an eclectic text. Those who translate these versions may, based on the evidence, reserve the right to formulate their own final text, but in practice the text generally followed is *The Greek New Testament* published by the United Bible Societies.[8]

The first question to ask in choosing the "best" Bible translation, then, is, "What is the textual base that underlies the translation? What text-critical theory was used to establish that base text?" This, however, is only the first issue. Another significant criterion to consider is the translator's approach to his or her work. In other words, what was the translation theory that he or she used when translating the original Hebrew, Aramaic, or Greek text into English?

Translation Theory

Rather than asking, "What is the *best* version?" the more conscientious inquirer may ask, "Which is the *most accurate* version?" The best answer might still be, "It depends." The problem here is with the definition of the word *accurate*. When any document is translated from one language to another, readers surely want an accurate translation, whether the document is a personal letter, a history book, a poem, a play, a treaty, or the Bible. Translating, however, is a complex task. A well-worn but truthful axiom illustrates the point: "Much gets lost in the translation." This complexity in translation is precisely why aspiring ministerial candidates are encouraged to learn Hebrew and Greek. Without a personal knowledge of biblical languages, the minister will be left to "pin his faith on other people's sleeves."[9] Given all of the complexities of translation, it remains the Bible translator's goal to produce the most accurate rendering of the original text.

Producing an "accurate" translation might seem like a straightforward operation, but consider just *one* problem: poetry. Much of the Bible, including large sections of the prophets, is poetic. Poetry by definition uses figures of speech to convey its message. Can we be sure that a figure of speech used in the Bible and "literally" translated will have the same impact on the modern audience as it had on the ancient readers? People who learn modern foreign languages are continually baffled by the vast array of figures of speech that are the common stock of any language. Should we expect any less of a problem when we are dealing with the original languages of the Bible?

Every Bible translator has to deal with two languages. One is the language of the ancient text—the *source* language (Hebrew, Aramaic, or Greek). The other is the language of the modern reader—the *receptor* language (which might be English, French, German, etc.). The translator's task is to reproduce the most accurate rendering of the source language in the receptor language. In producing the translation, the translator must decide what "accuracy" means. Does it mean that one must faithfully reproduce the wording and grammar of the source text? That is, must one be most concerned with a word-for-word translation of the source text? Or, does one show greater sensitivity to the receptor language, converting the meaning of the source text into forms (words and grammar) that the receptor or reader will more readily understand? In almost all nonbiblical translating today, the latter alternative is followed: the translator is most interested in the reader's understanding. Nevertheless, in Bible translation strong arguments can be made that the translator should be most interested in faithfulness to the specific forms of the original text.

In reality, few translators strictly follow one extreme or the other. Nevertheless, it is helpful to think of each particular Bible translation as falling somewhere on a spectrum as it relates to translation theory. On one side of the spectrum are those translations that follow a more literal translation theory or, as some call the theory, *formal equivalence*. The translator who espouses this theory will be most closely tied to the source text. On the other end of the spectrum is a theory commonly called *paraphrase*. Here, the translator's goal is primarily driven by sensitivity to the receptor language and to the readers' understanding. In this case, the translator shows little concern for the form of the original text, but restates the original words in another form, which he or she believes will convey the author's intended impact on his audience. Between these two poles, we may place the theory that has become known as *dynamic* or *functional equivalence*. The translator who uses dynamic equivalence attempts to balance his or her concern for a literal reproduction of the original form with a similar concern for the reader's understanding.

Translations that are produced based on any one of these theories may all be able to lay claim to the label "accurate." However, each translation has a different target of accuracy in mind, either a most accurate rendi-

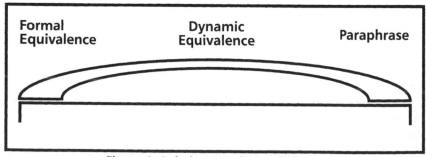

Figure A: Relative translation theories

tion of the *form* of the original text, a most accurate rendition of its *meaning* for the reader, or, as much as is possible, a most accurate balance of both. To confuse matters, not only does each theory have a claim to accuracy, but each, by overly strict adherence to its approach, may also contribute to inaccuracy. We will examine the issues of accuracy and inaccuracy as we consider the two most prominent approaches to translation theory: formal equivalence and dynamic equivalence.

Formal Equivalence

A literal translation is one in which the translator seeks to reproduce, in the receptor language, the word order, sentence structure, and grammar of the source language.[10] These translators seek formal equivalence, that is, an equivalent reproduction in the receptor language of each word and grammatical form in the source language.[11] For example, in the NT the attempt is made to translate each specific Greek word with a similar, specific English word. The translator strives to translate Greek verbs with English verbs and to translate Greek nouns with English nouns. In addition, translators using this method often seek to translate a word in the original language consistently with the same word in the receptor language whenever it appears. Furthermore, whenever words that do not explicitly appear in the original must be added to give the intended meaning of the author, they are placed in italics. Finally, little, if any, attempt is made to interpret the original words or grammar for the reader. One may call this a "word-for-word" translation theory.

A literalistic, word-for-word translation has a distinct advantage over other translations on the spectrum: the English Bible reader may be reasonably assured that he or she has a consistent reproduction of the original.[12] The serious student has an excellent resource for study.

One must affirm, however, that no Bible translator holds to a strict application of the literal method of translation. Take, for example, Ephesians 2:14–15a. A strictly literal approach to word order would result in the following translation: "He for is the peace of us, the one having made the both one and the dividing wall of the fence having destroyed, the enmity in the flesh of him, the law of the commandments in decrees having nullified." The only place one would find a "translation" even remotely similar to this word order would be in an interlinear Bible, in which the English words are placed directly under the words of the Greek text. More realistically, the KJV, which is largely a literal type of translation, renders these words, "For he is our peace, who hath made both one, and hath broken down the middle wall of partition *between us,* having abolished in his flesh the enmity, *even* the law of commandments *contained* in ordinances." Obviously, then, some liberties must be taken even in a word-for-word type of translation. Even so, with literal translations, a deliberate attempt is made to maintain the original word order as much as is possible in the receptor language.

Dynamic Equivalence

In recent decades, some people have maintained that adherence to the literal method might actually lead, at times, to a failure to communicate successfully the intended meaning of the biblical author. As was noted earlier, even practitioners of the literal method recognize this problem. The goals of the literal method might be laudable, but what if they get in the way of comprehensible communication? The problem is that rigid adherence to the literal method might reproduce a form of English that no one speaks today, thus making the Bible seem like a distant dialect.[13] Literal correspondence might result in a woodenly rigid translation that is more Greek-like than English. The theory of dynamic equivalence has sought to address these issues.

Eugene A. Nida and Charles R. Taber summarize the philosophy of dynamic equivalence: "Translating consists in reproducing in the receptor language the closest natural equivalent of the source-language message, first in terms of meaning and secondly in terms of style."[14] Meaning, then, takes precedence over form. Consequently, with this theory, conscious effort is made to reproduce not just the words of the idiom or metaphor, but the meaning of the idiom or metaphor. For example, the translator who employs the method of dynamic equivalence would not slavishly translate the English idiom "frog in the throat," word-for-word into another language. He or she would rather try to convey, in the receptor language, the notion of a throat condition that produces hoarseness. The translator would also seek to use monetary, weight, and time equivalents with which the modern reader is familiar instead of terms such as *denarius, talent,* and *ninth hour,* as are found in the original text. Italics would be eliminated from the translation because the added words are necessary for a proper understanding of the meaning. This translator would likewise feel free to use verbal nouns in place of nominal verbs and vice versa. For example, "I possess faith [noun] in God" may be rendered "I believe [verb] in God."[15]

From one perspective, the dynamic equivalence theory appears to be more reasonable than stringent, word-for-word correspondence. The average reader would agree that dynamic equivalent translations read more quickly and clearly and promote better understanding. However, a question remains: Does the reader actually end up with the original author's intent in all cases? This question is crucial to translation theory. The problem is that all translations are, by the nature of the case, interpretive. The more a translator departs from the literal method, the more interpretive he or she gets in the attempt to reproduce the meaning of the original text.

Take, for example, the matter of the genitive case. The genitive case in Greek is literally translated in English by the preposition *of* in combination with the following noun: for example, "a man *of* peace" or "the house *of* God." Literal translations frequently resist the notion of *interpreting* the genitive ("of + noun") construction; they choose rather to simply mirror it word for word. This practice leaves many readers scratching their heads when a more interpretive translation would, in theory, clarify the original author's meaning. For example, "body of sin" in Romans 6:6 surely means "sinful body," does it not? The "crown of life" in Revelation 2:10 must certainly mean the "crown which consists of life," correct? The "message of the cross" in 1 Corinthians 1:18 is surely the "message about the cross" just as the "faith of Christ" in Galatians 2:20 is "faith in Christ." "Not necessarily," some people would demur. "How can you be so sure about your *interpretation?*" Is the "love of Christ" that constrains me "Christ's love for me" or "my love for Christ" (2 Cor. 5:14)? Can translators be so sure of the interpretation that they are willing to put their conclusion not only in a commentary but also in a translation? Herein lies the main problem with the translation theory of dynamic equivalence. A dynamic equivalent translation that is meant to clarify the author's meaning might, in reality, misinterpret the author's intent.

Another example of the complexity of translation theory involves the rendering of participles. Participles are verbals ending in *-ing* that generally function as adverbs or adjectives: "The man collapsed while *running*" or "The *running* man collapsed." Literal translations, again, frequently reproduce the *-ing* word without clarifying its meaning. But is that helpful? Did Jesus mean, "Go make disciples, baptizing them and teaching them," or did He mean "Go make disciples *by means of* baptizing and teaching them" (Matt. 28:19–20)? Did Paul intend to say, "these, not having the law, are a law to themselves" or "these, *even though* they do not have the law, are a law to themselves" (Rom. 2:14)? Were the people who came to John to be baptized "confessing their sins," baptized *"as* they confessed their sins," or baptized *"because* they confessed their sins" (Matt 3:1)? Who decides these issues? It may be argued that although a literal translation might not be understandable, at least the reader, not a translator, gets to make the interpretive decision. However, that argument begs the question: Will average readers take the necessary steps to make an intelligent decision in these matters when reading a literal, word-for-word translation?

Another example will illustrate the problem of translation theory: theological terms. Does the average reader understand what Paul means by the literal rendering "the flesh"? Would it make better sense to use a translation such as "sinful nature," or is the rendering "selfish desires" preferable? Does the average reader know, with good understanding, the meaning and significance of the following theological terms: *propitiation, redemption, atonement, reconciliation, justification?* Leaving aside the average reader, what about the child, the immigrant, and the totally unchurched person? Will such people even understand an apparently simple theological term such as *grace?* Will common, post-Christian men or women think of "God's unmerited favor" when they read the word *grace,* or do visions of accomplished ballerinas come to their minds? Would a rendering such as "God's great kindness" give them a better, more accurate understanding of the word, or has the translator overstepped the proper bounds?

Perhaps, it might be argued, a dictionary appended to the Bible could best address the problem; but why not put the definition in the text where it is more likely to be read? If a reader is not going to study grammar to figure out the various uses of the genitive case or of participles, can we expect him or her to consult a theology text or an appended dictionary to assist in understanding theological terms? On the other hand, what if the translator's rendering is not precisely right? Has the translator done more harm than good?

One of the most overlooked and yet most important elements of discourse is conjunctions: *and, but, therefore, then, for,* etc. In an attempt to simplify language for the reader, dynamic equivalent translations and paraphrases shorten sentences in the original and, consequently, often leave out conjunctions. But when the conjunctions are left out, we no longer know that this statement is inferred from that one, or that this outcome is the intention of that purpose; that this outcome is the result of that statement, or that this statement is the reason for that statement. In other words, the author's argument might be lost and the understanding of the Word of God, the very thing the translation was intended to achieve, might be lost along with it.

These questions and comments are not meant to confuse the issue. Rather, they illustrate two points. First, all Bible believers should hesitate to be overly dogmatic about the merits of any one translation theory, as if either formal equivalence or dynamic equivalence was inherently the better theory. Both methods have strengths and weaknesses. Second, it is clear that a translation's "accuracy" might depend on the use for which a translation is intended. Before turning to that issue, however, it might prove helpful to identify where modern translations fit on the translation theory spectrum. A discussion of the issue of inclusive language would also be appropriate.

A Survey of Modern Translations

Where do twentieth-century translations fit on the spectrum of translation theories, with formal equivalence on one end of the scale and paraphrases on the other? The following survey deals with only a few of the more prominent examples available today, and that in cursory fashion.[16]

Formal Equivalent Translations

Beginning with the formal or literal end of the spectrum, the first prominent, modern translation, a revision of the KJV, was the American Standard Version (ASV, 1901). This version is very literal, following in the tradition of the KJV. Perhaps its main distinguishing feature is its use of an eclectic text, a departure from the TR of the KJV. In its day, the ASV was highly respected by many fundamentalists.[17]

A revision of the ASV, initiated by its copyright holder, was published through the efforts of an interdenominational team of scholars from 1946–52.[18] That revision was the Revised Standard Version (RSV). The RSV was for years the standard Bible used in mainstream denominations. It typically was also the translation most commonly cited by a broad spectrum of biblical scholars. Evangelicals and fundamentalists, however, generally have held it in suspicion, and with good reason. For example, "virgin," as translated in the King James Version of Isaiah 7:14, became "young

woman" in the RSV. "Christ, who is over all, God blessed forever" became ". . . Christ. God who is over all be blessed for ever" (Rom. 9:5).
"Propitiation" became "expiation" (Rom. 3:25; 1 John 2:2; 4:10). Many
people concluded that these renderings were not the result of careful
scholarship but rather were attacks on the person and work of Christ by
liberal theologians. In spite of these deficiencies, however, the RSV is, for
the most part, a good, literal translation, often more readable than other
versions such as the New American Standard Bible (NASB). Yet, being a
half-century old, the RSV is showing its age. Its vocabulary and grammar
are outdated by current English usage.

Some of the concerns with the RSV, both theological and linguistic, were
addressed in the major revision of the RSV, the New Revised Standard Version (NRSV, 1989). The chair of the translation committee was the respected
scholar Bruce Metzger. The main departure from the RSV, however, was
the NRSV's use of gender-neutral language.[19] The NRSV is quickly becoming
the standard text of mainstream denominations and is also, like the RSV
before it, becoming the choice of many biblical scholars.

The NASB (1960–1971), like the RSV, was a revision of the ASV. The
NASB is a literal translation produced by evangelical translators. Like the
RSV, it is not nearly as literalistic as the ASV. Unlike the RSV, it is free of
renditions that are offensive to evangelicals and fundamentalists. In those
circles, the NASB has become the Bible of choice for many teachers, students, pastors, and laypeople who want a Bible that follows a literal translation theory yet updates the English. For a time, before the recent onset
of the King James-Only controversy, it looked as if the NASB would eclipse
the KJV in popularity. The version controversy and the issuing of other
modern versions seems to have slowed the popularity of the NASB. The
only major change which was made in the updated NASB (1997) was the
abandonment of Elizabethan pronouns (thee, thou, etc.) which had been
retained in the original NASB whenever the writer or speaker in the text
was addressing God.

The final literal translation to be considered is the New King James
Version (NKJV; 1979, 1982). Unlike the RSV, NASB, and NRSV—all of which
were revisions or descendants of the 1901 ASV—the NKJV is, as its name
indicates, a revision of the KJV. Like the KJV, it is based on the TR. However, because of its significant departures from the KJV in its wording,
additional marginal notes, etc., the NKJV does not satisfy those who have
strong feelings for the KJV. On the other hand, because it is based on the

TR, neither does it satisfy those who desire a Bible based on an Eclectic Text. Nevertheless, it remains a popular choice in some circles.[20]

Dynamic Equivalent Translations

The New International Version (1973–1978) is the first prominent modern version that is not a revision connected to the KJV (through the ASV). It was produced by an international team of English-speaking, evangelical scholars and its copyright is held by the International Bible Society (hence, the name New International). It is intended for private and public reading. To that end, literary consultants contributed to the translation process with the goal of producing a translation with dignity and beauty, yet one that would be readable by ordinary people. Although the NIV is often labeled a dynamic equivalent translation in popular circles, this author agrees with the judgment that "its method is an eclectic one with emphasis for the most part on a flexible use of concordance and equivalence."[21] In other words, it technically falls somewhere between formal and dynamic equivalent translations, probably a little closer to dynamic equivalence.[22] The New International Reader's Version (NIrV, 1998) is based on the NIV but contains shorter words and shorter sentences, and sometimes it expands the text to explain more difficult words. These changes were designed to make the NIV, which reads at an average adult reading level, more understandable for those with only elementary reading skills.[23]

The American Bible Society has been and continues to be a proponent of dynamic equivalent translations. A significant indication of this commitment was its publication of Today's English Version (TEV), also marketed as the Good News Bible (1966–1971). The Contemporary English Version (CEV) is another recent example (1995). These versions are designed to be read by those with little, if any, religious background or little formal education. The artist's line drawings in the TEV, which attempt to depict biblical events or concepts, are distracting to a number of people. Some of the marginal notes in the CEV unquestioningly adopt the conclusions of liberal mainstream scholarship.

A couple of evangelical forays into the dynamic equivalent arena are noteworthy. The New Century Version (1986, 1988) was originally targeted at children as young as those on a third-grade instructional level. It has since been marketed to adult audiences as well. The New Living Translation (NLT, 1996) was produced by a well-known group of evangelical scholars as a translation in its own right and a revision of the extremely popular Living Bible (LB, 1962–71). The NLT translators targeted the reading level of a junior high student.

Paraphrases of the Bible

The LB is one of the best examples of a paraphrase. Kenneth Taylor used the ASV as the basic text, which he reworded. The entire Bible was paraphrased in sections, beginning with the NT epistles, which were published as the *Living Letters*. A more recent attempt at paraphrase is *The Message* by Eugene H. Peterson. This is an on-going work that began in 1993. Unlike the LB, *The Message* is a rewording of the original Hebrew and Greek.

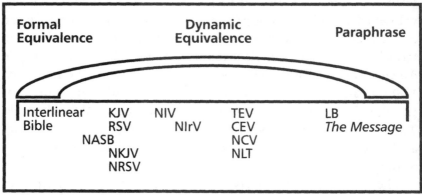

Figure B: Translations according to their relative translation theories

Inclusive Language

An issue that is not confined to any one translation theory is that of inclusive language. For example, one of the stated goals of the literal NRSV is that "masculine-oriented language should be eliminated as far as this can be done without altering passages that reflect the historical situation of ancient patriarchal culture."[24] Likewise, the dynamic equivalent NLT and CEV have the goal of gender-inclusive language. The use of inclusive language became an especially volatile issue in the spring of 1997, when it was revealed that the International Bible Society was considering an inclusive language edition of the popular NIV. Such an edition previously had been produced for readers in Great Britain. The ensuing debate resulted in a halt to any immediate plans to press ahead with this idea.

To the extent that it clarifies the biblical author's intended meaning, gender-inclusive language is a worthwhile goal. For example, the Greek word *anthropos,* in virtually all situations, stands for humanity, not members of the male sex. Another word, *aner,* is generally used for a male person. In a day in which English usage has evolved to exhibit greater gender-inclusiveness, no good reason exists to insist on translating *anthropos* as "man" or "mankind." To do so might even result in an understanding of the text that the author did not intend. In numerous places in Scripture the linguistics of biblical times resulted in the use of terms that, although they never were meant to exclude women, if used today would create confusion. For instance, in many contexts the Greek word *adelphoi,* "brothers," was used to designate both male and female believers. In those cases, an appropriate gender-neutral equivalent should be sought today. Other examples might be cited.

Still, the translator must be careful not to make gender-inclusive changes that alter the sense of the original, doing so just for the sake of avoiding offense to certain ideological elements within society. For example, the context of Matthew 9:9 makes clear that the person in view is a male.[25] It is unnecessary to eliminate the word *man* (NIV), as the NLT and CEV do.

One of the greatest obstacles to those who are attempting to produce gender-neutral translations is the absence, in English, of a gender-neutral third person singular personal pronoun. Like all other languages, English can refer to "she," "he," "her," or "him." Unlike some languages, however, English does not have a word that will stand for both genders at the same time. Frequently, this problem can be solved by using a word such as *one* (e.g., "one who loves" for "he or she who loves"). Often, however, this approach does not work. The temptation is to replace the singular form "he" with a plural pronoun (e.g., "they who love"). One might argue, on the other hand, that such a procedure alters the nuance of meaning. Balance is needed. No reason exists to insist on male-oriented language when a gender-neutral translation would best reflect the meaning of the original text. Nevertheless, the translator must be careful not to alter the true sense of a passage simply to avoid offending someone or to appease adherents of a feminist ideology.[26]

Intended Use of Translations

It might be best to conclude that the value of a translation is based primarily on its intended use, either the use intended by the translator or the use intended by the reader. In other words, different translations are appropriate for different purposes. For example, it is unfair to criticize negatively a translation for being a poor Bible for serious study when the translation was designed for use in evangelistic outreach or for use by elementary readers.

For increasing numbers of people today, the need for relevant vocabulary and current idiomatic expression will dictate the use of one of the modern translations. Few Americans realize that when John "suffered" Jesus (Matt. 3:15) he actually "agreed with" Jesus. Even fewer probably know that "to fetch a compass" (Acts 28:13) means "to set sail." In addition, what does it mean to "lay apart superfluity of naughtiness" (James 1:21)? What is the "the flower of her age" (1 Cor. 7:36b)? What are "fruits meet for repentance" (Matt. 3:8)? How does one "devour widows' houses" (Luke 20:47)? What are "the lively oracles" (Acts 7:38b)?[27] Much of the language used in the KJV, a good deal of which was taken over without change from Tyndale's translation, no longer communicates accurately to twenty-first century people.

No sound argument exists for objecting to the individual who desires to use the KJV because of its beauty or for some equally important reason. However, before one chooses a particular Bible to recommend to another person, especially a new believer, it might be wise to take this test. Go to a library and take one of William Shakespeare's plays off the shelf. Read it without consulting any explanatory notes or marginal helps. The unchurched person, the immigrant, the child, the television addict, and the secularized professional will read older versions such as the KJV with a similar degree of difficulty.

Which of the modern versions should one recommend? Which Bible is the best translation? It depends upon how a person expects to use the Bible. For the serious student, a literal translation might be the best. The serious student desires a close, consistent translation of words to do word studies and other steps of biblical exegesis. The serious student wants to diagram sentences in order to trace the author's argument. He or she appreciates the literal translation because it maintains important connections marked by conjunctions. It so closely resembles the underlying Greek and Hebrew original that the author's argument can be faithfully traced, especially by means of a sentence diagram. These features make the literal translation a good choice for serious study and, thus, for public teaching and preaching. The preacher does not have to expend time explaining the argument contained in the original languages; he simply needs to explain the text as it is already translated for the congregation.

The modern translation that best suits the needs of the serious Bible student is probably the NASB, in particular the updated edition. A serious drawback of the NASB, however, is the way in which virtually all publishers format this version. Each verse is indented as though it were a separate paragraph. Verse divisions, of course, were not inspired. The actual unit of thought in most written discourse is the paragraph or the stanza.[28] However, in the NASB, the paragraphs are not clearly marked. The editors have identified paragraphs by printing, in bold, the numbers of the verses which begin paragraphs, but the bold print is not always easy to distinguish. Furthermore, for most readers this feature is not sufficient to overcome the natural inclination to read each indented verse as a separate paragraph. For this reason, the reader may incorrectly be led to think in terms of verses instead of the discourse units of paragraphs and larger sections. The serious student, in private study, noting the bold verse numbers that mark the paragraphs, might be able to overcome this shortcoming. The teacher in the classroom might be able to cope as well. The public preacher and teacher of popular audiences, on the other hand, might not choose the NASB for this reason.[29]

If a literal translation were the version of choice for serious study, the choice for evangelism and initial instruction in the Bible would probably be a dynamic equivalent translation. The most effective evangelist is the Bible itself, and the most effective means of evangelism is, perhaps, Bible distribution. Unfortunately, we cannot assign a teacher to accompany every Bible that is distributed. The people whom Christians hope to reach today—the unchurched person, the post-Christian individual, the child, the homeless person—need a Bible that is free of difficult theological jargon, strings of dependent clauses, and college-level vocabulary. Yet, they also need one that conveys accurately the meaning of the original. A number of versions are available to meet this need, and the reader is directed to the previous section of this chapter for a survey of alternatives. A recent example produced by evangelical translators is the *New Living Translation.*

Paraphrases also have a place in the Christian's library. These are excellent tools for introducing inquiring people to the Bible. They also provide a useful, running commentary on the text. In addition, many seasoned believers have had the words of Scripture confront them in a new and fresh way with a paraphrase, or even with a dynamic equivalent translation.[30] If the impact on the reader is the same as that desired by the biblical author, we can certainly applaud the translator's efforts and recommend his or her work.

Does such a thing as an "all-purpose" Bible exist? Probably not. The NIV might provide the best balance between the literal and dynamic equivalent translation methods, leaning a little closer to the latter. It is appropriate for public teaching, for public and private reading, and for worship. In many cases, it might even be used for evangelism. The NIV promotes understanding through its formatting of paragraphs. Furthermore, the words of the original are rendered in good, aesthetically pleasing, idiomatic English. It is one of the few translations whose editors solicited the views of literary consultants. This attention to literary quality has made the NIV, for many people, the most suitable version for public reading and for private memorization. Furthermore, the NIV is the version used by many study Bibles and it forms the basis for most current commentaries designed for laypeople.

What a wealth lies before us! The English reader has available many Bibles that accurately present the Word of God and, at the same time, fulfill the need for a variety of uses. The question is whether we will use them. Has the wonderful multiplicity of versions contributed to a better understanding of God and His ways, or has debate over which version is the "best" led to the neglect of that which is most important? The best advice that anyone could give regarding the Word of God is this: "Just read it!" Whichever version(s) you choose to own, pick up your Bible and read it! Read it, meditate on it, and memorize it. It is a lamp to your feet and light for your path; it is more precious than gold and sweeter than honey. In it alone, with unmistakable clarity, you will find Him, whom to know is life eternal.

Chapter Notes

1. See chapter 2, "The Old Testament Text and the Version Debate," by Roy Beacham for a discussion of this issue.
2. See chapter 3, "The New Testament Text and the Version Debate," by W. Edward Glenny for a more in-depth treatment of this subject.
3. The story of Erasmus is well documented by William W. Combs, "Erasmus and the Textus Receptus," *Detroit Baptist Theological Journal* 1 (1996): 35–53.
4. Although this phrase, translated "received text," conveys a sense of authority, when it was first used in 1633 it meant little more than something

like "most popular." Appearing in the preface of that edition, it should be considered as something akin to the marketing blurbs that appear on the dust jackets of books today.

5. The "Eclectic Text" will be discussed in detail in the following paragraph. The NKJV, in its marginal readings, uses the abbreviation *M-Text* for majority text readings, and *NU-text* for the United Bible Societies' Eclectic Text readings. The *N* in *NU* stands for Nestle; the *U* stands for United Bible Societies. The use of *N* and *U* together is a recognition that the United Bible Societies' text, now in its fourth edition, is virtually the same as the Nestle-Aland Eclectic Text, now in its twenty-seventh edition. This latter text is published by the Deutsche Bibelgesellschaft under the name *Novum Testamentum Graece*.

6. A variation of this approach was championed by Harry A. Sturz in *The Byzantine Text-Type and New Testament Textual Criticism* (Nashville: Nelson, 1984), but Sturz's view is not considered in this chapter.

7. See chapter 3 by Edward Glenny for a discussion of this subjective factor in textual criticism. Often, the evidence gathered in this step is called "internal evidence" whereas matters of date, etc., are labeled "external evidence."

8. As was noted earlier, this text is essentially the same as the Nestle-Aland text.

9. The words in quotation marks are taken from the following statement: "Hebrew and Greek are the two eyes of a minister. Without them he cannot see for himself, but must pin his faith on other people's sleeves." This quotation was supplied by a former student, Darrell Post, and was attributed by him to Morgan Edwards.

10. For example, the following statement appears in the preface to the NASB: "The attempt has been made to render the grammar and terminology in contemporary English. When it was felt that the word-for-word literalness was unacceptable to the modern reader, a change was made in the direction of a more current English idiom. In the instances where this has been done, the more literal rendering has been indicated in the notes." One may compare the previous statement to the maxim followed by the translators of the NRSV and found in the preface of that version: "As literal as possible, as free as necessary." By the committee's own admission the NRSV "remains essentially a literal translation."

11. Throughout this discussion the labels "literal" and "formal equivalence" will be used interchangeably. Although most people familiar with the subject of Bible translation would place the NKJV in this category, the editors of the NKJV

prefer the term *complete equivalence*. See Arthur L. Farstad, *The New King James Version in the Great Tradition*, 2d ed. (Nashville: Nelson, 1989), 119–28. *Complete equivalence* is defined on page 124 as "basically the literal method updated to include scientific insights from *linguistic analysis*" (italics original).

12. Beginning Greek students know this well, quickly learning to work with an NASB or RSV nearby, despite their teacher's protests.

13. In the past, the author had occasion to minister to immigrants from Southeast Asia. These dear people struggled to learn two languages: contemporary English and the English of the KJV. Part of their problem, no doubt, was the archaic vocabulary of the KJV, but the literal method of translation followed by the KJV translators undeniably contributed to their problems of understanding the blessed Word of God.

14. Eugene A. Nida and Charles R. Taber, *The Theory and Practice of Translation* (Leiden: Brill, 1974), 12. This statement is remarkably similar to the principle often enunciated by Richard V. Clearwaters, the founder of Central Baptist Theological Seminary of Minneapolis: "A good translation will be the closest natural equivalent first in meaning and second in style."

15. With a bit of irony, the Contemporary English Version, which is a good example of dynamic equivalence, states the following in its preface: "Historically, many Bible translators have attempted in some measure to *retain the form of the King James Version*. But the translators of the *Contemporary English Version* (CEV) have diligently sought to *capture the spirit of the King James Version* by following certain principles set forth by its translators in the document 'The Translators to the Reader,' which was printed in the earliest editions" (italics original). The preface goes on to quote from portions of "The Translators to the Reader" and attempts to show how the CEV is the result of faithful adherence to these principles.

16. Some translations are not treated. For example, sectarian translations such as the New World Translation are not discussed. These translations reveal the theological biases of their translators and cannot be recommended. In addition, Roman Catholic and other translations that contain the Apocrypha cannot be recommended and are, therefore, not noted. Books are available that give much more detailed information about each version than that which is presented in this chapter. A good resource is Jack P. Lewis, *The English Bible from kjv to niv: A History and Evaluation*, 2d ed. (Grand Rapids: Baker, 1991).

17. For example, Richard V. Clearwaters, the founder of Central Baptist Theological Seminary of Minneapolis, wrote, "Honesty compels us to cite the

1901 American Revised as the best English Version of the original languages" (*The Great Conservative Baptist Compromise* [Minneapolis: Central Seminary Press, n.d.], 192).

18. The multiple dates here and in several of the following examples reflect the typical production of translations in stages, usually with the NT released first, followed by the OT a few years later. The copyright of the RSV is held by the Division of Christian Education of the National Council of Churches of Christ in the United States of America. The second edition was released in 1971.

19. See more on this issue below.

20. This may be due, in part, to its use in the popular AWANA youth program.

21. This quotation is from an International Bible Society publication as quoted by Calvin D. Linton, "The Importance of Literary Style in Bible Translation Today," in *The niv: The Making of a Contemporary Translation,* ed. Kenneth L. Barker (Grand Rapids: Zondervan, 1986), 20. The rest of the essays in this book are well worth reading.

22. This is also the judgment of Calvin D. Linton, who writes that "those advising from the periphery in matters of style sought constantly for such qualities of 'dynamic' equivalence as could be introduced without in any way compromising the highest fidelity to the content and form of the original." Ibid.

23. The KJV and NASB are both judged as hard to read by readability scales that measure factors such as sentence length and vocabulary (KJV: twelfth grade reading level; NASB: tenth grade reading level). The NIV, NRSV, and NKJV all fall within the average adult reading level (sixth to eighth grade). See the helpful booklet, *Text and Product Preview: Holy Bible, New Living Translation* (Wheaton: Tyndale, 1996), 38–39.

24. This quotation is from the preface of the NRSV.

25. "As Jesus went on from there, he saw a man named Matthew sitting at the tax collector's booth" (NIV). Compare this with the NLT, "As Jesus was going down the road, he saw Matthew sitting at his tax-collection booth," and the CEV, "As Jesus was leaving, he saw a tax collector named Matthew sitting at the place of paying taxes."

26. D. A. Carson provides an excellent treatment of this topic in *The Inclusive Language Debate: A Plea for Realism* (Grand Rapids: Baker, 1998).

27. The last four examples were taken from Nida and Taber, *Theory and Practice of Translation,* 6.

28. Paragraphing is particularly important in reading the NT epistles. As Gordon D. Fee suggests, a requirement for properly interpreting an epistle i to ask the following of each paragraph: "What is the point of the paragraph?" and "Why does [the author] now say this?" *New Testament Exegesis: A Handbook for Students and Pastors,* 2d ed. (Louisville: Westminster John Knox, 1993), 44. The same approach is found in Gordon D. Fee and Douglas Stuart, *How to Read the Bible for All Its Worth: A Guide for Understanding the Bible,* 2d ed. (Grand Rapids: Zondervan, 1993), 54–57. Setting poetry off in stanzas is important for, among other reasons, being able to note clearly the poetic lines of a poem and the parallelism that occurs between these lines, a crucial element to consider in interpreting poetry.

29. The RSV or NRSV, which are literal translations, are formatted to show clearly the paragraphs. This format is beneficial for the student. On the other hand, the apparent theological biases of the translators might cause some people to avoid these versions.

30. The habit of this author has been regularly to read different dynamic equivalent translations during times of private devotional reading. The intent is not to allow familiarity with the text to prevent the text from doing the reforming work for which it is intended.

An Appeal to Scripture

Kevin T. Bauder

ORTHODOX CHRISTIANS AFFIRM THAT God has preserved His Word. They acknowledge that God has accomplished this preservation through providential means. They recognize in the traditional Greek and Hebrew texts a substantial preservation of the words of the original documents. What they do not affirm, however, is that any one manuscript, manuscript group, or any single printed text preserves all of the words and only the words of the autographa. Such a specific affirmation clearly lies outside of the teaching of Scripture.

If the preservation of the Word of God depends upon the exact preservation of the words of the original documents, then the situation is dire. No two manuscripts contain exactly the same words. No two editions of the Masoretic Text contain exactly the same words. No two editions of the Textus Receptus contain exactly the same words. No two modifications of the King James Version contain exactly the same words, and the Bible nowhere tells us which edition, if any, *does* contain the exact words of the originals. These are not speculations; these are plain facts.

Confronted with these facts, King James–Only advocates are faced with one of two choices. Either they may specify, *a priori* and without biblical evidence, a single manuscript or edition of the Bible in which the exact words are preserved, or they may begin to qualify their insistence upon exact preservation.

Some of them choose the former alternative, usually naming a particular printed Greek or Hebrew text or else a particular edition of the King James Version that is supposed to contain all of the words, and only the words, of the originals. The problem for them lies in trying to justify their choice. They cannot base their conclusion upon any particular biblical promise, for even if the Bible does contain a promise of its own preservation, it never specifies where the preserved words are to be found. Nor do they seem to be able to base their conclusions upon strictly logical grounds. They argue that verbal inspiration is worthless without verbal preservation, but this does not settle the question of *where* the preserved words are to be found. Not having the preserved words is, after all, rather similar to having them but not knowing where they are. A special problem is created for those who try to make the King James Version into the measure by which the Greek and Hebrew texts are to be judged. The only way that the King James can sit in judgment over the Greek and Hebrew is if a second act of inspiration occurred in some particular edition of that translation. Some advocates of the King James Version do actually draw this conclusion, in stark contradiction of the claims of the Scriptures and of the King James translators themselves.

When confronted with the facts, however, most King James-Only advocates quickly begin to modify their insistence upon exact, word-for-word preservation. If they are pressed, they will admit that they do not have all of the words and only the words of the original in a single place. Instead, they will point out how similar most of the manuscripts are. While conceding that word-for-word accuracy is not possible, they insist that they can know *almost* exactly what the words of the originals must have been. They argue that the different editions of the Textus Receptus or the King James Version are *virtually* identical. They point out that the questionable passages are not very significant and that, in any case, all of the possible readings would be true doctrinally.

In spite of their passionate insistence upon the preservation of the words of Scripture, then, most King James-Only advocates are eventually willing to admit the possibility of an acceptable range of variation. They begin with the slogan, "We must have *all* of the words of God in order to have the Word of God," but they end up with the conclusion, "We must have *some* of the words of God in order to have the Word of God." The term *some* may be defined as "most," "all but a few," or even "all but one," but it remains "some" and not "all."

These King James-Only proponents, therefore, wish to have it both ways. They insist upon condemning the Ben-Asher Hebrew text, Codex Sinaiticus and Codex Vaticanus, the contemporary eclectic Greek texts, and the New American Standard Bible because they only contain some (not all) of the words of God. But they are willing to accept differences in the various editions of the Ben-Chayyim Hebrew text, of the Textus Receptus in Greek, and of the King James Version in English, even though no more than one edition of one of these documents can conceivably contain all of the words and only the words of God.

The King James-Only theory creates a sort of theological conundrum. It requires people to repudiate the very thing that it asserts. On one hand, if possession of the "Word of God" demands possession of the "very words of God," then those very words must be preserved somewhere exactly, or else the Word of God has been lost. On the other hand, most King James-Only advocates are forced to admit that God's people can actually make do with only *some* of God's words. This concession, however, supports the very position of those whom they oppose. People who use a Ben-Asher Hebrew text, a Nestle-Aland Greek text, or a New American Standard Bible insist that they, too, have *most* of the words of the original Scriptures—that is, *most* of the words of God. The proportion of words that are open to question is slight. The disputed passages are relatively insignificant. In any case, all of the various options support true doctrine.

In other words, if the King James-Only advocates were candid, most of them would have to admit to holding precisely the same theory as those whom they oppose. They would have to admit that the whole debate is merely an academic quibble over the percentage of acceptable variation. They might prefer the Textus Receptus over the Greek text of Westcott and Hort, but they would have to admit that their preference was based on a difference of *degree* and not a difference of *kind*.

Of course, such an admission would be fatal to the King James-Only movement. If its leaders were so candid, people would recognize that the whole debate amounts to a cyclone in a coffee cup. People would stop buying King James-Only books. They would no longer attend King James-Only schools. They would simply lose interest in the details and write off the debate as an arcane bit of pedantry more suited to the interests of the intellectuals.

That is what people *would* do if the King James-Only leaders *were* candid. In fact, the leaders are not about to allow that to happen. The movement survives, but only by clouding the issues and distracting people from the main point. It protects itself with an elaborate structure of theological illusions.

The Appeal to Faith

The first illusion is the appeal to faith. According to its leading defenders, the King James-Only movement is fundamentally a "faith position." Genuine, biblical faith, however, must rest in the promise of God. To be believed, the promise of God must be clearly revealed in the pages of Scripture itself. The question is not whether the Bible contains a promise that God will preserve His Word. King James-Only advocates go much further. They insist that God has preserved His words and preserved them exactly in a singular, identifiable, and accessible form. So the question is whether the Bible contains a promise that God will preserve, word for word, the text of the original documents of Scripture in a particular manuscript, textual tradition, printed text, or version. As this book has shown, the Bible contains no promise whatsoever that includes the preservation of all of the words of the autographa (without addition or deletion) in a single, publicly accessible source. Without such a promise, the appeal to faith does not rest in the promise of God, but in the untestable and unverifiable speculation of the King James-Only advocates themselves. Until they can produce a Scripture that (properly and contextually understood) *does* promise all that they assert, they have no legitimate right to appeal to faith.

The Appeal to Reason

The second illusion is the appeal to reason. The King James-Only advocates insist that belief in the preciseness of verbal inspiration (which we all affirm) is useless unless it is followed by exactness in verbal preservation (which the authors of this book do not affirm). While this argument from reason sounds plausible at first hearing, it actually runs counter to God's dealings in Scripture. With regard to God's *spoken* words, He has certainly *not* seen fit to preserve all of His words in a publicly accessible form. For example, God apparently revealed a sacrificial system to people before the Flood, but no record of those divine words has been preserved. In John's presence, God spoke through seven thunders, but then He explicitly forbade John to preserve those words in written form (Rev. 10:1–4). When the Scriptures tell us that not all of Jesus' "acts" were recorded (John 21:25), it logically follows that not all of His "words" were recorded either.

Even with regard to *written* words, it is demonstrably true that when someone's spoken words were later recorded in Scripture, the "exact" words spoken were not necessarily the very words that were used in Scripture. For example, when the Gospel writers recorded words that Jesus had spoken during His lifetime, these authors, under the influence of the Holy Spirit, recorded the *essence* of Jesus' words, not His *exact* words. This observation must be true because the recounting of Jesus' words by the Gospel writers do not *exactly* agree (compare, for example, Matt. 13:1–13 with Mark 4:1–13 word for word). We affirm wholeheartedly that the Gospel writers were accurately employing the exact words that God wanted them to use to record Jesus' speech under the perfect, supervisory ministry of the Holy Spirit. However, we also know that the Holy Spirit intended for these writers to record the *essence* of Jesus' speech, not His *exact* words, for that is what they did. Also, remember that Jesus and His disciples frequently quoted the Old Testament (OT) in other than *exact* words. They sometimes quoted the Septuagint, the Masoretic text, a free rendition, or a combination thereof. In God's method of propagating truth, it is apparent from the text of Scripture itself that He allowed some degree of latitude for the accurate and authoritative communication of that truth apart from the perfect preservation of all of the exact words in one particular place; and this latitude is observable even under the inspiration of the Holy Spirit.

God has not promised to preserve all of His spoken and written words in a publicly accessible form, nor has God always deemed public accessibility of His written revelation to be essential. In one case, the entire written revelation of God survived in a single manuscript that was *hidden* from public view (2 Kings 22:8; 2 Chron. 34:15). In all of the cases enumerated herein, God gave specific, verbal revelation, but He did not necessarily see fit to preserve all of the words and exactly the words in a publicly accessible form. The doctrines of inspiration and inerrancy (which are absolute truths) and the King James-Only proponents' postulate of perfect preservation (which is dubious speculation) are certainly not inextricable corollaries.

All parties to this debate acknowledge that God has superintended the choice of the precise words that would be used to communicate His truth. To accept this fact, however, is not to concede that God is obligated to preserve every word through which His truth has been revealed. He might preserve some words and He might permit some to be lost, depending upon His own purpose. The appeal to reason is not a sufficient ground for the King James-Only argument.

The Appeal to Evidence

The third illusion that attends the King James-Only position involves the evaluation of the actual evidence. King James-Only advocates are extremely reluctant to allow the empirical evidence to stand on its own merits. On the one hand, they are fond of insisting that "the majority rules" in textual matters. On the other hand, they are very careful about what they allow to count as a majority. For example, if all manuscripts of the ancient translations of the New Testament are counted, then manuscripts that support the Textus Receptus form a distinct minority. Moreover, according to the actual manuscript evidence, the manuscripts that support the Textus Receptus are not in the majority even of Greek manuscripts until the fourth century or even later. If the theory that "the majority rules" is correct, then the next two questions are, Majority of what? and, Majority from when?

The King James-Only movement can survive only by deploying a highly prejudicial definition of the word *majority*. Its defenders insist that very late Greek manuscripts be included in this majority but that very early translations be excluded from it. They revise history to explain the paucity of manuscripts that support the Textus Receptus before the fourth century. In fact, historical revisionism is a mainstay of the King James-Only argument. Their carefully reworked history is filled with heretics who deliberately miscopied the Scriptures; churches that rejected Alexandrian manuscripts; ecumenical councils that endorsed the Byzantine tradition; secret plots of Jesuits, Masons, Nazis, and Communists; and a variety of other irresponsible speculations, none of which can be shown to have happened.

The Appeal to Prejudice

King James-Only advocates advance their belief on the basis of a fourth illusion. Instead of demonstrating from Scripture and sound argument the clear location of all of the words and only the words of the autographs, they turn the debate into an *ad hominem* exposé of personalities associated with the Alexandrian and Western manuscripts. Into this discussion they drag the Alexandrian theologian Origen, any number of the medieval popes, and two textual scholars named B. F. Westcott and F. J. A. Hort. Conveniently, none of these people are still alive to defend themselves or to clarify their views.

The King James-Only advocates scour the writings of these individuals to discover any combination of words that sounds in the least heretical. They then present these citations to the unstudied public in tabloid fashion. Usually the argument runs something like this:

1. Roman Catholics hated and burned Bible believers during the Middle Ages and the Reformation;
2. Westcott and Hort display signs of sympathy for some Roman (or liberal, or spiritist) practices and teachings;
3. therefore, the manuscripts that Westcott and Hort handled must be tainted—even though those manuscripts were written a millennium and a half before Westcott and Hort ever touched them.

Ironically, the King James-Only proponents are not willing to apply the same argument to Erasmus, the original compiler of the Textus Receptus. Erasmus opposed the Reformation, remaining a faithful Roman Catholic priest until his death. In the writings of the King James-Only advocates, however, the Protestants Westcott and Hort are condemned for their incipient Catholicism whereas the Roman Catholic Erasmus is justified because of an imagined sympathy with the Reformation.

The problem with all of these fabricated histories and personal attacks is that they are virtually impossible to refute. The King James-Only advocates seem to be well aware that a universal negative can never be proven empirically. Can anyone prove that no ecumenical council ever addressed the difference between textual traditions? Can anyone prove conclusively that there is no Alexandrian Cult, stretching back to the time of Nimrod, that has set itself to corrupt and pervert the words and ways of God? Can anyone today prove that Origen, the medieval popes, and Westcott and Hort were not members of this cult? Of course not; such proof is logically impossible. The question ought to be whether sufficient evidence exists to indicate that these things are so, and that proof ought to be based mainly upon a fair reading of the documents that constitute the historical record. More than enough gossip has been spread in this debate. What is especially damaging is that the character of the people who handled the manuscripts is not really the issue at all. The issue is whether a single manuscript, family of manuscripts, printed text, or translation can be shown to contain all of the words and only the words of the original documents of Scripture.

The Appeal to Supernaturalism

The fifth illusion with which King James-Only advocates interject into this debate is their supposed repudiation of "naturalism." All parties to this debate agree that the Bible is a supernatural book, the writing of which was so overseen by the Holy Spirit that the resulting documents were indeed God-breathed and inerrant. Because of the Bible's supernatural origin, King James-Only advocates often argue that it should be exempted from any empirical evaluation at all. They insist that the textual critic who attempts to reconstruct the history of the copying of Scripture is guilty of treating the Bible "naturalistically." Quite often, the King James-Only proponents will compare the results of textual criticism with the results of literary and historical criticism as practiced by unbelieving men.

The fact is, a major difference exists between these critical methods. Literary and historical criticism attempt to answer questions about how the Bible was *written,* whereas textual criticism attempts to answer questions about how it was *copied.* All sides agree that the Bible was *produced* supernaturally; therefore, all sides reject destructive critical attempts to explain the *origin* of Scripture in purely natural terms. Just because the Bible was *produced* supernaturally, however, does not mean that it was *copied* supernaturally. People on both sides of the debate agree that God worked providentially to preserve His Word through the copying process. The key here is that providence is not miracle. A miracle involves the primary, direct intervention of God into otherwise natural processes whereas providence involves God's working secondarily or indirectly through natural processes themselves. In providential events, natural explanations are always possible, but they do not rule out God's oversight of the events.

Copies of the Scriptures did not appear miraculously out of thin air. They were produced through the labors of an army of scribes who grew tired, got distracted, and made mistakes. Unless one wishes to argue that inspiration is an ongoing phenomenon (only a few of the more extreme King James-Only advocates would argue this), then the possibility of mistakes in the copies must be admitted. The fact that every single manuscript of the New Testament differs from every other manuscript is proof that such mistakes did occur. Given these differences, only one of the manuscripts could possibly contain all of the words, and only the words, of the originals. Because all but one of the copies must contain mistakes, and because God has not revealed which copy is the perfect one (if any is), then the only legitimate way to decide which copies are better is to compare them. This comparative technique (properly called "textual criticism") is the method that we have affirmed throughout this book.

This practice of examining all of the available manuscript evidence is the method that King James-Only controversialists call "naturalism." They roundly denounce this "critical" method. In reality, however, they are forced to employ the very same method. They do not advance, on the basis of sound evidence, one particular manuscript as the perfect manuscript. They do not even suggest, on the basis of biblical evidence or logical reasoning, that one particular edition of the Textus Receptus or the King James Version is the word-for-word representation of the original documents of Scripture. What they actually do is to make comparisons between manuscripts or editions, and then take their best guess at which manuscript or edition best represents the original. In fact, this comparative technique is what the editors of those "best" manuscripts and editions did to produce their work. The King James-Only advocates, like the editors of their "best" texts, employ exactly the method that they denounce. The only difference is that the King James-Only advocates have decided beforehand that they will not allow some manuscripts to count as evidence. This approach is not any less naturalistic; it is just more biased.

The Appeal to Translation Theory

King James-Only controversialists also create illusions with regard to translation theory. Here their strategy is twofold: first, they demonize dynamic equivalence as an approach to translation, then they insist that all versions since the King James have employed it. Their argument fails on two counts. First, all translations, including the King James, unquestionably incorporate certain elements of dynamic equivalence into their work. Complete verbal and formal equivalence have never been maintained or even desired in any translation of the Bible, a fact that the King James translators themselves affirmed. Second, many of the more recent translations are at least as literal (verbally and formally equivalent) as the King James. The American Bible Union Version, Young's Literal Translation, the English Revised Version, the American Standard Version of 1901, the Revised Standard Version (with a few exceptions), and the New American Standard Bible are all as literal as the King James, and most of them are more literal. The translators of the King James Version aimed to produce a translation that would represent a balance between formal and dynamic equivalence. The modern version whose philosophy of translation most closely resembles the King James, given the clear statement of the King James translators themselves, is probably the New International Version. Bible version controversialists insist that the King James translators employed a superior translation theory, but the theory of those seventeenth-century translators has been shared by many other translators of many other versions since their day.

The Central Issue

The core issue in the King James-Only controversy is whether one must have the very words of God (*all* of the words and *only* the words of the autographa) to have the Word of God. The advocates of this theory are stymied by the fact that no two manuscripts, no two editions of the Masoreteic Text or Textus Receptus, and no two editions of the King James Version share all of the same words. Reasonable people ought to admit that the whole dispute is an academic quibble over percentages. Instead of making this admission, however, the leaders of the King James-Only movement attempt to shroud their theory in a veritable fog of unfounded speculations, unsupported assertions, and unsubstantiated accusations. As soon as their arguments are subjected to the bracing breeze of truth, however, the smoke clears and the central issue emerges again. Does possessing the Word of God depend upon the exact preservation of *all* of the words and *only* the words of the original documents of Scripture in an accessible form? If so, what text of Scripture teaches us this premise? Where are the exact words of the originals to be found, and what passage of Scripture assures us of the location of this accessible manuscript, manuscript tradition, published text, or version?

If the advocates of the King James-Only position cannot answer these questions with explicit, biblical, reasonable, and verifiable evidence, then they ought to stop defending their position as if it were a question of doctrine. They are certainly entitled to use the Ben-Chayyim Hebrew text, the Textus Receptus, and the King James Bible if they prefer to do so. We might even join them in that preference for any number of reasons. But they are no longer entitled to insist that the Ben-Chayyim is the only *permissible* Hebrew Old Testament, that the Textus Receptus is the only *permissible* Greek New Testament, or that the King James Version is the only *acceptable* representative of the Word of God in the English language. They have no legitimate right to condemn those who use a Ben-Asher Hebrew text, an eclectic Greek text, or a New American Standard Bible. Also, given the reliance of the King James Version and its underlying Greek and Hebrew texts upon textual criticism, it is hardly appropriate for King James-Only advocates to condemn textual critics as hypocrites or heretics.

Here, however, is the point at which the King James-Only movement crosses a moral and biblical line. The facts of the case indicate that the use of the King James Version and its underlying Greek and Hebrew texts is a matter of preference, and the superiority of those documents is a question for academic discussion. That discussion could be furthered if all parties would adopt a brotherly attitude and a humble recognition of the limitations of their own knowledge. Too often, however, the leaders of the King James-Only movement adopt the tactic of vilifying their opponents. This tactic is used not only by the extremists but also by the (relative) moderates.[1] Unfortunately, epithets such as *hypocrite, Pharisee, heretic, apostate, unregenerate,* and *leaven* become the final resort of those who cannot defend their theories by appealing to the facts.

If the accusations themselves were not so vitriolic and so grave, these King James-Only advocates might be regarded simply as a curiosity, as sort of eccentric but harmless old uncles. In fact, however, many King James-Only advocates repeatly issue these harsh charges in the presence of the whole Christian community. No honorable purpose can be served by the leveling of such irresponsible accusations. If the issue at hand were clearly doctrinal, their stern rebukes would be justified. However, as we have seen, the issue here is not the clear teachings of Scripture but the unverifiable suppositions of human teachers.

All of this leads to a very practical problem for those who do not hold the King James-Only position. Even if we wish to accommodate the King James-Only advocates, we are having more and more difficulty doing so. At times, it seems that every concession is met with demands for further concessions. Where the King James-Only controversialists have been able to gain control, we have watched them conduct faculty purges and divide ecclesiastical fellowships. They have shown a willingness to ruin people and organizations that they could not dominate. This puts a strain upon Christian fellowship. How, exactly, are we supposed to maintain warm and brotherly ties with people who continuously denounce us as apostates and hypocrites and who openly question our salvation? We continue to love our King James-Only friends and wish only the best for their ministries, but are we to be blamed if we suspect that the feeling is not mutual?

This question leads to two closing observations about the King James-Only movement. These observations are going to seem harsh, and we offer them with some hesitation. Nevertheless, the situation is so serious that a work of this sort would not be complete unless these evaluations were included.

The first observation is that, in spite of their claims to honor and reverence the Scriptures, the King James-Only advocates are really despising the Word of God. They do so at two levels. First, they despise the Word of God by basing their peculiar doctrines upon a highly speculative system of suggestions and inferences rather than upon the clear statements of the Bible. Second, they despise the Word of God by scorning many of the manuscripts and translations in which it has been preserved. They will not listen to God's voice when He speaks through an eclectic Greek text or a New American Standard Bible; indeed, most of them will not even submit to the authority of the New King James Version. These brethren need to remember what the translators of the King James Version wrote in "The Translators to the Reader."

> We do not deny, nay, we affirm and avow, that the very meanest translation of the Bible in *English* set forth by men of our [Protestant] profession . . . containeth the word of God, nay, is the word of God. . . . No cause therefore why the word translated should be denied to be the word, or forbidden to be current, notwithstanding that some imperfections and blemishes may be noted in the setting forth of it.[2]

We believe that the King James translators wrote the truth. Therefore, Christian charity places upon us an obligation to speak a word of warning to our brethren. A movement that rejects the Word of God as it has been preserved in *any* text or translation must base itself somewhere other than in Holy Writ. The King James-Only movement builds its core doctrines upon a speculative foundation outside of the Bible itself. We believe that a decision to base one's faith outside of the Bible is a dangerous move. Ultimately, our great fear is that the King James-Only movement might become a seed bed for more serious errors of faith and life.

Our second observation is that according to the New Testament understanding of heresy ("divisiveness"), the attitudes and actions of many leaders in the King James-Only movement are genuinely heretical. This situation creates both a practical concern and a biblical concern. Practically, the attempt to accommodate such divisive behavior will be disastrous for evangelical and fundamentalist institutions. Many King James-Only leaders have shown that they are not interested in peaceful coexistence. They have adopted a rule-or-ruin attitude. This attitude will corrode any fellowship within which it is permitted to flourish.

Biblically, the New Testament is very explicit about the way in which God's people are to respond to a person who displays such an attitude. The apostle Paul states quite clearly in Titus 3:10, "A man that is an heretick after the first and second admonition reject," or, as the passage is translated in the New King James Version, "Reject a divisive man after the first and second admonition." The New American Standard Bible renders the verse, "Reject a factious man after a first and second warning," and the force is brought out quite nicely in the New International Version: "Warn a divisive person once, and then warn him a second time. After that, have nothing to do with him." The leaders of the King James-Only movement have been warned far more than once or twice. Is it too much to suggest that the Word of God now speaks authoritatively about the stance that Christian leaders and institutions ought to take toward the factious element of the King James-Only movement?

We appeal to the Scriptures. The Bible constitutes our ultimate and sole authority. All who claim Christ must obey *fully* and defend *staunchly* the clear teaching of God's Holy Word, the Faith once for all delivered to His saints. We desire nothing more; we must accept nothing less. We must not elevate to the level of Scripture that which we only surmise. Biblical faith must never find its object in that which the Bible does not affirm. Our belief must be founded on the truth of God's revelation and on that revelation exclusively. To create another standard and to measure others by it is to degrade the true Standard and dishonor the great God who revealed it. An alternate standard assumes an alternate god. For us, the God of Scripture and His Word alone must stand.

Chapter Notes

1. Unfortunately, the use of abusive language and question-begging epithets characterizes even the relatively moderate wing of the King James-Only movement. In its video-taped series titled *The Leaven of Fundamentalism* (Pensacola, Fla.: Pensacola Christian College, 1998), Pensacola Christian College labels the use of textual criticism as a "leaven" and calls those who use the eclectic Greek text or the New American Standard Bible "Pharisees" and "sinful hypocrites." One of the more theologically moderate King James-Only advocates actually uses some of the most immoderate language: D. A. Waite repeatedly vilifies non-King James-Only fundamentalists as heretics, apostates, deceivers, blasphemers, false teachers, and hypocrites, and he openly questions their salvation. (See, for example, his books *Central Seminary Refuted on Bible Versions* [Collingswood, N.J.: Bible for Today Press, 1999]; and *Fundamentalist Distortions on Bible Versions* [Collingswood, N.J.: Bible for Today Press, 1999]). From a somewhat more extreme theological position, William P. Grady constantly derides fundamentalists who use modern versions such as the New American Standard as "Nicolaitanes," comparing them with the sect that the Lord Jesus condemned in the book of Revelation. Not satisfied with attacking the theological commitments of his opponents, he continually rebukes them for what he portrays as a lack of moral and physical courage. (See his book *Final Authority* [Schererville, Ind.: Grady, 1993]). In fairness, we must point out that not all King James-Only advocates resort to such caustic verbal abuse. Although Peter Van Kleeck does suggest that his opponents are not orthodox, he appears to be using the term *orthodoxy* in a restricted sense that entails adherence to the full system of faith as he defines it. (See "A 16th and 17th Century Exegetical and Theological Assessment of Central Baptist Theological Seminary's Perspective of the Bible Version Debate" [printed script of a public lecture delivered at the Midwest regional meeting of the Independent Baptist Fellowship of North America, Oak Creek, Wisc., 20 April 1998]). A recent publication by Charles L. Surrett displays a generally charitable spirit, although it repeats many of the mistakes of the King James-Only movement (see *Which Greek Text? The Debate Among Fundamentalists* [Kings Mountain, N.C.: Surrett Family Publications, 1999]). While we disagree with Van Kleeck and Surrett, we do believe

that meaningful conversation with them is possible. In this regard, we would not offer many of the criticisms against them that we do offer against the more abusive leaders of the King James-Only movement. We welcome and even seek meaningful conversation in this debate. We are sorrowed by the frequent use of unbiblical, vituperative language in this otherwise Christian forum and, thus, have sought to avoid using it ourselves.

2. From F. H. A. Scrivener, "The Translators to the Reader: Preface to the King James Version," in *The Authorized Edition of the English Bible (1611), Its Subsequent Reprints and Modern Representatives* (Cambridge: At the University Press, 1884), par. 13. A complete copy of "The Translators to the Reader" may be found in appendix C of this book.

Frequently Asked Questions in the Translation Controversy

Kevin T. Bauder

I am confused by some of the terms that I hear in this debate. What is the difference between an autograph and an apograph?

An autograph (pl. autographa) was the original biblical document that came from the human author. An apograph (pl. apographa) is any copy or translation of the original document, including copies or translations of copies.

How many of the autographa are still in existence?

None that we know of. As far as we can tell, God has not seen fit to preserve any of the original documents of Scripture.

How many of the apographa are in existence?

Because every copy of any part of the Bible constitutes some part of the apographa, it would be impossible even to estimate the number. We have many, many copies.

What is the difference between a manuscript and a text?

A manuscript (abbreviated MS; pl. MSS) is a handwritten copy of some part of the Hebrew Old Testament or the Greek New Testament. A text is a published edition of the Old Testament in Hebrew or the New Testament in Greek. A published text is normally compiled by comparing several manuscripts.

How many manuscript copies of the Bible exist?

The numbers are not firm, because researchers are still discovering manuscripts of the Old and New Testaments. For the sake of simplicity, let's restrict our discussion to manuscripts of the New Testament. In 1967, the number of extant Greek manuscripts stood at 5,255. In the ensuing years, that number has grown. Some estimates now range up to nearly 5,500 manuscripts. Not all of these are copies of the entire New Testament, however. Some of them are copies of only individual books. A few of them are just fragments of a page or so in length.

How similar are these manuscripts?

The short answer to this question is that they are very similar. Each manuscript, however, does show differences in the way that it was copied. Some manuscripts have more differences than others.

Some people are uncomfortable when they learn that differences exist between the manuscripts, but those people should realize three things. First, the differences affect only a small proportion of the words in the New Testament. At worst, less than 20 percent of the New Testament is open to any question at all. Most estimates are far less pessimistic than that. Second, most of the differences between manuscripts are over relatively minor matters such as spelling. Those differences do not alter the meaning of the text at all. According to F. H. A. Scrivener, only about seven words in one hundred may be regarded as real variants, and most of those do not significantly affect the interpretation of the text. Third, even where the meaning of the text is open to question, the different possibilities are all perfectly orthodox. At no point does a true doctrine of the faith hinge upon a disputed word or passage.

Are any of the manuscripts identical to each other?

To answer that question, one would have to examine all of the more than five thousand manuscripts in detail. I don't know of anyone who has ever done that, and I doubt that anyone ever could. Many scholars, however, have devoted their entire lives to comparing the manuscripts of the Greek New Testament. None of them has ever been able to demonstrate that any two Greek manuscripts are identical. We may conclude that, like snowflakes and fingerprints, every manuscript differs from every other manuscript in some respects. As we have seen, however, the differences are relatively minor.

Why are these manuscripts all different?

Changes could be introduced into a manuscript either intentionally or unintentionally. An unintentional alteration would be made when a copyist read one word but thought another word, or when a copyist accidentally skipped a word or section of text. An intentional alteration would be made when a copyist became convinced that an earlier copyist had made an unintentional change. A change could also occur if a copyist jotted an annotation into the margin of his manuscript (a frequent occurrence), and then a later copyist mistook it as part of the text.

Didn't heretics alter the text of some manuscripts to fit their theology?

That was a surprisingly rare occurrence. Many heretics superimposed a faulty interpretation upon the words of Scripture, but they generally left the words themselves alone. The heretics who wanted to tamper with the text of the Bible didn't just change a few words here and there. They rejected or rewrote whole books of the Bible, or inserted others. When they made such wholesale additions or deletions, it was very obvious. The early Christian leaders quickly placed these false teachers and their defective writings under theological quarantine by naming their names publicly and listing their defective writings. None of the reputable, modern printed editions of the Hebrew Old Testament or Greek New Testament uses these heretical writings as a basis for making changes in the text.

Don't some manuscripts (such as Sinaiticus and Vaticanus) reflect a heretical bias?

King James-Only advocates make this assertion frequently, but it is completely false. All of the major manuscripts (including Sinaiticus and Vaticanus) are entirely compatible with orthodox Christianity. They do not delete any doctrine of the faith or insert any alien doctrines. These manuscripts do not bear the marks of heretical tampering.

How do critics try to prove that Sinaiticus and Vaticanus are heretical?

First they piece together an imaginary story about heretical influences over the oldest manuscripts. Then they usually try to place the worst possible interpretation upon difficult readings that are found in these manuscripts. When dealing with the Textus Receptus, however, they place the most favorable interpretation upon the difficult readings. In fact, the actual readings in Sinaiticus and Vaticanus are completely compatible with Christian orthodoxy.

But doesn't Sinaiticus delete the resurrection from Mark's Gospel?

No, it does not. This accusation has been made by people who should know better. In fact, the Sinaiticus copy of Mark ends with the resurrection of Jesus and the assurance that the disciples would meet Him in Galilee.

What is textual criticism?

The term *criticism* is a little unsettling for some folks. It creates a fear that people are criticizing the Bible. In this context, however, the word *criticism* just means something like *careful thought*. Textual criticism is a careful or thoughtful attempt to restore as closely as possible the original wording of the Bible.

Why is textual criticism necessary?

First, because we no longer have access to the original documents that came from the hands of the biblical writers (the autographa). We have only copies (apographa). Second, because each of these copies appears to be different from all of the other copies. No two copies are alike. Although the differences between the copies are relatively minor, we are still interested in trying to discover exactly which words were in the originals. We want to get as close as we can to the very words of the inspired autographa. To do that, we have to compare the various copies. We can then make an informed choice about which variation is likely closest to the original.

What is the Textus Receptus?

The Textus Receptus (Latin for "received text") is the name for a series of printed editions of the Greek New Testament. The earliest of these editions was published by Erasmus, a Roman Catholic scholar who patched together his first text by comparing a handful of manuscripts. His manuscripts did not even contain the whole New Testament, so he supplemented them by translating some parts of the Latin Vulgate (the Latin Bible of the Roman Catholic Church) back into Greek. Erasmus revised his work several times as other manuscripts became available. It was then picked up by Robert Estienne (also known as Stephanus), who revised it several more times. Theodore Beza released eleven editions of this text, each of which was different from the others. The Elzevirs (uncle and nephew) also revised this text several times, and they were the first people to call it the Textus Receptus. The edition of the Textus Receptus that is currently published by the Trinitarian Bible Society is not identical with any of these earlier editions. It is based on the work of Frederick Scrivener, who compiled a new edition of the Textus Receptus in 1894 (it was reprinted in 1902). Scrivener used Beza's 1598 edition as his basic text but revised it by comparing it with other editions of the Textus Receptus and other published Greek texts and English translations.

Why were so many editions of the Textus Receptus necessary?

The editors of the Textus Receptus were constantly doing textual criticism. Erasmus started out with a handful of manuscripts, but he traveled the length and breadth of Europe, taking copious notes on biblical manuscripts wherever he could find them. With each succeeding edition, the editors of the Textus Receptus compared more and more Greek manuscripts and collated more and more of the differences between them. Every separate edition of the Textus Receptus bears testimony that ongoing textual criticism is a necessary activity.

Is the Textus Receptus an exact copy of the autographa?

Because no two editions of the Textus Receptus are identical, no more than one of them could provide an exact copy of the originals. The Bible itself offers no guarantee that any of them is exact.

What about the edition that the King James translators used? Couldn't it be the exact copy?

The King James translators did not use a single edition of the Textus Receptus. They relied mainly on Beza's fifth edition but corrected it in about two hundred instances. They referred to various editions as published by Erasmus, Stephanus, and Beza. The Elzevirs (who actually named the Textus Receptus) did not publish their editions until after the completion of the King James Version. Some people do claim that Beza's fifth edition is virtually identical with the autographa. The key word here is *virtually*. Such people must admit that even the best edition of the Textus Receptus is not an *exact* copy of the originals. Almost no one tries to argue that any single edition of the Textus Receptus contains all of the words, and only the words, of the inspired originals. Therefore, even those people who grant a special place to the Textus Receptus are forced to do textual criticism.

Aren't the majority of the manuscripts in very close agreement?

Actually, *all* of the manuscripts (including Sinaiticus, Vaticanus, and similar copies) are in quite close agreement. No one is parading manuscripts that differ seriously from one another.

Haven't I read that recent editions of the Greek New Testament differ from the Textus Receptus in more than five thousand places? How can you call that "close agreement?"

I have not personally counted the differences, but one man who reveres the Textus Receptus claims that the more recent Greek editions differ from the Textus Receptus in 5,604 places. The issue is what constitutes a difference. Should we count every word? Every letter of every word? Should changes in spelling be counted? When detractors attack the current editions of the Greek New Testament, they usually count the differences so as to get the highest number possible. But when they count differences among the various editions of the Textus Receptus (or even the King James Version), they will minimize the number. For instance, the same man who counted the 5,604 differences was told that the current King James Version of the Bible differs from the original 1611 King James in tens of thousands of places. He replied that only 421 of those places were "apparent to the ear" when the King James was read aloud by a modern reader. In other words, differences that would be counted when criticizing a current edition of the Greek New Testament would not be counted when evaluating different editions of the Textus Receptus or the King James Bible. The truth is that the overwhelming majority of differences between Greek manuscripts are very minor. What remarkable is not the difference but the agreement.

But don't some manuscripts differ more than others?

Yes. Many of the most ancient uncials and papyri (these are the oldest manuscripts) tend to have more differences than most of the more recent manuscripts. Moreover, they tend to resemble each other in the places in which they differ from the majority.

Why would a textual critic follow the minority of manuscripts rather than the great majority? The majority couldn't be wrong, could it?

People evaluate biblical manuscripts much like they evaluate rumors. Some people believe a rumor just because they hear it repeated a lot. Other people want to know where the rumor came from before they will believe it. Most of us would recognize that a widespread rumor might be true, but its being widespread is not what makes it true. The same thing is true of manuscripts. Just because a reading has been copied widely does not mean that it was the original reading. Many scholars believe that manuscripts from the fourth century should be trusted more than manuscripts from the fourteenth century because fourth century manuscripts were copied a full millennium closer to the source.

Didn't the early churches reject some of these ancient manuscripts? If the manuscripts had been used, they would have been copied, right?

From the fifth century, the manuscripts that tend to agree with the Textus Receptus (call them the "majority manuscripts") were most widely used in the Christian communities. That does not necessarily mean that the minority manuscripts were rejected, however. For the most part, these minority manuscripts were used in Africa and Western Europe. Historical events in those parts of the world resulted in a decreased use of the Greek New Testament. In Africa, for example, the rise of Islam cut short the opportunities of Christians to perpetuate the Word of God. Muslims often burned Christian manuscripts when they could find them. In Western Europe, people spoke Latin instead of Greek. Naturally, Latin manuscripts were the ones that were used and copied the most. Only in the Byzantine Empire were Greek manuscripts copied in great quantities. No historical evidence exists to prove that the churches ever deliberately rejected any manuscripts of the Bible. The early churches certainly were not in the habit of denouncing biblical manuscripts or refusing to acknowledge them as the Word of God.

Hasn't God promised to preserve all of the words of Scripture?

Most careful interpreters would say that no such specific promise can be found in the Bible itself. In fact, even John Burgon—something of a hero to the King James-Only advocates—insisted that the Bible contains no promise of textual preservation. The passages that are supposed to contain this promise do not stand up to careful scrutiny. Without exception, they appear to be talking about something besides the written preservation of all of the words of Scripture.

Who were Hort and Westcott?

F. J. A. Hort and B. F. Westcott were British scholars who published a printed edition of the Greek New Testament in 1881. Their work built upon previous editions of the Greek New Testament and compared some of the newly discovered manuscripts. Their inclusion of the most ancient manuscripts was what distinguished their work and made it a reference point for all later editions of the Greek New Testament.

Didn't Hort and Westcott reject the Textus Receptus in favor of the manuscripts Sinaiticus and Vaticanus?

They believed that the Textus Receptus had been granted more authority than its faithfulness to the autographa warranted. They also believed that the two ancient manuscripts Sinaiticus and Vaticanus ought to be given great weight in determining the wording of the autographa, largely because those manuscripts were so much older than most of the manuscripts that were used to support the Textus Receptus.

Weren't Hort and Westcott apostates? Why would I want to take their word for anything?

The King James-Only advocates are fond of publishing personal attacks against Hort and Westcott, men who are no longer here to clarify their statements or to defend themselves. Most of these attacks are pure gossip interspersed with brief quotations taken out of context. Were Hort and Westcott apostates? Possibly they were. Certainly Erasmus, the original compiler of the Textus Receptus was an apostate. Erasmus rejected and fought against those who proclaimed salvation through faith alone and who labeled the pope as antichrist. He remained a loyal Catholic until the day of his death. Most biblical manuscripts and all printed editions have passed through some unclean hands. But the Word of God cannot be sullied by the hands that hold it. Erasmus did not invent anything new for the Greek New Testament, and neither did Westcott and Hort. All of these scholars worked with the manuscripts that they had, and all of them were most interested in getting as near to the autographa as they possibly could. Their theological biases simply do not enter into this question. Westcott and Hort were dealing with manuscripts that God had providentially preserved but that were not available to earlier editors of the Greek New Testament. No one has proven that they handled the manuscripts in bad faith. If, however, you are reluctant about Westcott and Hort, you do not have to take their word for anything. You have the right and the ability to learn Greek and to study the manuscripts for yourself. In fact, if you don't want to take *somebody* else's word on this issue, that is exactly what you must do.

What different translation theories lie behind different versions of the Bible?

Bible translations range along a spectrum. Although some people would differ with me, I define that spectrum in the following terms. At one extreme is *rigid literalism,* word-for-word translation that disregards the needs of the reader. Interlinear translations are an example of this. *Formal equivalent* translations (sometimes called *concordant* translations) are those that aim to get as close as possible to a word-for-word translation while maintaining comprehensibility in the reader's language. Such versions as Young's Literal Translation, the American Standard Version (1901), and the New American Standard Bible are concordant. *Combination* versions are those that remain word oriented but also try to maintain good style in the readers' language. The King James is one such version; so are the New International (which is slightly less strict than the KJV) and the New Berkeley. *Dynamic equivalence* is a rather vague term that is used to describe versions that seek word meanings and sentence structures that will communicate the same thing to the modern reader that the word meanings and sentence structures communicated to the original readers. The Contemporary English Version is an example of dynamic equivalence, and some parts of the NIV probably are as well.

At the opposite extreme from rigid literalism is *paraphrase,* which attempts to reproduce the tone, rhythm, events, and ideas of the original writers in the language of the reader. Paraphrases are really interpretations rather than translations. Paraphrases include *The Living Bible* by Kenneth Taylor and *The Message* by Eugene Peterson.

Does the King James Bible reflect a superior translation theory?

All translators must do a balancing act. On the one hand, they must maintain faithfulness to the originals that they are translating. On the other hand, they must translate so that their readers will be able to understand what the original says. The words and structures of one language can almost never be transferred intact to another language. The King James translators recognized this fact. In "The Translators to the Reader," they said that they tried to express the "sense" or meaning of the original, even at the cost of some measure of imperfection in the translation. That practice is similar to the translation philosophy behind the New International Version. The New American Standard Bible is considerably more precise in reflecting the verbal and formal structures of the original languages than is the King James. The translation theory and techniques of the King James translators were not even unique, let alone superior.

Weren't the translators of the King James Version better equipped than modern scholars for the task of putting God's Word into the English language?

The King James translators remain unparalleled in certain ways. They were scholars whose breadth of study far exceeded that of most modern Bible translators. They were learned across a range of disciplines. They studied classical languages from their youth. They were at home in the thought of the philosophers as well as the biblical writers. They were masters of the Western intellectual tradition. Moreover, they were superb English stylists. They were humanists (in the proper sense of the term) of the very first rank. For that reason, the King James Version remains without peer as a work of simplicity, dignity, and grandeur, and it is in general a very faithful translation. As great as those scholars were, however, they lived at a time when linguistics was in its infancy. The knowledge of Hebrew was just being recovered in Europe. Even the understanding of certain Greek structures was relatively naïve. The ensuing four hundred years have brought major advances in our grasp of the biblical languages. Modern translators might sometimes be inferior to the King James translators in their breadth of learning, but they surpass them as masters of biblical Hebrew, Aramaic, and Greek. The net result is that some modern versions, although lacking the literary dignity of the King James, nevertheless surpass it in their precision and faithful adherence to the meaning of the original languages.

Don't the great Protestant confessions of faith teach the preservation of Scripture?

The Westminster Confession contains the following declaration (chap. 1, par. 8):

> The Old Testament in Hebrew (which was the native language of the people of God of old), and the New Testament in Greek (which at the time of the writing of it was most generally known to the nations), being immediately inspired by God, and by his singular care and providence kept pure in all ages, are therefore authentical. . . .

This language is echoed by other evangelical confessions. All evangelical Protestants acknowledge the providential preservation of the Scriptures. What these confessions do not do is to articulate a particular manuscript, group of manuscripts, or printed text within which the Scriptures have been preserved to the exclusion of all other manuscripts and texts. The authors of the Westminster Confession knew about the diversity within the Greek and Hebrew manuscripts. They even knew about manuscripts with readings similar to those of Sinaiticus and Vaticanus. When they wrote their confession, however, they were careful not to exclude *any* manuscripts from the category of providential preservation. To every indication, the authors of the great Protestant confessions would have recognized all Greek or Hebrew manuscripts and texts as the Word of God, the preserved Scriptures of the Old and New Testaments.

Is the current King James Version identical with the 1611 King James?

No. The King James Version has gone through several editions, many of which made changes in spelling or wording. The King James that most of us use today is actually the 1769 revision. It differs from the original King James translation of 1611 in more than seventy thousand particulars. Of course, none of those changes significantly alters the meaning of the text, but that is just the point. To the extent that we recognize the King James Version as the Word of God, we must admit that the preservation of God's Word does not depend upon an absolute preservation of every word and letter, especially not in a single printed text or version.

Does textual criticism attack or demean the King James Version?

The King James New Testament was translated mainly (though not exclusively) from the Textus Receptus. The Textus Receptus was compiled by using the techniques of textual criticism, although those techniques were sometimes hastily applied. In other words, the King James Version relies directly upon textual criticism. Far from attacking the King James, therefore, textual criticism is part of the equipment that enabled the King James translators to do their work so well. The purpose of textual criticism is not to attack the fine work that has been done in the past but to improve upon it. Textual criticism is important because we take the Bible seriously. Remember what textual criticism does: it is a thoughtful attempt to restore as nearly as possible the exact wording of the original documents of Scripture. This is an effort that should be applauded by all of those who truly love God's Word.

Is the King James Version a reliable translation?

Yes, it is a very reliable translation. The editors of the Revised Standard Version claimed in their preface that the King James "has grave defects." That is simply not true. A person who reads, understands, and believes the King James Version will not be led into error but into truth.

Then why not just use the King James? Why bother with other versions at all?

In fact, some of us do still treasure and use the King James. What we find, though, is that we must constantly stop to explain the difficult English before we can get to the actual meaning of the text. Other good versions are useful for three reasons. First, we have many more manuscripts at our disposal than the King James translators did, and some modern versions might help to get us closer to the readings of the original documents of Scripture. Second, some versions (for instance, the New American Standard) are much more precise than the King James if precision is defined in terms of verbal and formal equivalence. Third, Jacobean English is now a foreign language to most people. Some of the modern translations use more readable English without sacrificing faithfulness to the original Hebrew, Aramaic, and Greek.

Is the King James-Only movement cultic?

When someone asks such a question, definitions become very important. What exactly is a cult? This is a notoriously difficult question to answer. Part of the problem is that we actually use the term in two different senses.

In the narrower sense, a nominally Christian theology becomes cultic when it attempts to redefine orthodoxy. Jehovah's Witnesses are cultic because they remove the deity of Christ from the definition of orthodoxy. Mormons are cultic because they substitute a false view of the nature of God within their understanding of orthodoxy. Clearly, the King James-Only movement is rarely if ever cultic in its handling of these doctrines. But it sometimes alters the definition of orthodoxy in another way. Although it does not delete essential elements from the definition of orthodoxy, it sometimes adds elements. This is precisely what happens when the exclusive use of the King James Version (or the Textus Receptus or the Ben-Chayyim Hebrew text) is made a test of orthodoxy. A mere preference for the King James or the Textus Receptus would not be cultic in and of itself, even if it is a very strong preference. However, to say that those who use any other translation or any other Greek or Hebrew text have endangered the faith and are not orthodox is cultic. Sadly, one does find this attitude among some (though not all) King James-Only advocates.

In the broader sense, a religious movement might become cultic in the way that it secures the loyalty of its followers and challenges its opponents. How do its leaders react when questioned or criticized? Do they encourage their followers to question and examine their own fundamental principles, or do they require that their followers accept their dicta "by faith"? Does the movement revolve around a small nucleus of powerful leaders whose accountability to others is shadowy? How do its leaders meet opposition? Do they demonize their opponents? Do they shout them down or do they offer reasonable responses? How do they handle evidence? Do they ensure that they tell the whole story, or do they suppress facts that would contradict their teachings? Judged by these criteria, not everyone associated with the King James-Only movement would be cultic, but some of them would be.

Is the King James-Only movement heretical?

The answer to this question depends upon what is meant by the word *heresy* and *heretical*. In the broadest sense of the term, any departure fro~ true biblical teaching, no matter how small, is a heresy. On this defi~

tion, probably all of us hold some heretical beliefs, for all of us make mistakes in our understanding of God's Word. In the narrower, more technical sense of the term, however, a heresy is the denial of some cardinal doctrine of the faith. Based on this definition, only those who deny the fundamentals would be heretical. To be a heretic and to be an apostate would be the same thing. By the broad definition, the King James-Only movement is heretical, but so are the rest of us. By the narrow definition, the King James-Only movement is, for the most part, not heretical at all.

The New Testament definition of heresy, however, differs from both of the preceding definitions. The Greek term for heretic is *hairetikos*. It refers to a person who is factious or divisive. In the New Testament, therefore, a heretic is a person who causes unnecessary divisions among the brethren. This gives us a criterion for saying that large sections of the King James-Only Movement are very heretical.

People who prefer to use the King James Bible (or the Textus Receptus or the Ben-Chayyim Hebrew text) have a right to hold and advance their opinion. What they do not have a right to do is to question the integrity or spiritual standing of brethren who disagree with them. When they begin to throw around terms such as *apostate* and *hypocrite,* when they engage in name-calling and innuendo, when they question the salvation of their opponents, and when they represent their brethren as enemies of the faith, then they are engaging in genuinely heretical activity.

Some people say that they accept the King James as the best version or the Textus Receptus as the best text "by faith." Is this appeal to faith legitimate?

Faith is legitimate only when it rests in a sufficient object. When Christian truth is at stake, the legitimate ground of faith must be the promise and character of God. If God says that the King James is the only reliable version of the Bible in the English language, then we should take Him at His word. If God promises that He will preserve all of His words without addition or alteration in a particular printed text, then we ought to revere that printed text. The truth is, however, that God never made either of these promises. The faith of the King James-Only advocates rests not in the promise of God but in a highly rational system of their own devising. The Bible nowhere says that verbal inspiration demands verbal preservation. The Bible nowhere teaches that we must have all of God's words to have His Word. The Bible nowhere endorses a particular manuscript, tradition, or printed text as the perfectly preserved Word of God. Therefore, the faith of the King James-Only advocates is not in God's character or promise but in their own system.

These people are sometimes accused of being bibliolaters, of worshipping a particular version of the Bible. I disagree. They are not worshipping any version of the Bible. Their movement would be far less ominous if its adherents were really marked by loyalty to the Word of God. What they are worshiping is their own system, a theological construct of their own devising. In fairness, I should note that most of us place loyalty to system before loyalty to Scripture at some points, even though we might not be aware that we are doing so. But we ought to try to ensure that we are really defending Scripture, and not just our system, before we begin to call our brethren liars, fools, hypocrites, and apostates. The appeal to faith is appropriate, but only when faith is properly grounded in the promise of God as revealed in His Word.

Fundamentalism and the King James-Only Position

Larry D. Pettegrew

The following material is an excerpt from the book The Bible Version Debate: The Perspective of Central Baptist Theological Seminary. *This current book constitutes a major revision and republication of that earlier work. What follows is a brief discussion of the King James-Only issue as it has surfaced in the circles of biblical fundamentalism in the past few decades along with a clear refutation of the idea that historic fundamentalists held to a King James-Only position.*

Biblical fundamentalists love the King James Bible. For the most part, they preach and teach out of it and believe it to be an excellent English translation that has stood the test of time. In recent years, however, a new belief, the King James-Only position, has infiltrated historic fundamentalism. The King James-Only teaching is based on the hypothesis that the King James Version of the Bible is the only inspired and inerrant English Bible. This view holds that all other English translations are the work of the devil or are New Age Bibles. Even non-English Bibles must be translated out of the King James Version rather than the Greek and Hebrew.

Biblical fundamentalists have been a little reluctant to speak out against the King James-Only viewpoint—and for good reasons. Not only do most fundamentalists love and respect this translation but also some fundamentalists believe that the Greek manuscripts and Greek text from which the King James New Testament was translated are generally superior to those used by the translators of the New International Version and the New American Standard Bible.

The disagreement over Greek texts is a legitimate matter of discussion. To be sure, it is a highly technical issue. Most of the people who are dogmatic on one side or the other probably have never seen a New Testament Greek manuscript, and many of them cannot read Greek. Still, this is a valid matter for serious and careful study.[1]

Unfortunately, some of the people who are arguing for a certain Greek text apparently are only using the argument concerning the Greek text as a sophisticated cover for their real concern. The real issue for them is that only the King James Version is God-breathed, and all other English translations are New Age Bibles or worse. This view is obvious because many of these people reject the *New* King James Bible, although it is translated from the Greek text to which they are committed.

Fundamentalists have also been reluctant to expose the King James-Only position because some modern alternatives to the King James Bible have been unacceptable. The last generation of fundamentalists took a strong position against the Revised Standard Version, for example, because it translated some key doctrinal passages unfairly. This experience developed a mindset in many fundamentalists that inclined them to be suspicious of new translations.

Sometimes fundamentalists have also struggled to explain to the people in the pew, in nontechnical language, the problems of all translations without at the same time weakening people's respect for the authority of the Bible. Most Americans are particularly disadvantaged in this regard because they do not study other languages. Consequently, they do not understand the process and headaches of translating from one language to another. From a purely literary perspective, it is also difficult to give up the classic beauty of the English language so nobly incorporated in the style of the King James Bible.

In spite of the fundamentalists' rightful respect for the King James Version, they must not allow bad doctrine into their churches. The King James-Only position is based on a heterodox view of the inspiration and preservation of the Bible and is, consequently, nonfundamentalist and nonevangelical. The Bible clearly teaches that one of the serious responsibilities of pastors is to protect their sheep from wrong doctrine (Acts 20:28–31).

Fundamentalists Are Not Necessarily King James-Only

Occasionally, a King James-Only advocate insists that anyone who uses any version of the Bible other than the King James is departing from fundamentalism. This accusation simply is not true to the facts of history. Fundamentalist leaders have favored the King James Bible, and some, as we have already noted, have preferred the Greek text behind the King James to other Greek texts; but fundamentalists historically have not been adherents to the King James-Only theory.

What have fundamentalists taught about the inspiration of Bible versions? Church historians believe that fundamentalism as an American movement grew out of the nineteenth-century revivals and Bible conferences. In 1878, the greatest of the Bible conferences, the Niagara Bible Conference, published a twelve-point confession of faith. Concerning inspiration, the Niagara men wrote the following article:

> We believe "that all Scripture is given by inspiration of God," by which we understand the whole of the book called the Bible; nor do we take the statement in the sense in which it is sometimes foolishly said that works of human genius are inspired, but in the sense that the Holy Ghost gave the very words of the sacred writings to holy men of old; and that His Divine inspiration is not in different degrees, but extends equally and fully to all parts of these writings, historical, poetical, doctrinal and prophetical, and to the smallest word, and inflection of a word, provided such a word is found in the original manuscripts.[2]

These embryonic fundamentalists emphasized that it was the "original manuscripts" that were God-breathed.[3]

Ten years later, Wayland Hoyt wrote the following in the book *The Inspired Word,* edited by the well-known conservative A. T. Pierson:

> What is that for which Inspiration is to be claimed? King James' version? Certainly not. The Canterbury revision? No. The Douay version? Of course not. The Bishops' version, the Genevan, Cranmer's, Tyndall's, Wyckliff's, in German Luther's—any one

of the versions which have ever been made at any time or anywhere—
is Inspiration to be claimed for all or any of these? By no means.
Well, then, of the most ancient and precious manuscripts which we
possess—the Ephraem palimpsest in the imperial library at Paris,
the Alexandrian codex in the British Museum, the Vatican codex
in the Vatican, or most ancient possibly, and most complete of all,
the Sinaitic codex at St. Petersburg—of these most venerable and
inestimably valuable manuscripts is Inspiration to be claimed? . . .
Neither for versions nor for manuscripts is Inspiration to be claimed.
Inspiration is to be claimed only for the primal sacred autographs.[4]

James M. Gray, early fundamentalist president of Moody Bible Institute, was one of the writers of *The Fundamentals.* He wrote that inspiration
concerned the autographs:

Let it be stated further in this definitional connection, that the
record for whose inspiration we contend is the original record—
the autographs or parchments of Moses, David, Daniel, Matthew, Paul or Peter, as the case may be, and not a particular
translation or translations of them whatever. There is no translation absolutely without error, nor could there be, considering
the infirmities of human copyists, unless God were pleased to
perform a perpetual miracle to secure it.[5]

We could fill several pages with quotations from fundamentalists such
as James Brookes, the Father of American Dispensationalism; L. W.
Munhall; D. L. Moody; R. A. Torrey; C. I. Scofield; and many other
revered men of God from the late nineteenth and early twentieth centuries. All of these early fundamentalists have said something like what
R. A. Torrey, D. L. Moody's successor, said:

No one, as far as I know, holds that the Authorized Version, or
any English translation of the Bible, is absolutely infallible and
inerrant. The doctrine held by me and by many others who have
given years to careful and thorough study of the Bible is, that the
Scriptures *as originally given* were absolutely infallible and inerrant, and that our English translation is a *substantially* accurate
rendering of the scriptures as originally given.[6]

The main fundamentalist organization in the 1920s was the World's Christian Fundamental Association, led primarily by W. B. Riley. Its confession of faith begins with these words:

> I. We believe in the Scriptures of the Old and New Testament as verbally inspired of God, and inerrant in the original writings, and that they are of supreme and final authority in faith and practice.[7]

Clearly, the founders and early leaders of fundamentalism never accepted the view that the King James is the only inspired English translation. Likewise, the main leaders of fundamentalism in more recent history taught that inspiration and inerrancy extended only to the original autographs. John R. Rice, a long-time leader of a large segment of fundamentalism through the *Sword of the Lord* and his Sword Conferences, commented on translations as follows:

> A perfect translation of the Bible is humanly impossible. The words in one language do not have exactly the same color and meaning as opposite [corresponding] words in another language, and human frailty and imperfection enter in. So, let us say, there are no perfect translations. God does not inspire particular translations, although He may illuminate and give spiritual wisdom to the translator.[8]

Stewart Custer, former chairman of the Bible department of Bob Jones University, explains the matter similarly: "The final court of appeal in all theological disputes must be to the text of the original Greek and Hebrew manuscripts. Conservatives are not contending for the infallibility of any translation, but only for the infallibility of the original documents."[9] It is not correct, therefore, to suggest that one is more of a fundamentalist if he believes in the King James-Only theory. He is actually less of a fundamentalist.

Chapter Notes

1. Interestingly, this debate centers on only the New Testament, although hundreds of Hebrew manuscripts exist through which God has preserved the Old Testament autographa. King James-Only adherents often say that

God has preserved the Old Testament autographa through the Masoretic Text, implying that only one of them exists. However, there is no single Masoretic Text. See chapter 2, "The Old Testament Text and the Version Debate," by Roy E. Beacham.

God has preserved the text of the autographa of the New Testament in the mass of available Greek manuscripts in much the same way as He did the Old Testament autographa. Serious textual criticism is necessary to determine which readings are superior. The preservation of Scripture has been normally accomplished through providence rather than through miracle. This fact is evidenced by the various commands not to add to or subtract from the Word of God (Deut. 4:2; 12:32; Rev. 22:18–19, etc.). Historically, God providentially, rather than miraculously, preserved the text of the Old Testament. For example, the books of the law at one time were lost for almost fifty years before they were found again in the temple (2 Kings 22:8ff.; 2 Chron. 34:14–16).

The doctrine of preservation does not teach that God has perfectly preserved His Word without any corruption in (1) one group of manuscripts or (2) one solitary manuscript. Bible scholars say that as of 1980, fifty-five hundred Greek manuscripts have been examined and no two of them have 100 percent agreement. The most similar manuscripts disagree six to ten times in each chapter, and even the Byzantine set of manuscripts has five different subgroups within its family. Most (at least 95 percent) of the variants are insignificant, dealing with minor matters of Greek spelling and the like.

If only one manuscript perfectly preserves the original, which one is it and how could this fact be demonstrated? We believe that God has providentially preserved the King James Version and the manuscript tradition on which it is based; but He has also providentially preserved the other Old and New Testament manuscripts. No manuscript or group of manuscripts can be proved to be the exclusive possessor of the original text. This fact is the reason for engaging in textual criticism. Consequently, it is clear to us that textual study of all of the manuscripts is the most responsible procedure to follow.

2. "Declaration of Doctrinal Belief of Niagara Bible Conference," *The Truth* 20 (1894): 509–11.

3. Some people might argue that the inspiration and inerrancy of lost documents are not significant. We believe that the inspiration and perfection of the autographa greatly affect all copies and translations of the autograp

Inspiration and inerrancy act as foundation stones on which all copies and translations must be built. The abundant manuscripts and versions available today are not fallible copies of a fallible original. The perfect original is essential to the soundness and certainty to the Bibles of the present day. But beyond this, biblical proof for the inerrancy of the autographa exists, but not for the inerrancy of the copies.

4. W. Hoyt, "Questions Concerning Inspiration," in *The Inspired Word,* ed. A. T. Pierson (London: Hodder and Stoughton, 1888), 14.

5. J. Gray, "The Inspiration of the Bible—Definition, Extent and Proof," in *The Fundamentals* (Los Angeles: The Bible Institute of Los Angeles, 1917), 2:12–13.

6. R. A. Torrey, *Is the Bible the Inerrant Word of God?* (New York: George H. Doran, 1922), 76.

7. W. B. Riley, *The Conflict of Christianity with Its Counterfeits* (Minneapolis: W. B. Riley, n.d.), 132.

8. John R. Rice, *Our God-Breathed Book—The Bible* (Murfreesboro, Tenn.: Sword of the Lord Publishers, 1969), 376.

9. Stewart Custer, *Does Inspiration Demand Inerrancy?* (Nutley, N.J.: Craig Press, 1968), 88.

The Translators to the Reader: Preface to the King James Version[1]

The best things have been calumniated

1 Zeal to promote the common good, whether it be by devising anything ourselves, or revising that which hath been laboured by others, deserveth certainly much respect and esteem, but yet findeth but cold entertainment in the world. It is welcomed with suspicion instead of love, and with emulation instead of thanks: and if there be any hole left for cavil to enter, (and cavil, if it do not find a hole, will make one) it is sure to be misconstrued, and in danger to be condemned. This will easily be granted by as many as know story, or have any experience. For was there ever any thing projected, that savoured any way of newness or renewing, but the same endured many a storm of gainsaying or opposition? A man would think that civility, wholesome laws, learning and eloquence, synods, and Church-maintenance, (that we speak of no more things of this kind) should be as safe as a sanctuary, and out of shot, as they say, that no man would lift up the heel, no, nor dog move his tongue against the motioners of them. For by the first we are distinguished from brute beasts led with sensuality: by the second we are bridled and restrained from outrageous behaviour, and from doing of injuries, whether by fraud or by violence: by the third we are enabled to inform and reform others by the light and feeling that we have attained unto ourselves: briefly, by the fourth, being brought together to a parle face to face, we sooner compose our differences than by writings, which are endless: and lastly, that the Church be sufficiently provided for is so agreeable to good reason and conscience, that those mothers are holden to be less cruel, that kill their children as soon as they are born, than those nursing fathers and mothers (wheresoever they be) that withdraw from them who hang upon their breasts (and upon whose breasts again themselves do hang to receive the spiritual and sincere milk of the word) livelihood and support fit for their estates. Thus it is apparent, that these things which we speak of are of most necessary use, and therefore that none, either without absurdity can speak against them, or without note of wickedness can spurn against them.

2 Yet for all that, the learned know that certain worthy men have been brought to untimely death for none other fault, but for seeking to reduce their countrymen to good order and discipline: and that in some Commonwealths it was made a capital crime, once to motion the making of a new law for the abrogating of an old, though the same were most pernicious: And that certain, which would be counted pillars of the State, and patterns of virtue and prudence, could not be brought for a long time to give way to good letters and refined speech; but bare themselves as averse from them, as from rocks or boxes of poison: And fourthly, that he was no babe, but a great clerk, that gave forth, (and in writing to remain to posterity) in passion peradventure, but yet he gave forth, that he had not seen any profit to come by any synod or meeting of the Clergy, but rather the contrary: And lastly, against Church maintenance and allowance, in such sort as the ambassador and messengers of the great King of kings should be furnished, it is not unknown what a fiction or fable (so it is esteemed, and for no better by the reporter himself, though superstitious) was devised: namely, that at such time as the professors and teachers of Christianity in the Church of Rome, then a true Church, were liberally endowed, a voice forsooth was heard from heaven, saying, Now is poison poured down into the Church, &c. Thus not only as oft as we speak, as one saith, but also as oft as we do any thing of note or consequence, we subject ourselves to every one's censure, and happy is he that is least tossed upon tongues; for utterly to escape the snatch of them it is impossible. If any man conceit that this is the lot and portion of the meaner sort only, and that princes are privileged by their high estate, he is deceived. As *the sword devoureth, as well one as another,* as it is in *Samuel;* nay, as the great commander charged his soldiers in a certain battle to strike at no part of the enemy, but at the face; and as the king of *Syria* commanded his chief captains *to fight neither with small nor great, save only against the king of Israel:* so it is too true, that envy striketh most spitefully at the fairest, and at the chiefest. *David* was a worthy prince, and no man to be compared to him for his first deeds; and yet for as worthy an act as ever he did, even for bringing back the ark of God in solemnity, he was scorned and scoffed at by his own wife. *Solomon* was greater than *David,* though not in virtue, yet in power; and by his power and wisdom he built a temple to the Lord, such a one as was the glory of the land of Israel, and the wonder of the whole world. But was that his magnificence liked of by all? We doubt of it. Otherwise why do they lay it in his son's dish, and call unto him for easing of the burden? *Make, say they, the grievous servitude of thy father, and his sore yoke, lighter.* Belike he had charged them with some levies, and troubled them with some carriages; hereupon they raise up a tragedy, and wish in their heart the temple had never been built. So hard a thing it is to please all, even when we please God best, and do seek to approve ourselves to every one's conscience.

The highest personages have been calumniated

3 If we will descend to later times, we shall find many the like examples of such kind, or rather unkind, acceptance. The first Roman Emperor did never do a more pleasing deed to the learned, nor more profitable to posterity, for conserving the record of times in true supputation, than when he corrected the Calendar, and ordered the year according to the course of the sun: and yet this was imputed to him for novelty and arrogancy, and procured to him great obloquy. So the first Christened Emperor, (at the leastwise, that openly professed the faith himself, and allowed others to do the like) for strengthening the empire at his great charges, and providing for the Church, as he did, got for his labour the name *Pupillus,* as who would say, a wasteful Prince, that had need of a guardian or overseer. So the best Christened Emperor, for the love that he bare unto peace, thereby to enrich both himself and his subjects, and because he did not seek war, but find it, was judged to be no man at arms, (though in deed he excelled in feats of chivalry, and shew so much when he was provoked) and condemned for giving himsel his ease, and to his pleasure. To be short, the most learned Emperor of former times, (at the least, the greatest politician) what thanks had he for cutting off the superfluities of the laws, and digesting them into some order and method? This, that he hath been blotted by some to be an Epitomist, that is, one that extinguished worthy whole volumes, to bring his abridgments into request. This is the measure that hath been rendered to excellent Princes in former times, even, *cum benè facerent, malè audire,* for their good deeds to be evil spoken of. Neither is there any likelihood that envy and malignity died and were buried with the ancient. No, no, the reproof of *Moses* taketh hold of most ages, *You are risen up in your fathers' stead, an increase of sinful men. What is that that hath been done? that which shall be done: and there is no new thing under the sun,* saith the wise man. And St. Stephen, *As your fathers did, so do ye.*

His Majesty's constancy, notwithstanding, calumniation, for the survey of the English translations

4 This, and more to this purpose, his Majesty that now reigneth (and long and long may he reign, and his offspring for ever, *Himself and children and children's children always*) knew full well, according to the singular wisdom given unto him by God, and the rare learning and experience that he hath attained unto; namely, that whosoever attempteth any thing for the publick, (specially if it pertain to religion, and to the opening and clearing of the word of God) the same setteth himself upon a stage to be glouted upon by every evil eye; yea, he casteth himself headlong upon pikes, to be gored by every sharp tongue. For he that meddleth with men's religion in any part meddleth with their custom, nay, with their freehold; and though they find no content in that which they have, yet they cannot abide to hear of altering. Notwithstanding his royal heart was not daunted or discouraged for this or that colour, but stood resolute, *as a statue immoveable, and an anvil not easy to be beaten into plates,* as one saith; he knew who had chosen him to be a soldier, or rather a captain; and being assured that the course which he intended made much for the glory of God, and the building up of his Church, he would not suffer it to be broken off for whatsoever speeches or practices. It doth certainly belong unto kings, yea, it doth specially belong unto them, to have care of religion, yea, to know it aright, yea, to profess it zealously, yea, to promote it to the uttermost of their power. This is their glory before all nations which mean well, and this will bring unto them a far most excellent weight of glory in the day of the Lord Jesus. For the Scripture saith not in vain, *Them that honour me I will honour:* neither was it a vain word that *Eusebius* delivered long ago, That piety towards God was the weapon, and the only weapon, that both preserved *Constantine's* person, and avenged him of his enemies.

The praise of the Holy Scriptures

5 But now what piety without truth? What truth, what saving truth, without the word of God? What word of God, whereof we may be sure, without the Scripture? The Scriptures we are commanded to search. *John* 5. 39. *Isaiah* 8. 20. They are commended that searched and studied them. *Acts* 17. 11. and 8. 28, 29. They are reproved that were unskilful in them, or slow to believe them. *Matth.* 22. 29. *Luke* 24. 25. They can make us wise unto salvation. 2 *Tim.* 3. 15. If we be ignorant, they will instruct us; if out of the way, they will bring us home; if out of order, they will reform us; if in heaviness, comfort us; if dull, quicken us; if cold, inflame us. *Tolle, lege; tolle, lege;* Take up and read, take up and read the Scriptures, (for unto them was the direction) it was said unto S. *Augustine* by a supernatural voice. *Whatsoever is in the Scriptures, believe me,* saith the same S. *Augustine, is high and divine; there is verily truth, and a doctrine most fit for the refreshing and renewing of men's minds, and truly so tempered, that every one may draw from thence that which is sufficient for him, if he come to draw with a devout and pious mind, as true religion requireth.* Thus S. *Augustine.* And S. *Hierome, Ama Scripturas, et amabit te sapientia,* &c. Love the Scriptures, and wisdom will love thee. And S. *Cyrill* against *Julian, Even boys that are bred up in the Scriptures, become most religious,* &c. But what mention we three or four uses of the Scripture, whereas whatsoever is to be believed, or practised, or hoped for, is contained in them? or three or four sentences of the Fathers, since whosoever is worthy the name of a Father, from Christ's time downward, hath likewise written not only of the riches, but also of the perfection of the Scripture? *I adore the fulness of the Scripture,* saith *Tertullian* against *Hermogenes.* And again, to *Apelles* a heretick of the like stamp he saith, *I do not admit that which thou bringest in* (or concludest) *of thine own* (head or store, *de tuo*) without Scripture. So Saint *Justin Martyr* before him; *We must know by all means* (saith he) *that it is not lawful* (or possible) *to learn* (any thing) *of God or of right piety, save only out of the Prophets, who teach us by divine inspiration.* So Saint *Basil* after *Tertullian, It is a manifest falling away from the faith, and a fault of presumption, either to reject any of those things that are written, or to bring in* (upon the head of them, ἐπεισάγειν) *any of those things that* are not written. We omit to cite to the same effect S. *Cyrill,* Bishop of *Jerusalem* in his 4. *Cateches.* Saint *Hierome* against *Helvidius, Saint Augustine* in his third book against the letters of *Petilian,* and in very many other places of his works. Also we forbear to descend to latter Fathers, because we will not weary the reader. The Scriptures then being acknowledged to be so full and so perfect, how can we excuse ourselves of negligence, if we do not study them? of curiosity, if we be not content with them? Men talk much of εἰρεσιώνη, how many sweet and goodly things it had hanging on it; of the Philosopher's stone, that it turneth copper into gold; of *Cornu-copia,* that it had all things necessary for food in it; of *Panaces* the herb, that it was good for all diseases; of *Catholicon* the drug, that it is instead of all purges; of *Vulcan's* armour, that it was an armour of proof against all thrusts and all blows, &c. Well, that which they falsely or vainly attributed to these things for bodily good, we may justly and with full measure ascribe unto the Scripture for spiritual. It is not only an armour, but also a whole armoury of weapons, both offensive and defensive; whereby we may save ourselves, and put the enemy to flight. It is not an herb, but a tree, or rather a whole paradise of trees of life, which bring forth fruit every month, and the fruit thereof is for meat, and the leaves for medicine. It is not a pot of *Manna* or a cruse of oil, which were for memory only, or for a meal's meat or two; but as it were a shower of heavenly bread sufficient for a whole host, be it never so great, and as it were a whole cellar full of oil vessels; whereby all our necessities may be provided for, and our debts discharged. In a word, it is a panary of wholesome food against fenowed traditions; a physician's shop (Saint *Basil* calleth it) of preservatives against poisoned heresies, a pandect of profitable laws against rebellious spirits; a treasury of most costly jewels against beggarly rudiments; finally, a fountain of most pure water springing up unto everlasting life. And what marvel? the original thereof being from heaven, not from earth; the author being God, not man; the inditer, the Holy Spirit, not the wit of the Apostles or Prophets; the penmen, such as were sanctified from the womb, and endued with a principal portion of God's Spirit; the matter, verity, piety, purity, uprightness; the form, God's word, God's testimony, God's oracles, the word of truth, the word of salvation, &c.: the effects, light of understanding, stableness of persuasion, repentance from dead works, newness of life, holiness, peace, joy in the Holy Ghost; lastly, the end and reward of the study thereof, fellowship with the saints, participation of the heavenly nature, fruition of an inheritance immortal, undefiled, and that never shall fade away: Happy is the man that delighteth in the Scripture, and thrice happy that meditateth in it day and night.

Translation necessary

6 But how shall men meditate in that which they cannot understand? How shall they understand that which is kept close in an unknown tongue? as it is written, *Except I know the power of the voice, I shall be to him that speaketh a barbarian, and he that speaketh shall be a barbarian to me.* The Apostle excepteth no tongue; not *Hebrew* the ancientest, not *Greek* the most copious, not *Latin* the finest. Nature taught a natural man to confess, that all of us in those tongues which we do not understand are plainly deaf; we may turn the deaf ear unto them. The *Scythian* counted the *Athenian,* whom he did not understand, barbarous: so the *Roman* did the *Syrian* and the *Jew:* (even S. *Hierome* himself calleth the *Hebrew* tongue barbarous; belike, because it was strange to so many:) so the Emperor of *Constantinople* calleth the *Latin* tongue barbarous, though Pope Nicolas do storm at it: so the *Jews* long before *Christ* called all other nations *Lognazim,* which is little better than barbarous. Therefore as one complaineth that always in the Senate of *Rome* there was one or other that called for an interpreter; so, lest the Church be driven to the like exigent, it is necessary to have translations in a readiness. Translation it is that openeth the window, to let in the light; that breaketh the shell, that we may eat the kernel; that putteth aside the curtain, that we may look into the most holy place; that removeth the cover of the well, that we may come by the water; even as *Jacob* rolled away the stone from the mouth of the well, by which means the flocks of *Laban* were watered. Indeed without translation into the vulgar tongue, the unlearned are but like children at *Jacob's* well (which was deep) without a bucket or something to draw with: or as that person mentioned by *Esay, to* whom when a sealed book was delivered with this motion, *Read this, I pray thee,* he was fain to make this answer, *I cannot, for it is sealed.*

The translation of the Old Testament out of the Hebrew into Greek

7 While God would be known only in *Jacob,* and have his name great in *Israel,* and in none other place; while the dew lay on *Gideon's* fleece only, and all the earth besides was dry; then for one and the same people, which spake all of them the language of *Canaan,* that is, *Hebrew,* one and the same original in *Hebrew* was sufficient. But when the fullness of time drew ne that the Sun of righteousness, the Son of God, should come into the world, whom God ordained to be a reconciliation through faith in his blood, not of the *Jew* only, but also of the *Greek,* yea, of all them that were scattered abroad; then lo, it pleased the Lord to stir up the spirit of a *Greek* Prince, (*Greek* for descent and language) even of *Ptolemy Philadelph* king of *Egypt,* to procure the translating of the book of God out of *Hebrew* into *Greek.* This is the translation of the *Seventy* interpreters, commonly so called, which prepared the way for our Saviour among the *Gentiles* by written preaching, as Saint *John Baptist* did among the *Jews* by vocal. For the *Grecians,* being desirous of learning, were not wont to suffer books of worth to lie moulding in kings' libraries, but had many of their servants, ready scribes, to copy them out, and so they were dispersed and made common. Again, the *Greek* tongue was well known and made familiar to most inhabitants in *Asia* by reason of the conquest that there the *Grecians* had made, as also by the colonies which thither they had sent. For the same causes also it was well understood in many places of *Europe,* yea, and of *Africk* too. Therefore the word of God being set forth in *Greek,* becometh hereby like a candle set upon a candlestick, which giveth light to all that are in the house; or like a proclamation sounded forth in the market-place, which most men presently take knowledge of; and therefore that language was fittest to contain the Scriptures, both for the first preachers of the Gospel to appeal unto for witness, and for the learners also of those times to make search and trial by. It is certain, that that translation was not so sound and so perfect, but that it needed in many places correction; and who had been so sufficient for this work as the Apostles or apostolic men? Yet it seemed good to the Holy Ghost and to them to take that which they found, (the same being for the greatest part true and sufficient) rather than by making a new, in that new world and green age of the Church, to expose themselves to many exceptions and cavillations, as though they made a translation to serve their own turn, and therefore bearing witness to themselves, their witness not to be regarded. This may be supposed to be some cause, why the translation of the *Seventy* was allowed to pass for current. Notwithstanding, though it was commended generally, yet it did not fully content the learned, no not of the *Jews.* For not long after *Christ, Aquila* fell in hand with a new translation, and after him *Theodotion,* and after him *Symmachus:* yea, there was a fifth and a sixth edition the authors whereof were not known. These with the *Seventy* made up the *Hexapla,* and were worthily and to great purpose compiled together by *Origen.* Howbeit the edition of the *Seventy* went away with the credit, and therefore not only was placed in the midst *by Origen,* (for the worth and excellency thereof above the rest, as *Epiphanius* gathereth) but also was used by the *Greek* Fathers for the ground and foundation of their commentaries. Yea, *Epiphanius* above-named doth attribute so much unto it, that he holdeth the authors thereof not only for interpreters, but also for prophets in some respect: and *Justinian* the Emperor, enjoining the *Jews* his subjects to use specially the Translation of the *Seventy,* rendereth this reason thereof, Because they were, as it were, enlightened with prophetical grace. Yet for all that, as the *Egyptians* are said of the Prophet to be men and not God, and their horses flesh and not spirit: so it is evident, (and Saint *Hierome* affirmeth as much) that the *Seventy* were interpreters, they were not prophets. They did many things well, as learned men; but yet as men they stumbled and fell, one while through oversight, another while through ignorance; yea, sometimes they may be noted to add to the original, and sometimes to take from it: which made the Apostles to leave them many times, when they left the *Hebrew,* and to deliver the sense thereof according to the truth of the word, as the Spirit gave them utterance. This may suffice touching the *Greek* translations of the Old Testament.

Translation out of Hebrew and Greek into Latin

8 There were also within a few hundred years after *Christ* translations many into the *Latin* tongue: for this tongue also was very fit to convey the law and the Gospel by, because in those times very many countries of the West, yea of the South, East, and North, spake or understood *Latin,* being made provinces to the *Romans.* But now the *Latin* translations were too many to be all good, for they were infinite; *(Latini interpretes nullo modo numerari possunt, saith S. Augustine.)* Again, they were not out of the Hebrew fountain, (we speak of the *Latin* translations of the Old Testament) but out of the *Greek* stream; therefore the *Greek* being not altogether clear, the *Latin* derived from it must needs be muddy. This moved S. *Hierome,* a most learned Father, and the best linguist without controversy of his age, or of any that went before him, to undertake the translating of the Old Testament out of the very fountains themselves; which he performed with that evidence of great learning, judgment, industry, and faithfulness, that he hath for ever bound the Church unto him in a debt of special remembrance and thankfulness.

The translating of the Scripture into the vulgar tongues

9 Now though the Church were thus furnished with *Greek* and *Latin* translations, even before the faith of *Christ* was generally embraced in the Empire: (for the learned know that even in S. *Hierome's* time the Consul of *Rome* and his wife were both Ethnicks, and about the same time the greatest part of the Senate also) yet for all that the godly learned were not content to have the Scriptures in the language which themselves understood, *Greek* and *Latin*, (as the good lepers were not content to fare well themselves, but acquainted their neighbours with the store that God had sent, that they also might provide for themselves) but also for the behoof and edifying of the unlearned which hungered and thirsted after righteousness, and had souls to be saved as well as they, they provided translations into the vulgar for their countrymen, insomuch that most nations under heaven did shortly after their conversion hear Christ speaking unto them in their mother tongue, not by the voice of their minister only, but also by the written word translated. If any doubt hereof, he may be satisfied by examples enough, if enough will serve the turn. First, S. *Hierome* saith, *Multarum gentium linguis Scriptura ante translata docet falsa esse quae addita sunt*, &c. i. *The Scripture being translated before in the language of many nations doth shew that those things that were added* (by Lucian or Hesychius) *are false.* So S. *Hierome* in the place. The same *Hierome* elsewhere affirmeth that he, the time was, had set forth the translation of the *Seventy, suae linguae hominibus;* i.e. for his countrymen of *Dalmatia.* Which words not only *Erasmus* doth understand to purport, that S. *Hierome* translated the Scripture into the *Dalmatian* tongue; but also *Sixtus Senensis,* and *Alphonsus a Castro,* (that we speak of no more) men not to be excepted against by them of *Rome,* do ingenuously confess as much. So S. *Chrysostome,* that lived in S. *Hierome's* time, giveth evidence with him: *The doctrine of S.* John (saith he) *did not in such sort* (as the Philosophers did) *vanish away: but the Syrians, Egyptians, Indians, Persians, Ethiopians, and infinite other nations, being barbarous people, translated it into their (mother) tongue, and have learned to be (true) Philosophers,* he meaneth Christians. To this may be added *Theodoret,* as next unto him both for antiquity, and for learning. His words be these, *Every country that is under the sun is full of these words* (of the Apostles and Prophets) *and the Hebrew tongue* (he meaning the Scriptures in the Hebrew tongue) *is turned not only into the language of the Grecians, but also of the Romans, and Egyptians, and Persians, and Indians, and Armenians, and Scythians, and Sauromatians, and, briefly, into all the languages* *which any nation useth*. So he. In like manner *Ulpilas* is reported by *Paulus Diaconus* and *Isidore*, and before them by *Sozomen*, to have translated the Scriptures into the *Gothic* tongue: *John* Bishop of *Sevil* by *Vasseus*, to have turned them into *Arabick* about the year of our Lord 717: *Beda by Cistertiensis*, to have turned a great part of them into *Saxon: Efnard by Trithemius*, to have abridged the French Psalter (as *Beda* had done the *Hebrew*) about the year 800: King *Alured* by the said *Cistertiensis*, to have turned the Psalter into *Saxon: Methodius by Aventinus* (printed at *Ingolstad*) to have turned the Scriptures into *Sclavonian: Valdo* Bishop of *Frising* by *Beatus Rhenanus*, to have caused about that time the Gospels to be translated into *Dutch* rhythme, yet extant in the library of *Corbinian: Valdus* by divers, to have turned them himself, or to have gotten them turned into *French* about the year 1160: *Charles* the fifth of that name, surnamed *The wise*, to have caused them to be turned into *French*, about 200 years after *Valdus* his time; of which translation there be many copies yet extant, as witnesseth *Beroaldus*. Much about that time, even in our King *Richard* the second's days, *John Trevisa* translated them into *English*, and many *English* Bibles in written hand are yet to be seen with divers; translated, as it is very probable, in that age. So the *Syrian* translation of the New Testament is in most learned men's libraries, of *Widminstadius* his setting forth; and the Psalter in *Arabick* is with many, of *Augustinus Nebiensis'* setting forth. So *Postel* affirmeth, that in his travel he saw the Gospels in the *Ethiopian* tongue: And *Ambrose Thesius* allegeth the Psalter of the *Indians*, which he testifieth to have been set forth by *Potken* in *Syrian* characters. So that to have the Scriptures in the mother tongue is not a quaint conceit lately taken up, either by the Lord *Cromwell* in *England*, or by the Lord *Radevil* in *Polonie*, or by the Lord *Ungnadius* in the Emperor's dominion, but hath been thought upon, and put in practice of old, even from the first times of the conversion of any nation; no doubt, because it was esteemed most profitable to cause faith to grow in men's hearts the sooner, and to make them to be able to say with the words of the Psalm, *As we have heard, so we have seen*.

The unwillingness of our chief adversaries that the Scriptures should be divulged in the mother tongue, &c.

10 Now the Church of *Rome* would seem at the length to bear a motherly affection towards her children, and to allow them the Scriptures in their mother tongue: but indeed it is a gift, not deserving to be called gift, an unprofitable gift: they must first get a license in writing before they may use them; and to get that, they must approve themselves to their Confessor, that is, to be such as are, if not frozen in the dregs, yet soured with the leaven of their superstition. Howbeit, it seemed too much to *Clement* the eighth that there should be any license granted to have them in the vulgar tongue, and therefore he overruleth and frustrateth the grant of *Pius* the fourth. So much are they afraid of the light of the Scripture, (*Lucifugae Scripturarum,* as *Tertullian* speaketh) that they will not trust the people with it, no not as it is set forth by their own sworn men, no not with the license of their own Bishops and Inquisitors. Yea, so unwilling they are to communicate the Scriptures to the people's understanding in any sort, that they are not ashamed to confess that we forced them to translate it into *English* against their wills. This seemeth to argue a bad cause, or a bad conscience, or both. Sure we are, that it is not he that hath good gold, that is afraid to bring it to the touchstone, but he that hath the counterfeit; neither is it the true man that shunneth the light, but the malefactor, lest his deeds should be reproved; neither is it the plain-dealing merchant that is unwilling to have the weights, or the meteyard, brought in place, but he that useth deceit. But we will let them alone for this fault, and return to translation.

The speeches and reasons, both of our brethren, and
of our adversaries, against this work

11 Many men's mouths have been open a good while (and yet are not stopped) with speeches about the translation so long in hand, or rather perusals of translations made before: and ask what may be the reason, what the necessity, of the employment. Hath the Church been deceived, say they, all this while? Hath her sweet bread been mingled with leaven, her silver with dross, her wine with water, her milk with lime? *(lacte gypsum malè miscetur, saith S. Ireney.)* We hoped that we had been in the right way, that we had had the oracles of God delivered unto us, and that though all the world had cause to be offended, and to complain, yet that we had none. Hath the nurse holden out the breast, and nothing but wind in it? Hath the bread been delivered by the Fathers of the Church, and the same proved to be *lapidosus,* as *Seneca* speaketh? What is it to handle the word of God deceitfully, if this be not? Thus certain brethren. Also the adversaries of *Judah* and *Hierusalem,* like *Sanballat* in *Nehemiah,* mock, as we hear, both at the work and workmen, saying, *What do these weak Jews,*

&c. *will they make the stones whole again out of the heaps of dust which are burnt?* *Although they build, yet if a fox go up, he shall even break down their stony wall.* Was their translation good before? Why do they now mend it? Was it not good? Why then was it obtruded to the people? Yea, why did the Catholicks (meaning Popish *Romanists*) always go in jeopardy for refusing to go to hear it? Nay, if it must be translated into *English,* Catholicks are fittest to do it. They have learning, and they know when a thing is well, they can *manum de tabula.* We will answer them both briefly: and the former, being brethren, thus with St. *Hierome, Damnamus veteres? Minimè, sed post priorum studia in domo Domini quod possumus laboramus.* That is, *Do we condemn the ancient? In no case: but after the endeavours of them that were before us, we take the best pains we can in the house of God.* As if he said, Being provoked by the example of the learned that lived before my time, I have thought it my duty to assay whether my talent in the knowledge of the tongues may be profitable in any measure to God's Church, lest I should seem to have laboured in them in vain, and lest I should be thought to glory in men (although ancient) above that which was in them. Thus S. *Hierome* may be thought to speak.

A satisfaction to our brethren

12 And to the same effect say we, that we are so far off from condemning any of their labours that travailed before us in this kind, either in this land, or beyond sea, either in King *Henry's* time, or King *Edward's,* (if there were any translation, or correction of a translation, in his time) or Queen *Elizabeth's* of ever renowned memory, that we acknowledge them to have been raised up of God for the building and furnishing of his Church, and that they deserve to be had of us and of posterity in everlasting remembrance. The judgment of *Aristotle* is worthy and well known: *If Timotheus had not been, we had not had much sweet musick: But if Phrynis (Timotheus his master) had not been, we had not had Timotheus.* Therefore blessed be they, and most honoured be their name, that break the ice, and give the onset upon that which helpeth forward to the saving of souls. Now what can be more available thereto, than to deliver God's book unto God's people in a tongue which they understand? Since of an hidden treasure, and of a fountain that is sealed, there is no profit, as *Ptolemy Philadelph* wrote to the Rabbins or masters of the *Jews,* as witnesseth *Epiphanius:* and as S. *Augustine* saith, *A man had rather be with his dog than with a stranger* (whose tongue is strange unto him). Yet for all that, as nothing is begun and perfected at th same time, and the latter thoughts are thought to be the wiser: so, if we building upon their foundation that went before us, and being holpen by their labours, do endeavour to make that better which they left so good; no man, we are sure, hath cause to mislike us; they, we persuade ourselves, if they were alive, would thank us. The vintage of *Abiezer,* that strake the stroke; yet the gleaning of grapes of *Ephraim* was not to be despised. See *Judges* viii. *verse 2. Joash* the king of *Israel* did not satisfy himself till he had smitten the ground three times; and yet he offended the Prophet for giving over then. *Aquila,* of whom we spake before, translated the Bible as carefully and as skilfully as he could; and yet he thought good to go over it again, and then it got the credit with the *Jews* to be called κατὰ ἀκρίβειαν, that is, accurately done, as St. *Hierome* witnesseth. How many books of profane learning have been gone over again and again, by the same translators, by others ? Of one and the same book of *Aristotle's* Ethics there are extant not so few as six or seven several translations. Now if this cost may be bestowed upon the gourd, which affordeth us a little shade, and which today flourisheth, but tomorrow is cut down; what may we bestow, nay, what ought we not to bestow, upon the vine, the fruit whereof maketh glad the conscience of man, and the stem whereof abideth for ever? And this is the word of God, which we translate. *What is the chaff to the wheat? saith the Lord. Tanti vitreum, quanti verum margaritum* (saith *Tertullian*), if a toy of glass be of that reckoning with us, how ought we to value the true pearl? Therefore let no man's eye be evil, because his Majesty's is good; neither let any be grieved, that we have a Prince that seeketh the increase of the spiritual wealth of *Israel;* (let *Sanballats* and *Tobiahs* do so, which therefore do bear their just reproof) but let us rather bless God from the ground of our heart for working this religious care in him to have the translations of the Bible maturely considered of and examined. For by this means it cometh to pass, that whatsoever is sound already, (and all is sound for substance in one or other of our editions, and the worst of ours far better than their authentick Vulgar) the same will shine as gold more brightly, being rubbed and polished; also, if any thing be halting, or superfluous, or not so agreeable to the original, the same may be corrected, and the truth set in place. And what can the King command to be done, that will bring him more true honour than this? And wherein could they that have been set a work approve their duty to the King, yea, their obedience to God, and love to his Saints, more, than by yielding their service, and all that is within them, for the furnishing of the work? But besides all this, they were the principal motives of it, and therefore ought least to quarrel it. For the very historical truth is, that upon the importunate petitions of the Puritans at his Majesty's coming to this crown, the conference at *Hampton Court* having been appointed for hearing their complaints, when by force of reason they were put from all other grounds, they had recourse at the last to this shift, that they could not with good conscience subscribe to the Communion book, since it maintained the Bible as it was there translated, which was, as they said, a most corrupted translation. And although this was judged to be but a very poor and empty shift, yet even hereupon did his Majesty begin to bethink himself of the good that might ensue by a new translation, and presently after gave order for this translation which is now presented unto thee. Thus much to satisfy our scrupulous brethren.

An answer to the imputations of our adversaries

13 Now to the latter we answer, that we do not deny, nay, we affirm and avow, that the very meanest translation of the Bible in *English* set forth by men of our profession (for we have seen none of theirs of the whole Bible as yet) containeth the word of God, nay, is the word of God: as the King's speech which he uttered in Parliament, being translated into *French, Dutch, Italian,* and *Latin,* is still the King's speech, though it be not interpreted by every translator with the like grace, nor peradventure so fitly for phrase, nor so expressly for sense, every where. For it is confessed, that things are to take their denomination of the greater part; and a natural man could say, *Verum ubi multa nitent in carmine, non ego paucis offendor maculis,* &c. A man may be counted a virtuous man, though he have made many slips in his life, (else there were none virtuous, for *in many things we offend all*), also a comely man and lovely, though he have some warts upon his hand, yea, not only freckles upon his face, but also scars. No cause therefore why the word translated should be denied to be the word, or forbidden to be current, notwithstanding that some imperfections and blemishes may be noted in the setting forth of it. For whatever was perfect under the sun, where Apostles or apostolick men, that is, men endued with an extraordinary measure of God's Spirit, and privileged with the privilege of infallibility, had not their hand? The Romanists therefore in refusing to hear, and daring to burn the word translated, did no less than despite the Spirit of grace, from whom originally it proceeded, and whose sense and meaning, as well as man's weakness would enable, it did express. Judge by an example or two.

14 *Plutarch* writeth, that after that *Rome* had been burnt by the *Gaul* they fell soon to build it again: but doing it in haste, they did not cast the streets, nor proportion the houses, in such comely fashion, as had been most sightly and convenient. Was *Catiline* therefore an honest man, or a good patriot, that sought to bring it to a combustion? or *Nero* a good Prince, that did indeed set it on fire? So by the story of *Ezra* and the prophecy of *Haggai* it may be gathered, that the temple built by *Zerubbabel* after the return from *Babylon* was by no means to be compared to the former built by *Solomon:* (for they that remembered the former wept when they considered the latter) notwithstanding might this latter either have been abhorred and forsaken by the *Jews,* or profaned by the *Greeks?* The like we are to think of translations. The translation of the *Seventy* dissenteth from the Original in many places, neither doth it come near it for perspicuity, gravity, majesty; yet which of the Apostles did condemn it? Condemn it? Nay, they used it, (as it is apparent, and as Saint *Hierome* and most learned men do confess) which they would not have done, nor by their example of using of it so grace and commend it to the Church, if it had been unworthy the appellation and name of the word of God. And whereas they urge for their second defence of their vilifying and abusing of the *English* Bibles, or some pieces thereof, which they meet with, for that Hereticks forsooth were the authors of the translations: (Hereticks they call us by the same right that they call themselves Catholicks, both being wrong) we marvel what divinity taught them so. We are sure *Tertullian* was of another mind: *Ex personis probamus fidem, an ex fide personas?* Do we try men's faith by their persons? We should try their persons by their faith. Also S. *Augustine* was of another mind: for he, lighting upon certain rules made *by Tychonius* a *Donatist* for the better understanding of the Word, was not ashamed to make use of them, yea, to insert them into his own book, with giving commendation to them so far forth as they were worthy to be commended, as is to be seen in St. *Augustine's* third book *De Doctrina Christiana.* To be short, *Origen,* and the whole Church of God for certain hundred years, were of another mind: for they were so far from treading under foot (much more from burning) the translation of *Aquila* a proselyte, that is, one that had turned *Jew,* of *Symmachus,* and *Theodotion,* both *Ebionites,* that is, most vile hereticks, that they joined them together with the *Hebrew* original, and the translation of the *Seventy,* (as hath been before signified out of *Epiphanius*) and set them forth openly to be considered of and perused by all. But we weary the unlearned, who need not know so much; and trouble the learned, who know it already.

15 Yet before we end, we must answer a third cavil and objection of theirs against us, for altering and amending our Translations so oft; wherein truly they deal hardly and strangely with us. For to whom ever was it imputed for a fault (by such as were wise) to go over that which he had done, and to amend it where he saw cause? Saint *Augustine* was not afraid to exhort S. *Hierome* to a *Palinodia* or recantation. The same S. *Augustine* was not ashamed to retractate, we might say, revoke, many things that had passed him, and doth even glory that he seeth his infirmities. If we will be sons of the truth, we must consider what it speaketh, and trample upon our own credit, yea, and upon other men's too, if either be any way a hinderance to it. This to the cause. Then to the persons we say, that of all men they ought to be most silent in this case. For what varieties have they, and what alterations have they made, not only of their service books, portesses, and breviaries, but also of their *Latin* translation? The service book supposed to be made by S. *Ambrose (Officium Ambrosianum)* was a great while in special use and request: but Pope *Adrian,* calling a council with the aid of *Charles* the Emperor, abolished it, yea, burnt it, and commanded the service book of Saint *Gregory* universally to be used. Well, *Officium Gregorianum* gets by this means to be in credit; but doth it continue without change or altering? No, the very *Roman* service was of two fashions; the new fashion, and the old, the one used in one Church, the other in another; as is to be seen in *Pamelius* a Romanist his preface before *Micrologus.* The same *Pamelius* reporteth out of *Radulphus de Rivo,* that about the year of our Lord 1277 Pope *Nicolas* the third removed out of the churches of *Rome* the more ancient books (of service) and brought into use the missals of the Friers Minorites, and commanded them to be observed there; insomuch that about an hundred years after, when the above named *Radulphus* happened to be at *Rome,* he found all the books to be new, of the new stamp. Neither was there this chopping and changing in the more ancient times only, but also of late. *Pius Quintus* himself confesseth, that every bishoprick almost had a peculiar kind of service, most unlike to that which others had; which moved him to abolish all other breviaries, though never so ancient, and privileged and published by Bishops in their Dioceses, and to establish and ratify that only which was of his own setting forth in the year 1568. Now when the Father of their Church, who gladly would heal the sore of the daughter of his people softly and slightly, and make the best of it, findeth so great fault with them for their odds and jarring; we hope the children have no great cause to vaunt of their uniformity. But the difference that appeareth between our translations, and our often correcting of them, is the thing that we are specially charged with; let us see therefore whether they themselves be without fault this way, (if it be to be counted a fault to correct) and whether they be fit men to throw stones at us: *O tandem major parcas insane minori:* they that are less sound themselves ought not to object infirmities to others. If we should tell them that *Valla, Stapulensis, Erasmus,* and *Vives,* found fault with their vulgar translation, and consequently wished the same to be mended, or a new one to be made; they would answer peradventure, that we produced their enemies for witnesses against them; albeit they were in no other sort enemies, than as S. *Paul* was to the *Galatians,* for telling them the truth: and it were to be wished, that they had dared to tell it them plainlier and oftener. But what will they say to this, That Pope *Leo* the tenth allowed *Erasmus's* translation of the New Testament, so much different from the Vulgar, by his apostolick letter and bull? That the same *Leo* exhorted *Pagnine* to translate the whole Bible, and bare whatsoever charges was necessary for the work? Surely, as the Apostle reasoneth to the *Hebrews,* that *if the former Law and Testament had been sufficient, there had been no need of the latter:* so we may say, that if the old Vulgar had been at all points allowable, to small purpose had labour and charges been undergone about framing of a new. If they say, it was one Pope's private opinion, and that he consulted only himself; then we are able to go further with them, and to aver, that more of their chief men of all sorts, even their own *Trent* champions, *Paiva* and *Vega,* and their own Inquisitors, *Hieronymus ab Oleastro,* and their own Bishop *Isidorus Clarius,* and their own Cardinal *Thomas a Vio Cajetan,* do either make new translations themselves, or follow new ones of other men's making, or note the Vulgar interpreter for halting, none of them fear to dissent from him, nor yet to except against him. And call they this an uniform tenor of text and judgment about the text, so many of their worthies disclaiming the now received conceit? Nay, we will yet come nearer the quick. Doth not their *Paris* edition differ from the *Lovaine,* and *Hentenius* his from them both, and yet all of them allowed by authority? Nay, doth not *Sixtus Quintus* confess, that certain Catholicks (he meaneth certain of his own side) were in such a humour of translating the Scriptures into *Latin,* that Satan taking occasion by them, though they thought no such matter, did strive what he could, out of so uncertain and manifold a variety of translations, so to mingle all things, that nothing might seem to be left certain and firm in them? &c. Nay further, did not the same *Sixtus* ordain by an inviolable decree, and that with the counsel and consent of his Cardinals, that the *Latin* edition of the Old and New Testament, which the Council of *Trent* would have to be authentick, is the same without controversy which he then set forth, being diligently corrected and printed in the printinghouse of *Vatican?* Thus *Sixtus* in his Preface before his Bible. And yet *Clement* the eighth, his immediate successor, published another edition of [1592] the Bible, containing in it infinite differences from that of *Sixtus,* and many of them weighty and material; and yet this must be authentick by all means. What is to have the faith of our glorious Lord *Jesus Christ* with yea and nay, if this be not? Again, what is sweet harmony and consent, if this be? Therefore, as *Demaratus* of *Corinth* advised a great King, before he talked of the dissensions among the *Grecians,* to compose his domestick broils; (for at that time his queen and his son and heir were at deadly feud with him) so all the while that our adversaries do make so many and so various editions themselves, and do jar so much about the worth and authority of them, they can with no show of equity challenge us for changing and correcting.

The purpose of the Translators, with their number, furniture, care, &c.

16 But it is high time to leave them, and to shew in brief what we proposed to ourselves, and what course we held, in this our perusal and survey of the Bible. Truly, good Christian Reader, we never thought from the beginning that we should need to make a new translation, nor yet to make of a bad one a good one; (for then the imputation of *Sixtus* had been true in some sort, that our people had been fed with gall of dragons instead of wine, with whey instead of milk;) but to make a good one better, or out of many good ones one principal good one, not justly to be excepted against; that hath been our endeavour, that our mark. To that purpose there were many chosen, that were greater in other men's eyes than in their own, and that sought the truth rather than their own praise. Again, they came, or were thought to come, to the work, not *exercendi causa,* (as one saith) but *exercitati,* that is, learned, not to learn: For the chief overseer and ἐργοδιώκτῃ under his Majesty, to whom not only we, but also our whole Church was much bound, knew by his wisdom, which thing also *Nazianzen* taught so long ago, that it is a preposterous order to teach first, and to learn after, yea that τὸ ἐν πίθῳ κεραμίαν μανθάνειν, to learn and practise together, is neither commendable for the workman, nor safe for the work. Therefore such were thought upon, as could say modestly with S. *Hierome, Et Hebraeum sermonem ex parte didicimus, et in Latino penè ab ipsis incunabulis,* &c. *detriti sumus; Both we have learned the Hebrew tongue in part, and in the Latin we have been exercised almost from our very cradle.* S. *Hierome* maketh no mention of the *Greek* tongue, wherein yet he did excel; because he translated not the Old Testament out of *Greek*, but out of *Hebrew*. And in what sort did these assemble? In the trust of their own knowledge, or of their sharpness of wit, or deepness of judgment, as it were in an arm of flesh? At no hand. They trusted in him that hath the key of *David*, opening, and no man shutting; they prayed to the Lord, the Father of our Lord, to the effect that St. *Augustine* did; *O let thy Scriptures be my pure delight; let me not be deceived in them, neither let me deceive by them.* In this confidence, and with this devotion, did they assemble together; not too many, lest one should trouble another; and yet many, lest many things haply might escape them. If you ask what they had before them, truly it was the *Hebrew* text of the Old Testament, the *Greek of* the New. These are the two golden pipes, or rather conduits, wherethrough the olive branches empty themselves into the gold. Saint *Augustine* calleth them precedent, or original, tongues; Saint *Hierome*, fountains. The same Saint *Hierome* affirmeth, and *Gratian* hath not spared to put it into his decree, That *as the credit of the old books* (he meaneth of the Old Testament) *is to be tried by the Hebrew volumes; so of the New by the Greek tongue*, he meaneth by the original *Greek*. If truth be to be tried by these tongues, then whence should a translation be made, but out of them? These tongues therefore (the Scriptures, we say, in those tongues) we set before us to translate, being the tongues wherein God was pleased to speak to his Church by his Prophets and Apostles. Neither did we run over the work with that posting haste that the *Septuagint* did, if that be true which is reported of them, that they finished it in seventy-two days; neither were we barred or hindered from going over it again, having once done it, like St. *Hierome*, if that be true which himself reporteth, that he could no sooner write any thing, but presently it was caught from him, and published, and he could not have leave to mend it: neither, to be short, were we the first that fell in hand with translating the Scripture into *English*, and consequently destitute of former helps, as it is written of *Origen*, that he was the first in a manner, that put his hand to write commentaries upon the Scriptures, and therefore no marvel if he overshot himself many times. None of these things: the work hath not been huddled up in seventy-two days, but hath cost the workmen, as light as it seemeth, the pains of twice seven times seventy-two days, and more. Matters of such weight and consequence are to be speeded with maturity: for in a business of moment a man feareth not the blame of convenient slackness. Neither did we think much to consult the translators or commentators, *Chaldee, Hebrew, Syrian, Greek,* or *Latin;* no, nor the *Spanish, French, Italian,* or *Dutch;* neither did we disdain to revise that which we had done, and to bring back to the anvil that which we had hammered: but having and using as great helps as were needful, and fearing no reproach for slowness, nor coveting praise for expedition, we have at the length, through the good hand of the Lord upon us, brought the work to that pass that you see.

Reasons moving us to set diversity of senses in the margin,
where there is great probability for each

17 Some peradventure would have no variety of senses to be set in the margin, lest the authority of the Scriptures for deciding of controversies by that show of uncertainty should somewhat be shaken. But we hold their judgment not to be so sound in this point. For though *whatsoever things are necessary are manifest,* as S. *Chrysostome* saith; and, as S. *Augustine, in those things that are plainly set down in the Scriptures all such matters are found that concern faith, hope, and charity:* yet for all that it cannot be dissembled, that partly to exercise and whet our wits, partly to wean the curious from loathing of them for their every where plainness, partly also to stir up our devotion to crave the assistance of God's Spirit by prayer, and lastly, that we might be forward to seek aid of our brethren by conference, and never scorn those that be not in all respects so complete as they should be, being to seek in many things ourselves, it hath pleased God in his Divine Providence here and there to scatter words and sentences of that difficulty and doubtfulness, not in doctrinal points that concern salvation, (for in such it hath been vouched that the Scriptures are plain) but in matters of less moment, that fearfulness would better beseem us than confidence, and if we will resolve, to resolve upon modesty with S. *Augustine,* (though not in this same case altogether, yet upon the same ground) *Melius est dubitare de occultis, quam litigare de incertis: It is better to make doubt of those things which are secret, than to strive about those things that are uncertain.* There be many words in the Scriptures which be never found there but once, (having neither brother nor neighbour, as the *Hebrews* speak) so that we cannot be holpen by conference of places. Again, there be many rare names of certain birds, beasts, and precious stones, &c. concerning which the *Hebrews* themselves are so divided among themselves for judgment, that they may seem to have defined this or that, rather because they would say something, than because they were sure of that which they said, as S. *Hierome* somewhere saith of the *Septuagint.* Now in such a case doth not a margin do well to admonish the Reader to seek further, and not to conclude or dogmatize upon this or that peremptorily? For as it is a fault of incredulity, to doubt of those things that are evident; so to determine of such things as the Spirit of God hath left (even in the judgment of the judicious) questionable, can be no less than presumption. Therefore as S. *Augustine* saith, that variety of translations is profitable for the finding out of the sense of the Scriptures: so diversity of signification and sense in the margin, where the text is not so clear, must needs do good; yea, is necessary, as we are persuaded. We know that *Sixtus Quintus* expressly forbiddeth that any variety of readings of their Vulgar edition should be put in the margin; (which though it be not altogether the same thing to that we have in hand, yet it looketh that way;) but we think he hath not all of his own side his favourers for this conceit. They that are wise had rather have their judgments at liberty in differences of readings, than to be captivated to one, when it may be the other. If they were sure that their high priest had all laws shut up in his breast, as *Paul* the second bragged, and that he were as free from error by special privilege, as the dictators of *Rome* were made by law inviolable, it were another matter; then his word were an oracle, his opinion a decision. But the eyes of the world are now open, God be thanked, and have been a great while; they find that he is subject to the same affections and infirmities that others be, that his skin is penetrable, and therefore so much as he proveth, not as much as he claimeth, they grant and embrace.

Reasons inducing us not to stand curiously
upon an identity of phrasing

18 Another thing we think good to admonish thee of, gentle Reader, that we have not tied ourselves to an uniformity of phrasing, or to an identity of words, as some peradventure would wish that we had done, because they observe, that some learned men somewhere have been as exact as they could that way. Truly, that we might not vary from the sense of that which we had translated before, if the word signified the same thing in both places, (for there be some words that be not of the same sense every where) we were especially careful, and made a conscience, according to our duty. But that we should express the same notion in the same particular word; as for example, if we translate the *Hebrew* or *Greek* word once by *purpose,* never to call it *intent;* if one where *journeying,* never *travelling;* if one where *think,* never *suppose;* if one where *pain,* never *ache;* if one where *joy,* never *gladness,* &c. thus to mince the matter, we thought to savour more of curiosity than wisdom, and that rather it would breed scorn in the atheist, than bring profit to the godly reader. For is the kingdom of God become words or syllables? Why should we be in bondage to them, if we may be free? use one precisely, when we may use another no less fit as commodiously? A godly Father in the primitive time shewed himself greatly moved, that one of newfangleness called κράββατον, σκίμπου, though the difference be little or none; and another reporteth, that he was much abused for turning *cucurbita* (to which reading the people had been used) into *hedera.* Now if this happen in better times, and upon so small occasions, we might justly fear hard censure, if generally we should make verbal and unnecessary changings. We might also be charged (by scoffers) with some unequal dealing towards a great number of good *English* words. For as it is written of a certain great Philosopher, that he should say, that those logs were happy that were made images to be worshipped; for their fellows, as good as they, lay for blocks behind the fire: so if we should say, as it were, unto certain words, Stand up higher, have a place in the Bible always; and to others of like quality, Get ye hence, be banished for ever; we might be taxed peradventure with S. *James* his words, namely, *To be partial in ourselves, and judges of evil thoughts.* Add hereunto, that niceness in words was always counted the next step to trifling; and so was to be curious about names too: also that we cannot follow a better pattern for elocution than God himself; therefore he using divers words in his holy writ, and indifferently for one thing in nature; we, if we will not be superstitious, may use the same liberty in our *English* versions out of *Hebrew* and *Greek,* for that copy or store that he hath given us. Lastly, we have on the one side avoided the scrupulosity of the Puritans, who leave the old Ecclesiastical words, and betake them to other, as when they put *washing* for *Baptism,* and *Congregation* instead of *Church:* as also on the other side we have shunned the obscurity of the Papists, in their *Azimes, Tunike, Rational, Holocausts, Praepuce, Pasche,* and a number of such like, whereof their late translation is full, and that of purpose to darken the sense, that since they must needs translate the

Bible, yet by the language thereof it may be kept from being understood. But we desire that the Scripture may speak like itself, as in the language of *Canaan,* that *it* may be understood even of the very vulgar.

19 Many other things we might give thee warning of, gentle Reader, if we had not exceeded the measure of a preface already. It remaineth that we commend thee to God, and to the Spirit of his grace, which is able to build further than we can ask or think. He removeth the scales from our eyes, the vail from our hearts, opening our wits that we may understand his word, enlarging our hearts, yea, correcting our affections, that we may love it above gold and silver, yea, that we may love it to the end. Ye are brought unto fountains of living water which ye digged not; do not cast earth into them, with the Philistines, neither prefer broken pits before them, with the wicked Jews. Others have laboured, and you may enter into their labours. O receive not so great things in vain: O despise not so great salvation. Be not like swine to tread under foot so precious things, neither yet like dogs to tear and abuse holy things. Say not to our Saviour with the *Gergesites,* Depart out of our coasts; neither yet with *Esau* sell your birthright for a mess of pottage. If light be come into the world, love not darkness more than light: if food, if clothing, be offered, go not naked, starve not yourselves. Remember the advice of *Nazianzene, It is a grievous thing* (or dangerous) *to neglect a great fair, and to seek to make markets afterwards:* also the encouragement of S. *Chrysostome, It is altogether impossible, that he that is sober* (and watchful) *should at any time be neglected:* lastly, the admonition and menacing of S. *Augustine, They that despise God's will inviting them shall feel God's will taking vengeance of them.* It is a fearful thing to fall into the hands of the living God; but a blessed thing it is, and will bring us to everlasting blessedness in the end, when God speaketh unto us, to hearken; when he setteth his word before us, to read it; when he stretcheth out his hand and calleth, to answer, Here am I, here we are to do thy will, O God. The Lord work a care and conscience in us to know him and serve him, that we may be acknowledged of him at the appearing of our Lord JESUS CHRIST, to whom with the Holy Ghost be all praise and thanksgiving. Amen.

Chapter Notes

1. From F. H. A. Scrivener, *The Authorized Edition of the English Bible (1611), Its Subsequent Reprints and Modern Representatives* (Cambridge: At the University Press, 1884), 267–304. Paragraph numbers have been added.

The Address of Thomas Armitage at the Founding of the American Bible Union
with an Introduction by Kevin T. Bauder

Kevin T. Bauder

THE AMERICAN BIBLE UNION, founded in 1850, was the product of two separate Bible society splits. The parent organization was the American Bible Society, which was founded in 1816 for the translation and dissemination of the Scriptures. In 1835, William Yates presented a Bengali translation of the Bible to the society for publication. The society refused to print Yates's version, however, on the ground that he had translated the Greek verb *baptizein* by a Bengali word that meant *to immerse*. Although the society had already published a comparable translation in Burmese (that of Adoniram Judson), it now ruled that such a rendering of *baptizein* made the work sectarian.

Many members of the American Bible Society were shocked by the refusal to publish Yates's translation. The society was supported by a large number of Baptists who favored the literal translation of *baptizein*. The question was not confined to Baptists, however. Key voices from other denominations also expressed the opinion that the Scriptures ought to be translated as literally as possible. In April of 1837 these dissenters left the American Bible Society to form their own organization, the American and Foreign Bible Society. Their stated intention was to propagate the most faithful translations available of the Scriptures throughout the world.

The new society was deeply divided from the very beginning. A large minority of its members reasoned that if *baptizein* should be translated in Bengali, then it should also be translated in English. This and other considerations led the minority party to press for a new, more faithful translation of the Bible into English. The debate over a new English translation continued within the American and Foreign Bible Society for nearly fourteen years. In 1850, however, the society adopted the official policy that its translation work would be restricted to languages other than English. In English-speaking countries the society would distribute the "commonly received" (King James) version.

The minority could not accept this decision, and once again a split ensued. Another Bible society was founded on June 10, 1850. It was called the American Bible Union. The new society immediately set about the work of translating the Bible into several languages, one of which was English.

Its detractors charged that the American Bible Union was simply a Baptist society, but that was not strictly true. Along with several varieties of Baptists, its translators included Anglicans, Old School Presbyterians, Disciples, Methodists, Associate Reformed Presbyterians, Episcopalians, and members of the German Reformed Church. The concern of the American Bible Union was not to promote any particular denomination but to promote the purest possible translations of the Scriptures into every language.

In keeping with this purpose, the English translators were given only two rules: (1) the exact meaning of the original must be represented with the greatest clarity possible, and (2) the King James Version would be the basis for revision, with no more departures from its wording than necessity demanded. The efforts of the Union progressed well and were rewarded with the publication of a new English version of the New Testament in 1865.

One man who was prominent from the beginning of the American Bible Union was Thomas Armitage. Armitage had been a Methodist Episcopal pastor but converted to Baptist convictions. He became a very influential Baptist minister in New York City. He is commonly regarded as the foremost Baptist historian of nineteenth-century America.

To Armitage, the word *baptizein* demanded immersion. Having passed through the soul-struggle of conversion from Methodism, he thought it inconceivable that any Baptist should defend the Authorized Version with its regular transliteration of *baptizein*. For more than thirty years, he labored to see a new version of the English Bible.

The following address was delivered by Thomas Armitage on the occasion of the founding of the American Bible Union in 1850. The address itself was directed to the president of the Union, Spencer H. Cone. It was prefaced by a resolution that Armitage was presenting to the assembled members. The address here presented is an exact copy of the published transcript.[1]

The work of the American Bible Union antedated the publication of Westcott and Hort's critical text, but the translators made use of all of the manuscripts and texts that were available to them. The work of the American Bible Union also antedated the introduction of theological liberalism into the United States. The orthodox credentials of its supporters and translators are beyond question. Its members were moved by only a passion for the purity of the Word of God.

Too often, those who are involved in the current Bible version controversy lack a historical perspective. The following address is reprinted in the hope that people on both sides of the debate will find instruction in the words of a preacher of the gospel who spoke to a similar issue a century and a half ago.

Address of Rev. Thos. Armitage

Resolved, that it is a high honor and privilege to be permitted of God to labor and give for the vindication and propagation of His truth, in any form, but especially so, as His truth is vindicated and propagated in circulating faithful versions of the Sacred Scriptures.

Mr. President: I rise at this late hour to move this interesting and important resolution.

Sir, it would be a waste of time to multiply arguments to prove this resolution true. Every wise man will at once admit that labor and benevolence are honorable under *all* circumstances.

When God said to Adam, "In the sweat of thy brow shalt thou eat thy bread all the days of thy life," there was much of mercy in that curse. God saw that it would be good for man to labor. It is one of the greatest blessings we enjoy. Labor is good for the body, good for the mind, good for men as individuals, as societies, as nations. It is good for the Universe to work; hence, action—useful motion—is, by God's appointment, the order of the Universe.

But, sir, labor in the cause of God is more noble than exertion in any other sphere; and benevolence in circulating the Word of God, pure, unobscured, is the noblest privilege of humanity.

Oh, what honor is this! The most wise and devout men who ever lived have so considered it, and have labored in this lofty sphere at great cost. They have done it at the cost of tribulation and loss of confidence; at the cost of honor and the sacrifice of friends; at the cost of their goods, which were "spoiled," and their lives, which were taken. They regarded themselves as honored and favored in suffering for Christ's sake, and they loved to do it. It was their agency to propagate, and vindicate the truth of God!

And is not the privilege and honor equally great as conferred upon us? Our Lord could easily have dispensed with them and us, and still have carried on His glorious work of giving His truth to the world. By a word He created man at first, physically and mentally, and for all we know to the contrary, He could without any agency of ours, have re-generated a fallen world, produced a "new creation," tenanted the upper regions, effectively and instantaneously by the alone nerve of His omnipotent arm.

I say then, that while labor and benevolence are honorable in any good cause, they bestow the highest honor, and afford the richest privilege, when summoned into the cause of God.

I grant you, sir, there may be responsibilities involved in such labor and giving, but after all, the "yoke is easy and the burden light." Now let us go a step further. This resolution says, that it is a special privilege, and a special honor to vindicate the Truth of God, in circulating faithful versions of the Scriptures in all lands.

It is not difficult, I think, to see the force of this proposition. See how wonderfully God is glorified in the circulation of faithful versions of His Word. True, He is glorified in the work of the Christian ministry, when faithfully discharged. He is glorified in the faith and practice of the Church when they accord with the teachings of inspired truth. But, sir, mind you, it is only as the gospel ministry declares the whole truth without obscurity, and it is only as the Church sends forth the rule of faith and practice as God gave it by the inspired pen, that these can fulfil their mission as God would have them, and that God can be glorified by them.

Sir, we have fearful evidence that the Church may err, that the ministry may err, and that creeds and decrees may become the veriest tissue of error, and instead of glorifying God, they may grieve Him, and obscure the truth, and lead men astray; but the unadulterated Word, never! Let God speak in His own voice, let every man read the mind of the Spirit in his own tongue, be it French, German, English, or whatever else, as exactly as the ancient Jew or Greek read it in theirs, and who shall not be led into "all truth?" And how will you better glorify God? And how shall truth be more triumphant?

Besides, sir, this is the most likely means to destroy infidelity; on this subject I scarcely dare trust myself. From a child, I have cherished an almost indescribable dread of infidelity. There is something so forlorn, so blasting, so destructive of human hope and happiness, so perfectly horrid, in the dogmas of infidelity; whether regarded in the light of time or eternity, that to me is only another name for infernality. And yet, sir, this same infernal system draws more support from the imperfections of Christian practice, and the unnecessary obscurities of Christian teaching, than from all other sources combined. Its very vitality is identified with the errors that have been permitted to gather around Christianity. Now sir, are we entirely guiltless in this matter? Can any man close his eyes upon the fact, that the defects of imperfect translations of the Sacred Scriptures, defects universally acknowledged but which all permit to remain; have not furnished opportunity for cavilers to impose upon the common mind the sophistries of skepticism? The heart of infidelity may be cold and hard, but yet it has an intellect. Skeptics may be as good linguists as the disciples of Christ, and as well qualified to search the original Scriptures, and compare them with translations of the same, so far as literary abilities qualify for this work; and when they detect errors, glosses, or obscurities, they are also well qualified to make what use of them best comports with their hatred of Christ and His cause, and what can we say in return, when they cast these into our teeth?

That man must be lamentably ignorant of the weapons of the enemy, who does not know that they rely upon this as one of their choicest and most successful issues, when they can succeed in raising it in the uncultivated and popular mind. The history of all their literature, and the spirit of all their controversy, attest this.

"Why," says the wily infidel, "if as your commentators, divines, ministers and literati, say, this passage is wrongly translated, and the passage is wrongly translated, how do you, unlettered people, know what is wrong and what is right, and guard against the impositions of priestcraft and cunning?

True, sir, this amounts to very little, with a man of education and established Christian principles, but it is not for these we plead, but for the "common people," who stumble at such difficulties, and what is worse than all, stumble unnecessarily. Could we but succeed in wresting from the foe this subtlety, certainly God would be glorified; and how can we more successfully do so than by securing as perfect a transcript of the original Scriptures for the common people as piety and learning can give? Besides, sir, do not incorrect versions of the Sacred Scriptures tend to produce discord in the Church of Christ, as well as to foster skepticism out of it? They create different standpoints from which men look differently at great principles, and looking at the same thing through different mediums, they get different impressions, imbibe different views, and as naturally maintain different theories, sometimes at the sacrifice of Christian union. One sect says, "our divines give this translation," and another, "our divines give that," and these translations give different senses, as if you could make the originals talk any way you pleased, and as if the only perfect rule of faith and practice had no one definite sense, or else that Christians are too dishonest to hear it without an interpreter. Sir, let us labor and let us give, to procure, if possible, such a translation of the Word of God as will give one sense, and but one, and that so clearly, as to enable the unlettered to understand the Word of God, without the use of note, or comment, or gloss, or of the living teacher, where the Spirit has designed no inexplicable mystery, to which we must submissively bow. And will not God be thus glorified, and Christian union promoted?

That our commonly received version of the English Scriptures does this, we cannot confidently declare. If we can, why the dissatisfaction with it which has always existed in the minds of the most godly and learned men, from the time it was given? Why the number of new translations, in part or in whole, by such men as Thomson, Scarlet, Wakefield, Dickinson, Wesley, Webster, A. Clark, Campbell, Macknight, Stewart, Doddridge, Lowth, Barnes, and multitudes of others? Why the piles of Comments, Notes, Essays, and Exegeses, either accompanying these translations or going forth alone, treating of the errors of this version, and seeking to remove them? And from whence has all this dissatisfaction arisen? Allow Dr. Macknight to give you an answer to that question. He says:

1. This version often differs from the Hebrew, to follow the LXX, if not the German translation; particularly in the proper names.
2. The translators, following the Vulgate Latin, have adopted many of the original words, without translating them, by which they have rendered their version unintelligible to a mere English reader. But they may have done this in compliance with the King's injunction concerning the old ecclesiastical words, and because by long use, many of them were as well understood by the people as if they had been English.
3. That by keeping too close to the Hebrew and Greek idioms, they have rendered their version obscure.
4. That they were a little too complaisant to the King in favoring his notion of predestination, election, witchcraft, familiar spirits, and so forth. But these, it is probable, were their own opinions, as well as the King's.
5. That their translation is partial, speaking the language of, and giving authority to, *one sect.* But this perhaps was owing to the restraint they were laid under by those who employed them.
6. That where original words and phrases admitted of different translations the *worst* translation, by plurality of votes, was put into the text, and the better was often thrown into the margin.
7. That notwithstanding all the pains taken in correcting this and the former editions of the English Bible, there still remain many passages mistranslated, either through negligence or want of knowledge; and that to other passages, improper additions are made which pervert the sense.

These and other reasons are alleged in favor of a new translation from the originals, and from these and additional reasons there has ever been a desire, on the part of many, to see this work undertaken. And, sir, Dr. Macknight does not stand alone. As far back as 1792, Dr. Newcomb, Bishop of Waterford, and Member of the Royal Irish Academy, published a thick octavo volume on this very subject, entitled *An Historical*

View of the English Biblical Translations, the Expedience of Revising by Authority our Present Translation, and the Means of Executing such a Revision.

I would refer you to the mass of testimony which he collected, from divines of great eminence, then deceased for the most part, but some were living, and approved his labor. Among them, Blackwall, in his sacred classics (1731) says:

> Innumerable instances might be made (in the English Bible) of faulty translations of the divine original, which either weaken its sense, or debase and tarnish the beauty of its language. A new translation can give no offence to people of sound judgment and consideration, because every body conversant in these matters, and unprejudiced, must acknowledge that there was less occasion to change the old version into the present, than to change the present version into a new one. Any scholar, who compares them, will find that the old one, though amended by this that we now use in several places, is yet equal to it in very many, and superior in a considerable number. Such an accurate and admirable translation, proved and supported by sound criticism, would quash and silence most of the objections of pert and profane cavilers, which chiefly proceed from their want of penetration and discernment of the connection of the argument, and their ignorance of the manner and phrase of the divine writings. It would likewise remove the scruples of many pious and conscientious Christians.
>
> In short, a faithful, just, and beautiful version of the books of God, will bring inexpressible advantage and pleasure, not only to devout Christians who do not understand the sacred original, but to the learned who can with judgment and high pleasure read them in the language that the Allwise God delivered them. Such a work will recommend itself to all men of true sense and judgment by its faithfulness and integrity; by its beautiful plainness and vigorous emphasis. It is with pleasure and a just veneration to the memory of our learned and judicious translators, that I acknowledge their version in the main, to be faithful, clear and solid.
>
> But no man can be so superstitiously devoted to them, but must own a considerable number of passages are *weakly* and

imperfectly, and not a few *falsely* rendered, and no wonder, for since their time there have been great improvements in the knowledge of antiquity, and advancements in critical learning.

Bishop Lowth—1758

To confirm and illustrate the Holy Scriptures, to evince their truth, to show their consistency, to explain their meaning, to make them more generally known and studied, more easily and perfectly understood by all; to remove the difficulties that discourage the honest endeavors of the unlearned, and provoke the malicious cavils of the half-learned; this is the most worthy object that can engage our attention, the most important end to which our labors in search of truth can be directed. And *here* I cannot but mention that *nothing* would more effectually conduce this end, than the exhibiting of the Holy Scriptures themselves to the people in a more advantageous and just light by an accurate revisal of our vulgar translation by public authority. This hath often been represented, and I hope will not always be represented in vain.

Matthew Pilkington—1759

Let us know, that many of the inconsistencies, improprieties, and obscurities which occur to any attentive reader of any of the versions, ancient or modern, are occasioned by the translators' misunderstanding of the true import of several Hebrew words and phrases. The consequence of the proof of this will be, showing the benefit and expediency of a more correct and intelligible translation of the Bible. No doubt but that the improvement of the English language was one of the considerations that induced King James to order a new version to be made, about forty years after that published and made use of in the time of Queen Elizabeth. It is now one hundred and forty years since that version was made, and will it not be thought, will it not be found upon examination, that our language has been more altered, and received greater improvements in the last one hundred and forty years than in the forty years preceding? And would not, consequently, a greater benefit arise now from a new version than could then be expected?

Purver—1764

It is well known that those called the living languages do alter. Hence it is necessary that new translations should be made from one time or century to another, accommodated to the present use of speaking and writing. This deference is paid to the heathen classics, and why should the Scriptures meet with less regard? Is it therefore to be more exposed to ridicule and contempt in this our libertine age? Let the preface of King James's translators be compared with Addison's writings; and see what difference of language there is in a hundred years.

Durrell—1772

Is it pretended that the times will not bear a new version? I answer by another question. Is the temper of the people different from that of their ancestors, at the distance of six generations?

On the introduction of the present version into our churches, in the year 1611, we hear of no tumult, clamor, or discontent. The same pacific disposition prevailed in the reign of Elizabeth.

To ascend higher would be unnecessary as to controvert the axiom, that similar causes always produce similar effects. The godly, the learned, the ingenuous, would doubtless rejoice; the gay, the thoughtless, the voluptuous, would still continue unaffected. But the caviler, the skeptic, the deist, would thereby find the sharpest and most trusty arrow of their quiver blunted; and the illiterate, who always depart reluctantly from old institutions, would soon be reconciled, when instead of an invasion of their property, they experienced that the old coin was only called in, in order that they might be repaid in new, of sterling value. The minds of the people cannot hereby be unsettled; all the leading articles of religion will remain undisturbed; neither will the ground of their faith and practice be ever so remotely affected.

Dr. Symonds—1789

The ambiguities in our version are very numerous, and sometimes too gross to be defended. Whoever examines our version in present use, with the least degree of attention, will find that it is ambiguous and incorrect, *even in matters of the highest importance*. There are some writers who fairly acknowledge these mistakes and imperfections, but strenuously maintain that to new-model or to revise our version would be a rash and dangerous experiment, as it might unhinge the minds of weak Christians, and disturb the public quiet. These arguments, which are the result of timidity rather than of prudence, have been adopted in all ages, and in all countries; and have been the perpetual obstacles to improvement in several parts of Europe. BUT IS ERROR EVER SO VALUABLE AN INHERITANCE THAT IT OUGHT NEVER TO BE RELINQUISHED? Can it be sanctified by the plea of a long prescription? There are other writers who warmly contend that our version is sufficiently clear and obvious in all things necessary to be delivered and practiced, and that therefore to alter it in the least degree would be a daring and mischievous innovation. On this point I will freely join issue with them, and rest the merits of the case upon a single argument. Hath not the misrepresentation of *one word* driven thousands of well-meaning Christians from holy communion? For the truth of this melancholy assertion, we may safely appeal to the masters of families, and to such as are concerned in parochial cures.

The last authority which I would cite is taken from Dr. Cummings, minister of the Crown Court church, London, in his *Manual of Bible Evidence for the People,* p. 164. He says:

I admit that our version is susceptible of improvement; but of such a nature, that if all the words in our translation which might be changed, were translated exactly as the original warrants, those great truths which are embodied in the standards of the Protestant churches, and which are proclaimed from every evangelical pulpit, would shine forth in yet more glorious and beautiful relief. Let me give another instance or two. In St. Paul's Epistle to Titus [2:13], we find these words: "Looking for the blessed hope and the glorious appearing of the great God and our Savior Jesus Christ." From reading these words, we might suppose the meaning to be: "Looking for the glorious appearing of the great God," [that is, God the Father], and secondly, "of our Savior Jesus Christ." But the literal translation of the verse, as any classical scholar well knows, is this: "looking for that blessed hope, and the glorious appearing of *Jesus Christ, our great God and Savior.*"

Again: in the Second Epistle of Peter, 1:1, we find these words: "Simon Peter, a servant and an apostle of Jesus Christ, to them that have obtained like precious faith with us, through the righteousness of God, and our Savior Jesus Christ." From reading these words, one would likewise suppose allusion to be made to God the Father, and to God the Son; but the literal translation is, "Through the righteousness of Jesus Christ, our God and Savior."

Along with these two, there are four other passages to which I might refer, did space permit, [viz.—Eph. 5:5; 2 Thess. 1:12; 1 Tim. 5:32; and Jude 4,] in all of which we find the very same phraseology mistranslated in our version, as if the two persons of the trinity were meant; but when corrected according to exact and accurate criticism, we have in these six passages most decided and intelligible proof of the essential Deity and Godhead of our Lord and Savior Jesus Christ.

I may show by reference to two or three specimens of a different class, what would be the result of such alterations of our authorized translation, as would render it more minutely literal.

He gives several other examples, and closes by saying:

Now what is the result of these alterations? Not that the doctrines we preach are impugned—not that the theology we hear from every evangelical pulpit is affected,—but that the *great truths of Christianity* are brought forth in a more brilliant and prominent glare.

No, sir, it is for this work of giving faithful versions of the Scriptures, that this Union is formed. And it well becomes an *American* Union to lead in such a holy enterprise. Yet, while it emanates in America, let it not be confined here. Give the movement catholicity. Let it embrace all denominations of Christians, in all lands, as far as individuals feel at liberty to unite with it.

I would not have the imprint of this "Union" stamped upon any version of the English Scriptures now in existence. Nor would I have it attached to any version whatever, until it is as perfect as man can conform it to the originals. Let us then move with deliberation. Let every eminent scholar in the world be consulted. Let every considerable library be ransacked in quest of truth. Let every accessible ancient manuscript be examined, and reexamined. And what matters it, if years intervene between the commencement and completion of this work? The more mature the production, the more perfect. And above all, sir, let us proceed kindly. Put away all wrath and malice. Whoever may honestly differ from us, let us treat them in a spirit worthy of our noble enterprise; let us not throw obstructions in the way of other Bible associations, but let us prosecute our labors with constancy, catholicity, liberality, deliberation, love; and God, even our fathers' God, will be with us and bless us.

Chapter Notes

1. William Wyckoff and C. A. Buckbee, eds., *A Documentary History of the American Bible Union* (Louisville: Bible Revision Assoc., 1857), n.p. This history consists of the collected journals of the American Bible Union. It is a major source of information on its proceedings. The other major source is Thomas Armitage, *A History of the Baptists* (New York: Bryan, Taylor and Co., 1887), 893–918.

Bibliography

Aland, Kurt. *The Text of the New Testament: An Introduction to the Critical Editions and to the Theory and Practice of Modern Textual Criticism.* 2d edition. Trans. Erroll R. Rhodes. Grand Rapids: Eerdmans, 1989.

———. "The Text of the Church?" *Trinity Journal* 8 (1987): 131–44.

Aland, Kurt, and Barbara Aland, eds. Kurzgefasste Liste der grieschen Handschriften des Neuen Testaments. *Arbeiten zurneutest-amentlichen Textforschung.* Band 1. Hawthorne, N.Y.: Walter de Gruyter, 1994.

Alford, Henry. *The New Testament for English Readers.* 4 vols. Reprint, Grand Rapids: Baker, 1983.

Archer, Gleason L., and G. C. Chirichigno. *Old Testament Quotations in the New Testament: A Complete Survey.* Chicago: Moody, 1983.

Armerding, Carl E. *The Old Testament and Criticism.* Grand Rapids: Eerdmans, 1983.

Armitage, Thomas. *A History of the Baptists.* New York: Bryan, Taylor and Co., 1887.

———. *History of the Baptists.* 2 vols. Reprint, Minneapolis: James & Klock, 1977.

Bainton, Roland. *Erasmus of Christendom.* New York: Charles Scribner's Sons, 1969.

Barker, Kenneth L. *The niv: The Making of a Contemporary Translation.* Grand Rapids: Zondervan, 1986.

Beekman, John, and John Callow. *Translating the Word of God.* Grand Rapids: Zondervan, 1984.

Black, David Alan. *New Testament Textual Criticism: A Concise Guide.* Grand Rapids: Baker, 1994.

———. *Using New Testament Greek in Ministry.* Grand Rapids: Baker, 1993.

Brotzman, Ellis R. *Old Testament Textual Criticism.* Grand Rapids: Baker, 1994.

Bruce, F. F. *The Books and the Parchments.* London: Pickering and Inglis, 1950.

———. *The Books and the Parchments.* Rev. ed. Westwood, N.J.: Revell, 1963.

Burgon, John William. *The Revision Revised.* London: John Murray, 1883. Reprint, Paradise, Pa.: Conservative Classics, n.d.

Carleton, James. *The Part of Rheims in the Making of the English Bible.* Oxford: Oxford University Press, 1902.

Carson, D. A. *The Inclusive Language Debate: A Plea for Realism.* Grand Rapids: Baker, 1998.

———. *The King James Version Debate: A Plea for Realism.* Grand Rapids: Baker, 1979.

Catalog of Central Baptist Theological Seminary, Minneapolis, Minn., 1996–1998.

Charlesworth, James H., ed. *The Old Testament Pseudepigrapha.* 2 vols. New York: Doubleday, 1985.

Clearwaters, R. V. "Bible Versions." Central Bible Workshop, 23 April 1974.

———. *The Great Conservative Baptist Compromise.* Minneapolis: Central Seminary Press, n.d.

Combs, William W. "Erasmus and the Textus Receptus." *Detroit Baptist Seminary Journal* 1, no. 1 (spring 1996): 35–53.

———. "The Preface to the King James Version and the King James-Only Position." *Detroit Baptist Seminary Journal* 1, no. 2 (fall 1996): 253–67.

Cone, Edward Winfield, *The Life of Spencer H. Cone.* New York: Sheldon, Blakeman, & Co., 1857.

Craigie, Peter C. *Psalms 1–50.* Waco, Tex.: Word, 1983.

Cross, Frank Moore. "The Text Behind the Hebrew Bible." In *Understanding the Dead Sea Scrolls.* Ed. Hershel Shanks, 139–155. New York: Random House, 1992.

———. "Light on the Bible from the Dead Sea Caves." In *Understanding the Dead Sea Scrolls.* Ed. Hershel Shanks, 156–66. New York: Random House, 1992.

Custer, Stewart. *Does Inspiration Demand Inerrancy?* Nutley, N.J.: Craig Press, 1968.

Darlow, T. H., and H. F. Moule, comps. *Historical Catalogue of the Printed Editions of the Holy Scripture in the Library of the British and Foreign Bible Society.* Vol. II. Part II. London: British and Foreign Bible Society, 1903–1911.

D'Aubigne, J. H. Merle. *History of the Reformation of the Sixteenth Century.* 1846. Reprint, Grand Rapids: Baker, 1976.

"Declaration of Doctrinal Belief of Niagara Bible Conference." *The Truth* 20 (1894): 509–11.

DeHaan, Mart. "Translations." Radio Bible Class Ministries, April 1996. <search.gospelcom.net/rbc/td/04-1996/bta.html>. 19 December 2000.

Deist, F. E. *Towards the Text of the Old Testament.* Trans. W. K. Winckler. Pretoria, S. Africa: N. G. Kerkboekhandel Transvaal, 1978.

Delitzsch, Franz. *The Psalms.* Trans. Francis Bolton. 2 vols. Biblical Commentary on the Old Testament. Edinburgh: T & T Clark, 1894; Grand Rapids: Eerdmans, 1976.

Douglas, J. D., ed. *The New International Dictionary of the Christian Church.* Rev. ed. Grand Rapids: Zondervan, 1978.

Dunbar, David G. "The Biblical Canon." In *Hermeneutics Authority and Canon.* Ed. D. A. Carson and John D. Woodbridge, 295–360. Grand Rapids: Zondervan, 1986.

Ehrman, Bart D. "New Testament Textual Criticism: Quest for Methodology." M.Div. thesis, Princeton Theological Seminary, 1981.

Epp, Eldon Jay. "The Papyrus Manuscripts of the New Testament." In *The Text of the New Testament in Contemporary Research: Essays on the Status Quaestionis,* 3–21. Grand Rapids: Eerdmans, 1995.

Erickson, Millard J. *Christian Theology.* 3 vols. Grand Rapids: Baker, 1983.

Farstad, Arthur L. *The New King James Version in the Great Tradition.* 2d ed. Nashville: Nelson, 1989.

Fee, Gordon D. "Modern Textual Criticism and the Revival of the *Textus Receptus." Journal of the Evangelical Theological Society* 21 (1978): 19–33.

———. *New Testament Exegesis: A Handbook for Students and Pastors.* 2d ed. Louisville: Westminster/John Knox, 1993.

———. "Textual Criticism of the New Testament." In *Textual Criticism of the New Testament.* Ed. Eldon J. Epp and Gordon D. Fee, 3–16. Grand Rapids: Eerdmans, 1993.

————. "The Textual Criticism of the New Testament." In *The Expositor's Bible Commentary*. Ed. Frank E. Gaebelein, 1:417–33. Grand Rapids: Zondervan, 1979.

Fee, Gordon D., and Douglas Stuart. *How to Read the Bible for All Its Worth: A Guide for Understanding the Bible*. 2d ed. Grand Rapids: Zondervan, 1993.

Froude, J. A., *Life and Letters of Erasmus*. London: Longmans, Green, and Co., 1900.

Fuller, David Otis, ed. *Counterfeit or Genuine?* Grand Rapids: Grand Rapids International Publications, 1975.

————. *Which Bible?* 5th ed. Grand Rapids: Grand Rapids International Publications, 1975.

Geisler, Norman L., and William E. Nix. *A General Introduction to the Bible*. Rev. and expanded ed. Chicago: Moody, 1986.

Gill, John. *A Complete Body of Doctrinal and Practical Divinity: Or, a System of Evangelical Truths*. London: Mathews & Leigh, 1839.

————. *An Exposition of the New Testament*. Vol. 1. 1842–1854. Reprint, Grand Rapids: Baker, 1980.

Glassman, Eugene H. *The Translation Debate*. Downers Grove, Ill.: InterVarsity, 1982.

Goodspeed, Edgar J. "The Versions of the New Testament." In *Tools for Bible Study*. Ed. Balmer H. Kelly and Donald G. Miller, 111–26. Richmond: John Knox, 1956.

Grady, William P. *Final Authority*. Schererville, Ind.: Grady, 1993.

Grassmick, John. *Principles and Practice of Greek Exegesis*. Dallas: Dallas Theological Seminary, 1976.

Gray, James. "The Inspiration of the Bible—Definition, Extent and Proof." In *The Fundamentals*, 2:9–43. Los Angeles: The Bible Institute of Los Angeles, 1917.

Greene, W. C., trans. *Saint Augustine: The City of God Against the Pagans*. Vol. 6. London: William Heinemann, 1969.

Greenlee, J. H. *Introduction to New Testament Textual Criticism*. Rev. ed. Peabody, Mass.: Hendrickson, 1995.

Gromacki, Robert G. *Translations on Trial: Is Your Bible the Word of God?* Lincoln, Neb.: Back to the Bible, 1990.

Grudem, Wayne. *1 Peter*. Grand Rapids: Eerdmans, 1988.

Hastings, James. *A Dictionary of the Bible*. 5 vols. Edinburgh: T & T Clark, 1904.

Hills, Edward F. *Believing Bible Study.* Des Moines: Christian Research, 1967.

——. *The King James Version Defended!* 4th ed. Des Moines: Christian Research, 1984.

Hodges, Zane C. *A Defense of the Majority Text.* Dallas: Dallas Theological Seminary, n.d.

——. "Review of *The Bible Babel.*" *Bibliotheca Sacra,* October 1967.

Hodges, Zane C., and Arthur L. Farstad, eds. *The Greek New Testament According to the Majority Text.* 2d ed. Nashville: Nelson, 1985.

Hoyt, W. "Questions Concerning Inspiration." In *The Inspired Word.* Ed. A. T. Pierson, 8–30. London: Hodder and Stoughton, 1888.

Hudson, Gary. "The Real 'Eye Opener.'" *Baptist Biblical Heritage* 2, no. 1 (spring 1991).

——. "Why Dean Burgon Would Not Join the Dean Burgon Society." Pasadena, Tex.: Pilgrim, n.d.

Klein, R. W. *Textual Criticism of the Old Testament: The Septuagint after Qumran.* Philadelphia: Fortress Press, 1974.

Kutilek, Doug. *An Answer to David Otis Fuller: Fuller's Deceptive Treatment of Spurgeon Regarding the King James Version.* Pasadena, Tex.: Pilgrim, n.d.

——. "A Careful Investigation of Psalm 12:6–7." *The Biblical Evangelist* 17, no. 21 (14 October 1983).

——. "Erasmus and His Greek Text." *The Biblical Evangelist* 19, no. 19 (1 October 1985).

——. "Erasmus and His Theology." *The Biblical Evangelist* 19, no. 20 (16 October 1985).

——. *Erasmus: His Greek Text, and His Theology.* Hatfield, Pa.: Interdisciplinary Biblical Research Institute, 1986.

——. *J. Frank Norris and His Heirs: the Bible Translation Controversy.* Pasadena, Tex.: Pilgrim, 1999.

——. "The KJV Is a Copyrighted Translation." *Baptist Biblical Heritage* 4, no. 3 (October 1993): 5–8.

——. "Ruckman on Luther and 1 John 5:7." Unpublished article.

——. "Ruckmanism: A Refuge of Lies." *Baptist Biblical Heritage* 4, no. 4 (January 1994): 5–6.

——. "Ruckman's Phony 'Advanced Revelations.' " *The Biblical Evangelist* 24, no. 5 (May 1990): 1, 4–6.

——. "The Septuagint: Riplinger's Blunders, Believe It or Not." *Baptist Biblical Heritage* 5, no. 2 (3d quarter, 1994): 3–4, 12.

————. "Spencer H. Cone." *Frontline* 10, no. 1 (January–February 2000): 39.

————. "The Truth About the Waldensian Bible and the Old Latin Version." *Baptist Biblical Heritage* 2, no. 2 (summer 1991).

————. "The Unlearned Men: The True Genealogy and Genesis of King James-Onlyism." *Baptist Biblical Heritage* 5, no. 4 (1st quarter, 1995).

————. *Westcott and Hort vs. Textus Receptus: Which Is Superior?* Hatfield, Pa.: Interdisciplinary Biblical Research Institute, 1996.

————. "Wilkinson's Incredible Errors." *Baptist Biblical Heritage* 1, no. 3 (fall 1990).

Kutilek, Doug, and Gary Hudson. "The Great 'Which Bible?' Fraud." *Baptist Biblical Heritage* 1, no. 2 (summer 1990): 1, 3–6.

Lamsa, George M. *The Holy Bible from Ancient Eastern Manuscripts.* Philadelphia: A. J. Holman, 1957.

The Leaven of Fundamentalism. Video tape. Pensacola, Fla.: Pensacola Christian College, 1998.

Letis, Theodore P., ed. *The Majority Text: Essays and Reviews in the Continuing Debate.* Fort Wayne, Ind.: Institute for Biblical Textual Studies, 1987.

Lewis, Jack P. *The English Bible from kjv to niv: A History and Evaluation.* 2d ed. Grand Rapids: Baker, 1991.

Linton, Calvin D. "The Importance of Literary Style in Bible Translation Today." In *The niv: The Making of a Contemporary Translation.* Ed. Kenneth L. Barker. Grand Rapids: Zondervan, 1986.

McCune, Kevin L. "The Relationship of the Doctrine of Inspiration to Copies and Translations of the Autographa." Unpublished M. Div. thesis, Central Baptist Seminary, Plymouth, Minn., 1981.

McRay, J. R. "Canon of Bible." In *Evangelical Dictionary of Theology.* Ed. Walter A. Elwell, 140–41. Grand Rapids: Baker, 1984.

Manly, Basil, Jr. *The Bible Doctrine of Inspiration.* Reprint, Harrisonburg, Va.: Gano Books, 1985.

Marcus, Ralph, trans. *Josephus.* Vol. 7. Cambridge, Mass.: Harvard University Press, 1986.

Merrill, Eugene H. *Deuteronomy.* Nashville: Broadman and Holman, 1994.

Metzger, Bruce. *The Text of the New Testament: Its Transmission, Corruption, and Restoration.* 3d ed. New York: Oxford University Press, 1992.

Metzger, Bruce, and Roland E. Murphy, eds. *The New Oxford Annotated Bible: New Revised Standard Version.* New York: Oxford Press, 1994.

Minton, Ron. "The Making and Preservation of the Bible." 9th ed. An unpublished notebook available from the author at Piedmont Baptist College Graduate Division, 716 Franklin Street, Winston-Salem, N.C. 27101.

"New Revised Standard Version Bible: God's Word for all People." A pamphlet published by the New Revised Standard Version Bible, Bible Translation and Utilization, New York, NY.

The New Testament: The Greek Text Underlying the English Authorized Version of 1611. London: The Trinitarian Bible Society, 1977.

Nida, Eugene A., and Charles R. Taber. *The Theory and Practice of Translation.* Leiden: Brill, 1974.

Osburn, Carroll D. "The Greek Lectionaries of the New Testament." In *The Text of the New Testament in Contemporary Research: Essays on the Status Quaestionis.* Ed. Bart Ehrman and Michael Holmes, 61–74. Grand Rapids: Eerdmans, 1995.

Pache, René. *The Inspiration and Authority of Scripture.* Chicago: Moody, 1969.

Pickering, Wilbur N. *The Identity of the New Testament Text.* Rev. ed. Nashville: Nelson, 1997.

———. "An Evaluation of the Contribution of John William Burgon to New Testament Textual Criticism." Th.M. thesis, Dallas Theological Seminary, 1968.

Price, Ira Maurice. *The Ancestry of Our English Bible.* 2d rev. ed. Ed. William A. Irwin and Allen P. Wikgren. New York: Harper and Brothers, 1949.

Price, James A., *The King James-Only Controversy in American Fundamentalism Since 1950.* Unpublished Th. D. dissertation, Temple Baptist Seminary, 1990

———. "King James-Only View of Edward F. Hills." *Baptist Biblical Heritage* 1, no. 4 (winter 1990–1991).

———. "KJV Issues." Electronic Mail to R. E. Beacham, 1 May 1996. Transcript in the library of Central Baptist Theological Seminary of Minneapolis, Minneapolis, Minn.

Quasten, Johannes, *Patrology.* 3 vols. Utrecht, Neth.: Spectrum, n.d.

Ray, James Jasper, *God Wrote Only One Bible.* Rev. ed. Junction City, Ore.: Eye Opener, 1970.

Rice, John R. *Our God-Breathed Book—The Bible.* Murfreesboro, Tenn.: Sword of the Lord Publishers, 1969.

Riley, W. B. *The Conflict of Christianity with Its Counterfeits.* Minneapolis: W. B. Riley, n.d.

Roberts, Alexander, and James Donaldson, ed. *The Ante-Nicene Fathers*. Vol. 1, *The Apostolic Fathers with Justin Martyr and Irenaeus*. Reprint, Grand Rapids: Eerdmans, 1979.

Robinson, Maurice A., and William G. Pierpont, eds. *The New Testament in the Original Greek According to the Byzantine/Majority Textform*. Atlanta: Original Word, 1991.

Ruckman, Peter. *The Christian's Handbook of Manuscript Evidence*. Pensacola: Pensacola Bible Institute, 1970.

————. *Problem Texts*. Pensacola: Pensacola Bible Institute, 1980.

Sawyer, James M. "Evangelicals and the Canon of the New Testament." *Grace Theological Journal* 11, no. 1 (spring 1991): 29–52.

Schaff, Philip, ed. *The Creeds of Christendom*. Vol. 2. Rev. David S. Schaff. 6th ed. Reprint, Grand Rapids: Baker, 1983.

————. *History of the Christian Church*. Vol. 7. Reprint, Grand Rapids: Eerdmans, 1974.

Schaff, Philip, and Henry Wace, eds. *A Select Library of the Nicene and Post-Nicene Fathers of the Christian Church*. Vol. 7. 2d Series. Reprint, Grand Rapids: Eerdmans, 1989.

Scrivener, F. H. A. *A Plain Introduction to the Criticism of the New Testament*. 4th ed. London: George Bell and Sons, 1894.

————. *A Plain Introduction to the Criticism of the New Testament*. 2d ed. Cambridge: Deighton, Bell, and Co., 1874.

————. "The Translators to the Reader: Preface to the King James Version." In *The Authorized Edition of the English Bible (1611)*. Cambridge: At the University Press, 1884.

Spurgeon, Charles Haddon. *The Greatest Fight in the World*. Reprint, Pasadena, Tex.: Pilgrim, 1990.

Strousse, Thomas M. "Fundamentalism and the Authorized Version." A paper presented at the National Leadership Conference, Landsdale, Pa., February 1996.

Sturz, H. A. *The Byzantine Text Type and New Testament Textual Criticism*. Nashville: Nelson, 1984.

Surrett, Charles L. *Which Greek Text? The Debate Among Fundamentalists*. Kings Mountain, N.C.: Surrett Family Publications, 1999.

Swete, Henry Barclay, *An Introduction to the Old Testament in Greek*. Rev. Richard Rusden Ottley. 1914. Reprint, New York: Ktav, 1968.

Text and Product Preview, Holy Bible: New Living Translation. Wheaton, Ill.: Tyndale House, 1996.

Thomas, Robert L. "Bible Translations: The Link Between Exegesis and Expository Preaching." *The Masters Seminary Journal* 1, no. 1 (spring 1990): 53–73.

———. *Revelation 8–22: An Exegetical Commentary*. Chicago: Moody, 1995.

Torrey, R. A. *Is the Bible the Inerrant Word of God?* New York: George H. Doran, 1922.

Tov, Emanuel. *Textual Criticism of the Hebrew Bible*. Minneapolis: Fortress, 1992.

Van Kleeck, Peter. "A 16th and 17th Century Exegetical and Theological Assessment of Central Baptist Theological Seminary's Perspective of the Bible Version Debate." Public lecture delivered at the Midwest regional meeting of the Independent Baptist Fellowship of North America, Oak Creek, Wisc., 20 April 1998.

van Til, Cornelius. *The Doctrine of Scripture*. Ripon, Calif.: den Dulk Christian Foundation, 1967.

Waite, D. A. *Defending the King James Bible*. Collingswood, N.J.: Bible for Today Press, 1992.

———. *Central Seminary Refuted on Bible Versions*. Collingswood, N.J.: Bible for Today Press, 1999.

———. *Fundamentalist Distortions on Bible Versions*. Collingswood, N.J.: Bible for Today Press, 1999.

Wallace, Daniel B. "Some Second Thoughts on the Majority Text." *Bibliotheca Sacra* 146, no. 583 (July–September 1989): 270–90.

———. "The Majority Text Theory: History, Methods, and Critique." In *The Text of the New Testament in Contemporary Research: Essays on the Status Quaestionis*. Ed. Bart Ehrman and Michael Holmes, 297–320. Grand Rapids: Eerdmans, 1995.

———. "Inspiration, Preservation, and New Testament Textual Criticism." *Grace Theological Journal* 12, no. 1 (spring 1992): 21–50.

———. "The Majority Text and the Original Text: Are They Identical?" *Bibliotheca Sacra* 148, no. 590 (April–June 1991): 158–66.

Waltke, Bruce K., and M. O'Connor. *An Introduction to Biblical Hebrew Syntax*. Winona Lake, Ind.: Eisenbrauns, 1990.

Ware, Timothy. *The Orthodox Church*. New York: Penguin, 1964.

Warfield, B. B. *The Inspiration and Authority of the Bible*. Philadelphia: Presbyterian and Reformed, 1964.

Whiston, William, trans. *The Works of Josephus*. 4 vols. Reprint, Grand Rapids: Baker, 1979.

White, James R. *The King James Only Controversy.* Minneapolis: Bethany House, 1995.

Wilson, Robert Dick. *Studies in the Book of Daniel.* Vol. 1. Reprint, Grand Rapids: Baker, 1972.

————. *A Scientific Investigation of the Old Testament.* Chicago: Moody, 1959.

Wurthwein, Ernst. *The Text of the Old Testament.* Trans. Erroll F. Rhodes. Grand Rapids: Eerdmans, 1979.

Wyckoff, William, and C. A. Buckbee, eds. *A Documentary History of the American Bible Union.* Louisville: Bible Revision Assoc., 1857.

Yeivin, Israel. *Introduction to the Tiberian Masorah.* Trans. and ed. E. J. Revell. *The Society of Biblical Literature Masoretic Studies.* No. 5. Ed. Harry M. Orlinsky. Missoula, Mont.: Scholars Press, 1980.

Yonge, C. D. *The Works of Philo.* New updated ed. Peabody, Mass.: Hendrickson, 1993.

CPSIA information can be obtained
at www.ICGtesting.com
Printed in the USA
BVHW04s2247200318
511073BV00030B/378/P